Pseudo-Problems

Pseudo-Problems

How analytic philosophy gets done

Roy A. Sorensen

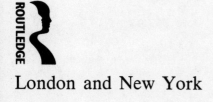

London and New York

First published 1993
by Routledge
11 New Fetter Lane, London EC4P 4EE

Simultaneously published in the USA and Canada
by Routledge
29 West 35th Street, New York, NY 10001

© 1993 Roy A. Sorensen

Printed in Great Britain by
T. J. Press (Padstow) Ltd, Padstow, Cornwall

British Library Cataloguing in Publication Data:
Sorensen, Roy A.
  Pseudo-problems
  I. Title
  160

ISBN 0–415–09464–X

A necessity I could not understand swept over me: I had to try again and again to imagine the edge of space, or its edgelessness, time with a beginning or end, and both were equally impossible, equally hopeless . . . Under an irresistible compulsion I reeled from one to the other, at times so closely threatened with the danger of madness that I seriously thought of avoiding it by suicide.

(Martin Buber)

We have accumulated around the terms 'force' and 'electricity' more relations than can be completely reconciled amongst themselves. We have an obscure feeling of this and want to have things cleared up. Our confused wish finds expression in the confused question as to the nature of force and electricity. But the answer which we want is not really an answer to this question. It is not by finding out more and fresh relations and connections that it can be answered; but by removing the contradictions existing between those already known, and thus perhaps by reducing their number. When these painful contradictions are removed, the question as to the nature of force will not have been answered; but our minds, no longer vexed, will cease to ask illegitimate questions.

(Heinrich Hertz)

This book is dedicated to my niece,

Kristen Judith Coulaz,

and my nephew,

Stephen Paul Coulaz.

Saltem hic liber in Latinam non conscribitur!

Contents

Acknowledgements

Pseudo-Problems has benefited from the comments and suggestions of John Carroll, Julia Driver, Carsten Hansen, John Richardson, Douglas Stalker, and anonymous referees. Since earlier drafts were also used in several classes on twentieth-century philosophy, the book has also been improved by points raised by my students.

Pseudo-Problems draws on some material that has previously appeared in writing or lectures. In particular, Chapter 2 draws heavily on 'Debunkers and assurers' (1991b). Parts of chapter 9 first appeared as 'Maximizing and mimicking' in reply to a paper by Henry Richardson at the Woodrow Wilson International Center in Washington DC, 22 May 1992. The tenth chapter draws on 'The egg came before the chicken' (1992b) by permission of Oxford University Press. The last chapter is based on 'What makes a problem deep?', which was presented at the ninth International Congress of Logic, Methodology, and Philosophy of Science in Uppsala, Sweden, 12 August 1991. I thank the respective editors and colloquium organizers for permission to incorporate this material.

Finally, I thank Adrian Driscoll for conducting this manuscript so professionally to print.

Roy A. Sorensen
New York City

Introduction

Hold this page in front of a mirror. Why does the mirror only reverse the letters of one of the words?

S	M
E	A
E	T

Presto! Our first pseudo-problem! The mirror really reverses *both* words. The symmetry of the letters in the second word makes the letters *look* the same after reversal.

The title of this book won a close competition between such rivals as *Quelling Queer Questions* and *How to Neither Win nor Lose Arguments*. Like all books on logic, rhetoric, and debate, this one concerns the structure of controversy and intellectual problems. Unlike them all, *Pseudo-Problems* is not concerned with winning debates or solving problems.

Instead the topic is the *selection* and *dissolution* of disputes and problems. I question questioned questions. Where do pseudo-problems come from? How did they achieve prominence in the twentieth century? How can these bogus questions be avoided? Is there an analogy between dissolution and Sextus Empiricus' *epoche* – or Jacques Derrida's deconstruction? Are solution and dissolution antithetical approaches or can they work in concert? Can a problem change into a-pseudo-problem? What about the reverse?

Pseudo-Problems drums out three myths about dissolution. The Myth of Neutrality is the belief that the dissolver is an impartial referee who calls off a dispute on independent, theory-neutral grounds. Ludwig Wittgenstein relished this role. Ever the outsider, ostentatiously ill read, his motto was 'Don't think; look and see.' I aim to level this mystique of intellectual privilege with the thesis that the dissolver is just another player in the game – just another hot cognizer who acts as a disinterested party to suit his own agenda. Common sense, science, metaphysics, and even one's general attitude toward conflict season the warm theory-ladenness of dissolution.

Thus I also oppose the Myth of Uniqueness – the belief that pseudo-problems are peculiar to philosophy. The antidote for this failure of nerve is metaphilosophical gradualism: philosophy differs from science in degree, not kind. Science and philosophy are composed of the same variables. The differences in their inputs create mutually illuminating contrasts. But they have *qualitative* kinship. Philosophy is *reassuringly* like science and science is *disturbingly* like philosophy. They are natural variations of the same drive to understand. Both science and philosophy gamble, so both have pseudo-problems. Both have evolved countermeasures, so both traffic in trade-offs.

Science triumphs by the way it controls research. Thus an understanding of how the gate-keepers sort issues into problems and pseudo-problems is a precondition of understanding how scientists answer so many questions. This understanding is deepened by a grasp of the distinction between the various kinds of defective inquiries. As long as pseudo-problems continue to be lumped together, we won't appreciate why scientists are picky about the proper characterization of the defect. We will also remain ignorant of the delicate craft behind deproblematization.

Since the credentials of the natural sciences are better established, I principally use science to illuminate philosophy. Although only a few centuries old, physics and biology are vastly larger than their parent discipline. When science sneezes, philosophy catches pneumonia. Through strength of numbers, more and more of the best philosophy has been driven by scientists: Ernst Mach, Pierre Duhem, Henri Poincaré, B. F. Skinner, Noam Chomsky, Richard Dawkins, E. O. Wilson. It is especially telling that Wittgenstein, a former engineering student, traced his ideas about dissolution to nineteenth-century physicists such as Ludwig Boltzmann and Heinrich Hertz. Indeed, Wittgenstein contemplated using Hertz's sermon about fishy forces (that opens this book) as the *Philosophical Investigations'* head quotation. He adopts and elaborates on their metaphors of entanglement, overextension, empty operations, false prisons, insanity, magic, witchcraft. Special effort shall be made to showcase Wittgenstein's scientific mentors.

As the Chinese say, those who drink should remember who dug

the well. So recognition will also be extended to the American pragmatists. True, the treatment of pseudo-problems by C. S. Peirce, William James, and John Dewey lacks the spit and polish of the German, Austrian, and British analytics. The Americans never had the virtues of high-minded hygiene. But their down and dirty concreteness also shielded them from the abrasive vices of strong cleansing agents. Furthermore, the pragmatist's articulation of the American preoccupation with practicality framed the reception and reconstitution of analytic themes.

And indeed, *Pseudo-Problems* is a book on analytic philosophy from an American perspective. I have learned much from British retrospectives. However, my book is aligned with the American tradition of problem-oriented philosophy. The idea is to incorporate the insights of the problem underminers into a general framework – to complement the yin of solution with the yang of dissolution.

Or perhaps it should be the *yin* of dissolution. The yin signifies the feminine aspect of the Way: cooperative, unifying, yielding. So one might expect this affinity to find expression in feminist scholarship. But there is only uneven confirmation. As an illustration, consider Carol Gilligan's (1982) psychological studies of female morality. She dwells on her subjects' tendency to reject forced choices, to conciliate, to find the unity in opposites. However, Gilligan also intimates that analytic tendencies (which are also crucial to dissolution) are alien to the female perspective. And indeed, much feminist writing gravitates back toward the organicism associated with Idealism – the very school of thought against which the analytics defined themselves.

No organicism for *Pseudo-Problems*! However, it does swim with other currents in contemporary philosophy. The book lives out a belief in semantic ascent and makes heavy use of H. P. Grice's theory of conversation. *Pseudo-Problems* is also intended to reflect the recent interdisciplinarianism. It draws on artificial intelligence, psychology, linguistics, and the history of science and is intended to be of interest to these neighbors of philosophy.

The theme of dynamism within (and without) analytic philosophy segues into the third misconception about pseudo-problems; the Myth of Absoluteness. There are many facets to this misconception. Part of this failure to relativize lies in the assumption that pseudo-problems are static, stable entities. My counter-theme will be that questions are opportunistically updated by new data, new theories, and shifting interests. For example, the seventeenth-century question of whether comets are inhabited has been reconstituted by new conceptions of life. Frequently, a problem is like a submerged block of salt which is losing about as many atoms as it is gaining. Is it dissolving into the water or crystallizing out of the water?

The Myth of Absoluteness also manifests itself in our insensitivity to the conventionality of pseudo-status and its consequent susceptibility to sheer stipulation and charismatic manipulation. At the core of the myth is the common belief that pseudo-problems are a natural kind such as trichinosis. Although the disease analogy is fertile, I shall argue that 'pseudo-problem' is too ambiguous to classify pathological research. *A fortiori*, this and other debunking expressions (bogus, false, phony) are too protean for a critique of philosophy. Yet Wittgenstein ruthlessly exploited their plasticity to body massage us into a repudiation of philosophy. My point is that the widening circle of flagellation emanating from Cambridge University was as much the effect of Wittgenstein's character as it was the product of his cogitation. He seized control of debunkers in a way that gives new meaning to *The World as Will and Representation*. (Schopenhauer is one of the few philosophers Wittgenstein admits reading.)

Happily, there is another term, 'dissolution', that does admit of principled classification. I develop this taxonomy in detail. This foundation for the constructive phase of this book supports my theory of dissolution by structuring a representative survey of pseudo-problems. The essential idea is that debate requires an invisible infrastructure of agreement between the disputants. Therefore, an outsider can crack a debate by refuting one of these underlying assumptions. I have kept this latter portion of *Pseudo-Problems* fairly modular. That way someone interested in a particular kind of pseudo-problem can dive into the most relevant chapter. 'For I approach deep problems like cold baths: quickly into them and quickly out again' (Nietzsche 1882/7: §381).

I hope that this book will have the practical effect of reducing misadventures with pseudo-problems. Studies of problem solving only give passing reference to the need to check whether the problem is healthy. More than pieties about 'well-defined' problems are needed to absorb the lessons taught by the logical atomists, the positivists, and the ordinary language philosophers. A comprehensive flowchart of problem solving should contain a side-branch for pseudo-problem detection. Homage is due to the Sultans of pseudo-problems.

I also hope that *Pseudo-Problems* will curb the rejection of genuine problems and thus ease analytic philosophy's penchant for intellectual repression. Ignorance of dissolution's fine structure makes for coarse scars and reactionary overcompensation. The traumatized work of injured metaphysicians assumes the over-secured character of a Roman edifice. Ancient architects lacked an accurate knowledge of safety factors and so had to err ponderously on the side of caution to insure against collapse. Thus they wasted time and treasure on anxious over-building. 'Risky' projects languished. Our ideal is to avoid waste on both sides of the problem/pseudo-problem divide. This balanced theory of dissolution will then let us rise secure but unencumbered in a sounder amalgam of responsibility and grace.

1 Question quality control

If therefore philosophy were to succeed in creating a system such that in all cases mentioned it stood out clearly when a question is not justified so that the drive towards asking it would gradually die away, we should at one stroke have resolved the most obscure riddles and philosophy would become worthy of the name of queen of the sciences.

(Ludwig Boltzmann)

One sure way to avoid dialectical dead ends is to never try to solve a problem or win a debate. But the path of total abstention is also barren of the fruit that labor may bear. Just as fear of bad apples shouldn't make us forgo all apples, fear of wasteful debate shouldn't cow us into intellectual retirement. Instead, we should just be pickier about our apples.

Obviously this presupposes that pickiness pays – that examining apples prevents enough disappointment to justify the inspection. This assumption is best cast in the framework of quality control:

	Good issue	Bad issue
Judged good	☺ True positives	False positives
Judged bad	False negatives	☻ True negatives

The inspector is correct in the cases along the northwest diagonal, mistaken along the northeast diagonal. Giving a control group a discrimination test would measure our natural talent for spotting good problems and bad problems. Testing a 'treated' group – ones who had studied question quality – would give us the next set of numbers. Checking the difference would tell us whether study improves our ability to separate good disputes from bad ones. Possibly there would be no improvement at all. Maybe people are excellent natural evaluators of questions. Maybe only a minority are trouble prone. One of my Wittgensteinian professors went to teach in Hong Kong after finishing his training in England. The students proved immune to philosophical worries, so he had nothing to do.

But at a more general level, there is widespread belief that it pays to be choosy about whether to choose sides. Outsiders frequently criticize and ridicule the issues that engross others. Second, nearly all disputants experience remorse about entering some debates. And everyone abides by dispute policies designed to prevent and halt bad disputes: avoid the topics of religion and politics; clearly state the issue in contention; address factual differences before evaluative ones. So there is some initial evidence that it pays to be judicious about debate topics. Further evidence will flow in dribs and drabs as the study of pseudo-problems unfolds.

THE FASCINATION OF FALSE POSITIVES

The simplest quality control questions feature two options: accept the item or reject it. Ideally, all good items will be embraced and all bad ones spurned. Realistically, mistakes will be made. Some bad items will be accepted (false positives) and some good items will be rejected (false negatives).

In the case of issues, people give priority to sidestepping false positives, that is, bad questions. People are less worried about rejecting good questions. This asymmetry engages the distinction between act and omission; errors that lead to action tend to be worse than errors that lead to inaction.

The linguistic philosophy associated with Ludwig Wittgenstein is dedicated to the eradication of false positives. His disciples pictured themselves as having taken a crucial step back from philosophizing, the step needed to gain enough distance to question the activity itself. Suitably re-oriented, they concluded that instead of trying to answer the question, we should question the questions. This self-image shimmers through Frederich Waismann's summary:

> Previous philosophers have almost always directed their attention to the *answers* given in reply to philosophical questions. Their disputes were all concerned with these answers, their truth or

falsity, their proof or refutation. The new point of view differs from all the others in that, from the start, it ignores the answers and directs all its attention towards the questions. It is well known that we often think that we understand precisely what is meant by a question, whereas further examination shows us that we have deceived ourselves in thinking this and have been led astray by superficial linguistic analogies. The great mistake of philosophers up to now, which has led to so many misunderstandings, is that they have produced answers before seeing clearly the nature of the questions they have been asking. They seem to have been quite unaware of the possibility that the form of the question itself might conceal an error. This has meant that they have been satisfied by pseudo-solutions which, though they dazed the mind for a little while, could not stand the test of time.

(1965: 4)

Waismann shows off the method of dissolution by applying it to 'How do I know that my memory is reliable?' Offhand, the question seems elementary: just match memories against records and other traces. For example, my memory that Andy Warhol was shot a couple of days before Robert Kennedy can be checked by consulting New York newspapers from June 1968. My memory of feeding the cat this morning can be verified by a search for residual Meow-Mix. However, the *philosophical* questioner disallows these answers as question begging. How do I know that the records and traces are reliable indicators? If I check them against other records and traces, then curiosity is merely shuttled to these further indicators. If the records are justified by their congruence with past events, then how do I know that those past events took place? Ultimately, I must somewhere enlist memories. If I try to validate memory by making predictions from it, I face cold curiosity about how I know I made those predictions. So it appears that I have no justification for my belief in the reliability of memory.

Waismann calls a misdeal: the above line of reasoning robs 'reliable' of meaning by putting all memories into doubt. If the word is meaningful, then it will *contrast* with 'unreliable'; there will be some test that sorts reliable memories from unreliable ones. In its ordinary use, 'reliable' has this essential opposition because we call a memory reliable when it corresponds to records and traces. But the groggy generality of the philosopher's doubt disengages 'reliable' from such tests, ensuring that the skeptic 'does not know himself what he is asking'. Waismann compares 'Is not all memory (including that which we call reliable) perhaps unreliable?' with 'Are not all notes including those which we call low perhaps high?' He draws a sweeping lesson:

> We can now see how the problem dissolves. We do not say to the doubter, 'You are mistaken, for what you doubt is something which is a matter of fact'. We tell him instead, 'Your question has no meaning, for you have failed to give a meaning to the words of which it is made up'. Our conclusion would be in no way affected, however much he persisted that he meant something definite by his question. We should reply: 'Then tell us what it is that you mean. If you cannot do this, then do not imagine that there is a question . . .' This example shows very clearly how a philosophical problem arises. We first of all learn to use the word 'unreliable' in cases where it has a clear meaning, where it means the opposite of 'reliable'. Thinking that we understand the word, we then use it in the question 'Is *all* memory unreliable?' But in this case what does calling a memory unreliable distinguish it from? We have failed to notice how, by asking just this question, we have destroyed the meaning of the word 'unreliable'.
>
> (1965: 21–2)

Bracket the question of whether Waismann's treatment is correct. Dwell on his *general* picture of dissolution.

Waismann's paternal tone misleadingly suggests that the rejection of something as a pseudo-question puts one beyond the reach of the querists. The dissolver presents himself as neutral, as a mediator who makes a disinterested sortie into a confused, all too human imbroglio. But this anthropological detachment and its consequent authority may be challenged by shrewd controversialists. Just as bargaining theorists have come to represent mediators as just new players in a larger game, dissolvers are fruitfully pictured as new participants in a wider issue. Instead of being guardian angels, they are intellectual entrepreneurs acting on their own agenda. Theme: dissolution is theory-laden; dissolvers are up to their raised eyebrows in common sense, science, and philosophy. Little wonder that debaters normally (and correctly) perceive the dissolution as a challenge to their shared ground. They unite against the dissolver. No wonder that the refusal to debate an issue is often the most provocative response. For example, historians emphasize Galileo's policy of searching for mathematical descriptions of phenomena rather than causes because his 'mature refusal to enter into debates over physical causes epitomizes his basic challenge to Aristotelian physics', (Galileo 1632: xxviii).

LANGUISHING FALSE NEGATIVES

Scorn of silly disputes has pummeled up a colorful history of mistakenly maligned questions. The natural sciences contain the most compelling cases. Atmospherics was the object of derision at its inception in the seventeenth century. Members of the Royal Society were widely dismissed as eccentrics with little better to do than to 'weigh the air'. Jonathan Swift lampooned the organization when he wrote of the philosophers of Laputa busy in the attempt to make sunbeams out of cucumbers.

Academia has no monopoly on closed minds. At the turn of the century, Washington newspapers ridiculed Federal funding of research on the hypothesis that malaria is carried by mosquitos. History contains many bracing changes in received opinion about what is too ridiculous to dignify with discussion. Consider the reception of Richard Martin's proposed law to prevent the abuse of horses in 1821:

> when Alderman C. Smith suggested that protection should be given to asses, there were such howls of laughter that *The Times* reporter could hear little of what was said. When the Chairman repeated this proposal, the laughter was intensified. Another member said Martin would be legislating for dogs next, which caused a further roar of mirth, and a cry 'And cats!' sent the House into convulsions.
>
> (Turner 1964: 127)

Nevertheless, in the following year Martin prevailed with a similar bill. As John Stuart Mill observed 'All great movements go through three states: ridicule, discussion, adoption.'

Folks worry less about wrongly dismissing genuine issues but there is still *some* concern. Even strong believers in the act/omission distinction add qualifications. An agreement, such as a lifeguard's contract, can impose a duty to act. Even an ill-defined position of responsibility tends to undermine the protection afforded by passivity. Politicians who practice *laissez-faire* economics are regularly rebuked for doing nothing. Moreover, the act/omission distinction is blurred by the fact that a call for inaction is itself an act. Thus the deed of classifying a project as a pseudo-problem can be rude or reckless. Recall the rumpus over Senator William Proxmire's

'Golden Fleece Awards'. The 'awards' were for wasting tax dollars on inane research. Indignant scientists protested that rather than applying a valid measure of research quality, Proxmire merely belittled projects with funny sounding titles. 'Idle' curiosity reflects biological recognition of our tendency to exclude good questions. This unmotivated sort of inquiry compensates for our prejudice for passivity by fastening on questions that are normally filtered out. Thus idle curiosity has a scanning function even though the whimsical inquirer is not trying to give spurned questions a second chance.

Although linguistic philosophers concentrate on the exposure of pseudo-problems, they never entirely neglected pseudo-pseudo-problems. This is partly because they have a professional stake in defending themselves against other dissolutionists. In 1951, many of the issues raised in Anthony Flew's first anthology of ordinary language philosophy were lambasted as pedantic trifles. Reviewers complained that these new philosophers were 'selling their truthright for a mess of verbiage'. So in the next volume, Flew upholds the authenticity of the contributors' problems:

> Some verbal disputes are trivial and idle: it would indeed be trivial to criticize the same reviewer for using the word 'verbosopher' because it is a mongrel from mixed Latin and Greek parents. But other disputes about words are not trivial at all: sometimes even when all the facts are agreed much may depend on the decision as to which word to use: and much may reasonably be said for and against. Can it or can it not be called the action of a reasonable man? Are we to say he is sane or that he is insane? So not all disputes about words are *'mere* disputes about words'.
>
> (1965: 221)

Most philosophers rightly think that an adequate analysis of a long-standing problem must 'preserve' the problem in the sense that it account for the feeling of difficulty. If a dissolver portrays the perplexed as dunces, he tangles with the principle of charity (which instructs us to maximize the rationality of interpretees).

Nevertheless, any group that views itself as possessing an important body of knowledge takes a dim view of free debate on 'settled' issues. Hence, most religions and political ideologies ban some inquiries as wasteful and misleading. Ditto for science. Witness the hostility biologists beam against the proposal that creationism be given equal time with evolutionary theory. Fear of fracas led some scientific societies to ban debate even amongst professional scientists. The founders of the Geological Society wanted to prevent meetings from becoming a forum for interminable debate. One of their regulations specified that 'all questions on which there appears to be any difference of opinion be determined by ballot at the next ordinary meeting' (Woodward 1978: 23). Another prophylactic was to have secretaries rather than authors read papers. These anti-debate measures led to minute, unsystematic, detailed descriptions of strata and exotic rocks. Another result was boredom. Alarmed by the erosion of attendance and membership, the Geological Society began to allow a time for 'conversation', then informal debate, and finally permitted publication of debates after 1868. In addition to reviving the Geological Society, the repeal of debate prohibition enhanced the level of scientific work.

Ronald Curtis (1989) has used this episode to illustrate his thesis that scientific rationality can sprout from an invisible hand process. Just as stable prices are produced without design, traditions of critical inquiry arise without anyone intending to produce them. In the case of debate, the intentions may even run in an opposed direction. Scientists imbued with Baconian ideals, strive to establish hypotheses on the basis of indisputable evidence. Conflicts between these hypotheses are discovered, so the debate-averse scientists seek more evidence. As this cycle complicates the issue, more attention is devoted to the analysis of evidence, so debate eventually breaks to the surface. Thus the good news is that genuine problems can survive premature burial.

SUCCOR FOR SUCKERS?

The usual point of calling something a pseudo-problem is to discourage further dealings with it. And indeed, when Wittgenstein completed the *Tractatus*, he quit philosophy. The puzzle is that he came back. Wittgenstein's initial explanation was that he needed to mop up minor errors. The touch-up became a renovation and the renovation a demolition. Out of the detritus of logical atomism emerged a new discipline of dialectical jujitsu which Wittgenstein jigsawed into the *Philosophical Investigations*. However, the conversion never solved the motivational mystery because this latter work preserves the dissolutional thrust of the *Tractatus*.

Can philosophy get back in business by perking up the reputation of pseudo-problems? Upbeat debunkers say that pseudo-problems are not so bad. Indeed, in some circles pre-occupation with pseudo-problems is venerated as a sign of genius. Before arguing for the thesis that Freudian psychology is a pseudo-science, Frank Cioffi genuflects: 'A successful pseudo-science is a great intellectual achievement' (1970: 471). Stephen Barker denies that he belittles David Hume when he attacks the project of justifying inductive inference:

> One can regard the problem of induction as a conceptual con-
> fusion and yet still regard it as a deep and important confusion.
> There is nothing shallow or trivial about the problem as it appears
> in Hume's thought, and it is greatly to Hume's credit that he had
> the intellectual penetration without which he could not have
> fallen into his conceptual difficulties about induction. We do not
> necessarily denigrate a philosopher's achievement when we say
> that he was a victim of conceptual confusion. And we do not
> necessarily waste our own time when we devote lengthy study to
> the unravelling of pseudo-problems.
>
> (1974: 61)

Barker is right about there being brilliant pseudo-problems. But that is an incomplete rejoinder. We treasure brilliance for the questions it answers, not the pseudo-questions it foists upon us. It is not as if Hume were some precocious schoolboy whose clever error fore-shadows future insights. If induction is a brilliant pseudo-problem, then it is more like Hume led two centuries of our best minds on an expedition that only served to squander their wit on infertile ground. Things *diagnostic* of good things need not themselves be good. An adequate defense of pseudo-problems must explain how they cause improvements or how their suppression would cause harm.

Another qualm: if pseudo-problems were predictably helpful, then shouldn't we try to put ourselves under their spell? Unfortu-nately, you can't try to solve a problem that you regard as meaning-less. And in any case, if pseudo-problems did benefit us on average, how could we recognize their fertility? Recall the joke about the wife who begs a psychiatrist to cure her husband: 'He thinks he's a chicken!' 'That's terrible! How long has he been this way?' 'Two years.' 'Why didn't you see me sooner?' 'We needed the eggs.'

Wittgenstein operated on the conviction that all philosophical problems were pseudo-problems that had to be cured like diseases ('mental cramps'). Good philosophy is a matter of ridding ourselves of bad philosophy. Once the pathological philosophy is cured, philo-sophy is finished. Sure, the therapy can be complicated and require skill. But only in the way untying knots requires patience and skill.

The untied knot is merely returned to its original state. Nothing new is produced by this corrective process. Its point is to clear away the pseudo-problems that bedevil our thinking. Although this is a negative goal, it can still be of a great value. Just compare clarity (absence of confusion) with health (absence of disease).

But even those happy to concede the value of clarity will scout for cheaper ways to attain it. 'An ounce of prevention is worth a pound of cure.' So when John Wisdom wheeled out Wittgenstein's dissolutional themes in 1936, he explicitly raised the question of whether an anti-puzzlement drug should be prescribed (1969: 41). Wittgenstein would have rejected this psycho-pharmacological regimen: 'In philosophizing we may not *terminate* a disease of thought. It must run its natural course, and *slow* cure is all important' (1967: §382). There are four reasons for this conservative prognosis. First, Wittgenstein intimates that there is an ineffable insight to be obtained by first feeling the problem and then working through it. Something is *shown*. An east wind blows: 'Before you have studied Zen, mountains are mountains and rivers are rivers; while you are studying it, mountains are no longer mountains and rivers are no longer rivers; but once you have Enlightenment, mountains are once again mountains and rivers are rivers' (Suzuki 1956: xvi–xvii).

Second, Wittgenstein admired our tendency to soar afoul of linguistic limits. 'Go the bloody *hard* way' he told Rush Rhees (author of the aptly titled *Without Answers*). A philosopher is like a bird fluttering against the bars of its cage. The drive for free flight commands respect. Immanuel Kant spoke with similar tenderness of the bent of mind that leads to transgression of the limits of experience. Enchantment with lost causes is by no means confined to philosophers. Oliver Wendell Holmes voiced this romantic defeatism when he wrote: 'A man may fulfil the object of his existence by asking a question he cannot answer, and attempting a task he cannot achieve.'

The third reason for not taking the anti-philosophy pill is that it would destroy something else of value. This can be interpreted two ways. First, asking pseudo-questions might *cause* benefits. Many historians of science trace real sciences to pseudo-sciences. They say astrology led to astronomy, alchemy to chemistry, and phrenology to neurology. Perhaps you must ask the wrong questions to ask the right ones. Wrong questions may be needed to eliminate false paths or to root out hazards. (Sailors are fond of observing that every ship is a minesweeper – once!) And indeed, some pseudo-questions confer a negative service: they lead to intellectual jams that compel us to backtrack to an insight. Alasdair MacIntyre speculates that

The first steps toward producing a logical grammar of the verb 'to be' perhaps necessarily involved assimilating the different senses and uses of the words, and of consequently becoming caught up in paradox and learning how to free oneself. When Aristotle, in Book I of the *Metaphysics*, clarified earlier errors, he was able to do so only because he had learned from the efforts and missteps of Parmenides and Plato.

(1967: 273)

The theme of error as a necessary stepping stone has been applied by Paul Feyerabend (1965) to the history of physics. Other pseudo-questions entice us into inquiry by leading us to overestimate rewards. In *The Gay Science*, Friedrich Nietzsche sticks up for the misleading advertising:

Do you really believe that the sciences would ever have originated and grown if the way had not been prepared by magicians, alchemists, astrologers and witches whose promises and pretensions first had to create a thirst, a hunger, a taste for *hidden* and *forbidden* powers? Indeed, infinitely more had to be *promised* than could ever be fulfilled in order that anything at all might be fulfilled in the realms of knowledge.

(1882/7: §300)

A final qualm about the smart balm: there may be a *common cause* that generates philosophy and another effect that does have value. Johannes Kepler's career illustrates how an eccentric world view enhances the recognition of recondite patterns. For largely religious 'reasons', Kepler became a Pythagorean mystic who believed that the universe is governed by precise mathematical laws. This preconception led him to ask a zodiac of bizarre questions: what is the relationship between the color of a planet and its distance? If two planets form an angle *n* degrees at your birth, how is your life affected? How do musical harmonies relate to the 'harmonic' motion of planets? However, the very same math mania led him to an extremely fruitful question. For it led him to notice that planets nearer the sun orbit more frequently and so to query 'What is the precise relationship between orbital speed and distance from the sun? The answer is Kepler's second law: a line drawn from the sun to a planet passes over equal areas in equal times. Thank goodness there was no Gilbert Ryle around to disabuse Johannes of metaphysical misconceptions!

Revolutionaries triumph by superimposing an alien conceptual framework on recalcitrant data. Mechanists picture animals as machines, meteorologists treat air as a fluid, cognitive scientists operate as if the brain were a computer. The scientists go beyond casual metaphor; they push the analogy and then push some more. Forcing puzzling phenomena into familiar shapes leads to mixed results. It is impractical to demand that only good questions emerge from such ruthless reductionism. So pseudo-problems are an inevitable spillover of progress; the marketplace of ideas has its own form of pollution. As they say in Pittsburgh, it's the smell of progress. Of course, this does not make any particular pseudo-problem inevitable or permanent. In time, parsimony leads scientists to abandon the idle aspects of the model (that is, those that fail to stimulate further fruitful inquiry). Indeed, the revolutionary's original picture eventually bleaches out into literality. For example, Kepler originally viewed the solar system as a Christian allegory (sun = God, earth = Christ, space = Holy Ghost, etc.) but this spirituality was gradually bled out of Kepler's original vision to yield the dead matter picture of Victorian physics.

Pseudo-problems can be *good* news. They can be a sign that one of the preconditions of innovation has been satisfied. A loosening of constraints is frequently needed to shake a stifling mind-set. Restricted thinking proceeds safely but unambitiously, along straight, well-trodden paths. Our desire for the fruits of new thinking might lead us to encourage intellectual risk taking. In *Prose Observations*, Samuel Butler remarks: 'As all Feats of Activity are the more admired, the nearer they come to Danger, so is all Speculative wit the nearer it comes to Nonsense.' Conceptual crashes might even reassure us that our research policies are sufficiently tolerant just as occasional defaults reassure bankers that their loan policy is not overly cautious.

Even if we grant that philosophy bestows all of these bounties, it could not survive if everyone became persuaded that all philosophical problems are pseudo-problems. For once one becomes convinced that a question has no answer, one cannot try to answer it. Of course, one could go through the motions and pretend one is trying to answer it. But recognition of an impossibility precludes the attempt to bring it about.

Why did philosophers take such a keen interest in the possibility that philosophy was composed solely of pseudo-problems? Perhaps philosophers were fascinated by the prospect of total dissolution in the way mountaineers sitting on a precipice become entranced by the possibility of jumping into the abyss.

But before delving into motivating lunacies, note that philosophers have *rational* grounds for interest for Wittgenstein's debunking. (Dissolution is not de-worming.) Philosophers have a timeless wariness of traditional problems. Their grounds for circumspection are soberly inductive. The longer a problem resists solution, the more evidence we have that it will continue to resist solution. If a problem is insoluble, then something is wrong with either the problem or the people beset by the problem. In either case, we have ample reason to maintain flight distance. This wariness makes one receptive to efforts to show that large families of problems are defective. Wittgenstein's working hypothesis, that all traditional philosophical problems are pseudo-problems, can be seen as a bold generalization of traditional circumspection.

A second basis for interest in the thesis is that dissolution is a way of *rationally* resolving a problem. One can shut down disputes through various irrational and arational techniques. Bickering children can be separated or scolded into silence, scientific controversy can wind down by attrition, political opposition can be dispatched to re-education camps and psychiatric hospitals. But Wittgenstein wants us to hear the voice of reason. The philosopher is to be *argued out* of his problem. Contrast Wittgenstein's advice on the problem of induction, the external world, and personal identity with David Hume's. Skeptical worries plagued Hume in the study but they could be banished by a cheerful game of whist in the parlor. Whereas Wittgenstein tried to promote an insight, Hume extolled the therapeutic effects of submersion into everyday life. Wittgenstein strove for a state closer to Sextus Empiricus' *epoche* – tranquil indecision that results from a policy of matching each argument with an equally potent counterargument. But unlike Sextus Empiricus, Wittgenstein denies the existence of hidden answers.

Here is how things stand. Common sense and intellectual history give us ample reason to be interested in question quality. Since we have a stronger aversion to actively pursuing a bad question than failing to pursue a good one, this interest most strongly manifests itself as desire to avoid pseudo-problems. This nay-saying is tempered by two concerns. The major worry is that we want to minimize our rejections of good problems. The minor consideration is that there may be some benefits to pseudo-problems, so they needn't be as bad as they look.

The next step would appear to be the classification of pseudo-problems. For just as physicians make people healthy by studying diseases, thinkers purify their research by pigeonholing research flaws. However, taxonomy is premature until we are sure that the subject is free of ambiguity. Senses of words should not be confused with species of a genus. The next two chapters shall vindicate this caution by exposing the hyper-ambiguity of 'pseudo-problem'.

2 Get 'real'!

I don't want reality. I want magic.

(Blanche DuBois)

'Pseudo-problem': highly evocative, highly eviscerative, highly equivocal. That's why I shall devote this entire chapter to clarifying 'pseudo' and kindred expressions. Analysis of the complete expression, 'pseudo-problem' is reserved for chapter 3.

The mission of the hour is to establish that this circumspection is warranted. (This is in turn a subgoal toward the larger project of de-fanging Wittgensteinian metaphilosophy.) Immediate headway is made by noting that 'pseudo' belongs to a coven of terms huddled around the caldron of negation. Numbered among this dark clan are proven mischief-makers such as 'nothing', 'nonexistent', 'omission', and 'illusion'. The dangers posed by debunkers will be chronicled by examining their sway over a wide range of philosophical issues. Some of these controversies (free will, paternalism, forgery, false consciousness) will be addressed in passing. Others (false belief, false pleasure, perversion, pseudo-science) merit their own sections. One of this chapter's themes is that these apparently disparate issues are related, so the study of debunkers makes these topics mutually illuminating. Balancing the message of unity is another of diversity: debunkers are highly ambiguous and so entice the unwary into all manner of equivocation.

INFERENTIAL TRAFFIC CONTROL

W. C. Fields once said that scientists have discovered that the universe is composed of three elements: oxygen, nitrogen, and horse shit. Philosophers have not neglected this third element in their quest for a general description of the universe. But despite their long 'unmasking' tradition, they have yet to apply the strategy of semantic ascent to this subject – an omission I shall rectify forthwith. That is, my direct objects of study are debunking words: decoy, dummy, factitious, fake, false, mock, nominal, pseudo, phony, sham, specious, spurious, unreal. Debunkers also include nonwords such as scare quotes and phrases such as 'so-called'.

J. L. Austin gave debunkers passing notice in his study of 'real' and other words of assurance such as 'authentic', 'definitely', and 'true'. Debunkers and assurers should be studied together because assurers are inferential intimates; denying one tends to commit you to the other. They also have parallel semantic, syntactic, and pragmatic ambiguities. So it should be expected that insights about one group of words translate into insights about the other.

Substantive theories of 'real' and the redundancy theory

'Real' has been thought to designate a *property* such as permanence (Plato) or rationality (Hegel). It has also been defined as a relation. For example, Anthony Quinton (1962: 144) takes the real things to be those which it pays to monitor. Since changes in beliefs and desires alter what merits minding, Quinton's subjectivity entrains counterintuitive shifts in reality. The standard remedy for this onto-logical instability is to relativize the psychological states to an ideal observer. C. S. Peirce (1940: 247f.) is well known for defining reality in terms of the conclusions that would be reached by a community of ideal inquirers.

The redundancy theory of truth denies that 'true' has any semantic meaning (Horwich 1990, Grover 1992). This minimalism says that '*p* is true' and *p* have the same truth conditions. Consequently, 'true' can be eliminated from the language without *semantic* loss. My position is that the core usage of every assurer is devoid of semantic meaning. Thus it is a generalized redundancy theory.

Be true to 'true'! Distinguish absence of meaning from negative meaning. When my look-alike, Roland Hall (1963), characterized 'real' as an excluder term, he only meant to deny that it designates a property. 'Sober' is an excluder because it is equivalent to 'not drunken', 'idle' because it means 'not working'. Hall's thesis is that although 'real' has no positive meaning, it does have meaning as an 'openly ambiguous' attributive term. I differ. My thesis is that 'real' has neither positive nor negative meaning.

Redundancy theorists admit that 'true' has senses in which it is not redundant. For example, tires are true when properly aligned and lovers are true when faithful. The redundancy thesis for 'true' only targets one broad pattern of usage that has been the site of heavy metaphysical transactions. The same can be said for other assurers, such as 'real' (and 'really' and 'reality'). In one peripheral sense, 'real' means 'very'. (Actually, I'll try to finesse this sense away later but let's keep things simple for now.) Thus some hot baths are not hot enough to be real hot baths. This intensifier sense of 'real' is only philosophically interesting insofar as it sows confusion. For example, a conflation of the intensifier and metaphysical usages gives fallacious support to the doctrine that there are degrees of reality. The conflation also misleads us into thinking that only extreme instances of *F*-ness are *F*s (Blose 1980). Psychological egoists exploit this perfectionist temptation when challenging us chumps for an example of altruism unsullied by the prospects of a subtle *quid pro quo*.

Is 'real' *ambiguous*? Compare it to 'darn'. In 'Scrotella must darn socks', 'darn' means mending by stitching. But in 'Darn those mice!', 'darn' functions as a semantically meaningless expletive. There aren't two *senses* to 'darn', so there is no ambiguity. Damn it. Well, let's coin another word to mark this duality of use. Call a term 'semisemous' (on analogy with polysemous) when it has both a meaningful and a meaningless usage. Thus 'darn' and 'well' – and 'real' – are semisemous words. Each has two usages but only one of those usages is a sense.

The redundancy theory shocks those who take ' "*p*" is true = p' to imply that 'true' is as meaningless as 'prue'. But this semantic eliminativist credits 'true' with syntactic roles. 'True' as uttered in response to an assertion, is an abbreviated repetition such as 'Ditto' and 'Amen'. Really! Relate 'true' to pronouns of laziness such as 'it' in 'Mia likes her dog; it is a pit bull.' 'It' can also function as a variable as in 'If anything moves, shoot it.' The same role is filled by 'true' in 'Everything Abe said is true.' 'Real' is the lazy man's adjective just as 'thing' is his linguistic crutch for a noun. Advertisers combined these surrogates into a masterpiece of nondescription: 'Coke is the real thing.'

Responding 'True' also has a pragmatic dimension: one is thereby performing the speech act of *endorsing* the previous utterance. To appreciate how 'true' can have pragmatic meaning without semantic meaning, compare it to the device of emphasis. (There are a few semantic theories of emphasis but they are refuted in Boer 1979.) The truth conditions of 'Bubba is big' and 'Bubba is *big*' are identical but they have different conditions under which they may be asserted. A parallel point can be made on behalf of 'Who the heck is she?' Adding 'the heck' after an interrogative pronoun does not affect which question is asked but it does increase the force of query. (Notice that this interrogative punch can be strengthened by selecting stronger interpolations: where the devil is she? how the hell did she get loose? why the #%+$@* did she do that?) When I stress Bubba's bigness, I invite my audience to believe that Bubba is a clear case of a big man, that he is not being counted big on some technicality. Assurers gravitate toward the most salient paradigms, hence locutions such as 'If you think the Mrs is big at the end of her second trimester, just wait until she's truly pregnant!' Just as emphasis comes in degrees, assurers come in degrees. Calling something an *F par excellence* is stronger than calling it a real *F*. The hierarchy continues: paradigm, exemplary, authentic, genuine, model, standard, plain, ordinary. These vary in how thickly they lubricate inferences from the thing's *F*-ness. This variation in degrees of assurance provides a second fallacious source for the degrees of reality doctrine.

Arresting inferences

Another fertile comparison is between assurers and 'catalyst words': although, anyhow, but, even, however, nevertheless, yet. Catalyst words are primarily devoted to the efficient transfer of information. They do not constitute information. As H. P. Grice (1989) notes, 'She is poor but honest' has the same truth conditions as 'She is poor and honest'. However, they are not pragmatically synonymous because 'but' signals that what follows is contrary to the conversational drift. Assurers and debunkers also convey conventional implicatures. They are pragmatic devices that encourage and discourage inferences.

Assurers are simpler than debunkers because they have no semantic meaning at all. (Debunkers are enriched kinds of negation, hence they are not semantically redundant.) The truth conditions for '*x* is a real *F*' are identical to those of '*x* is an *F*'. Consequently, all real *F*s are *F*s and all *F*s are real *F*s. Of course, if I step up to a stranger and aver that my watch is real (without any previous context of doubt), then I have spoken infelicitously (but not falsely!). The explanation is that '*x* is *F*' and '*x* is a real *F*' (or '*x* is really *F*') have different assertability conditions. When you describe *x* as a real *F*, you implicate that *x* is free of the sort of peculiarities that imperil inferences from its *F*-ness. The same idea explains how obvious tautologies can be (pragmatically) informative. When an instructor says of a fluorescent condom, 'It is what it is', he encourages his audience to go by appearances and soothes worries about hidden divergences from familiar condoms.

The role of 'real' is to regulate inference. When you know *x* is *F*, you are always entitled to infer what is strictly implied by '*x* is *F*'. But we are usually interested in making looser inferences. The fact that something is a car does not guarantee it can outrun a dachshund. Being a pear does not necessitate edibility. But these properties are associated by statistical correlation, stereotype, and norms. The heuristic function of 'real' is to assure us that inferences to these less tightly linked properties will go well. If I describe a race as a real race and you learn that it was fixed, then you can complain that I have misled you but you cannot literally say the rigged race was not a race.

As in politics, assurances in one area tend to be at the expense of neighboring areas. The assurer in 'Chris admired Ronald Reagan but he was a real Democrat' stifles the inference that Chris voted for Reagan. Inferential space is crowded. Assurers tend to have an indirect debunking effect because making room for the inferences from *F* crowds out inferences from *G*.

Debunkers differ from assurers in that they contribute to truth conditions. (Thus 'phooey' doesn't qualify as a debunker because its negativism is nonsemantic.) Debunkers also have several philosophically significant senses that are much prone to conflation. These semantic divisions track the pragmatic and syntactic ambiguities of denial. Study of logic reinforces the picture of denial being solely concerned with the truth-value of what was said. But sometimes denial is denial of the *assertability* of a statement. If I say your Toyota Corolla equals or exceeds my Ford Escort's fuel efficiency, then you might deny my claim on the grounds that the Corolla's fuel efficiency clearly exceeds the Escort's. This kind of denial cannot be aimed at flipping a truth-value. For it entails the truth of what I said! A second point: saying '*x* is not *F*' conveys the implicature that *x* is apt to be misclassified as an *F*. Thus the use of a debunker is only appropriate when the speaker has evidence that there is the danger of error. This explains the absurdity of 'My parrot is a pseudo-oyster.' It also explains how something can fail to be a sham *F* without being a real *F*: jam is not sham spam but nor is jam real spam. Thirdly, we must also be wary of the *syntactic* duality of '*b* is not *F*'. In the previous paragraph, we read '*b* is not *F*' as $(\exists x)(x = b \;\&\; \sim Fb)$. But it also has the weaker reading $\sim(\exists x)(x = b \;\&\; Fb)$, which can be made true by *b* not existing.

Debunkers aim at avoiding error rather than getting truth

Most words serve the positive goal of getting truth. They add information that produces new true beliefs or remove inferential friction. Debunkers serve the negative goal of avoiding error. Error is reduced by both prevention and remedy. Since an ounce of prevention is worth a pound of cure, we append warning labels (bogus, phony, unreal) to the menacing term – nipping the error in the bud. The point is to post a cognitive danger zone. Debunkers are the warning flares of language. They are myth markers.

As Kent Bach (1984) points out, our cognitive limitations require that we engage in default reasoning. Instead of proceeding explicitly from premises to conclusion, we adopt the first idea that comes to mind as long as it is not followed by the thought of a reason against it or another explanation. This 'inference to the first unchallenged alternative' works well because we are sensitive to the signs that warrant second thoughts. We can proceed automatically because alarms will sound when the intellectual terrain becomes rugged. If alerted, we only delve into suspicious areas. So our reasoning will still have a ragged texture because the routine steps are skipped and because we break off reasoning when things settle down. Our detection of cognitive hazards is imperfect. We overlook warning signs and make reckless snap decisions. We can also become overly cautious and get bogged down in unproductive circumspection. My suggestion is that debunkers and assurers curtail these opposite errors. Debunkers put us in a heightened state of linguistic alert. Assurers bring us down to a more relaxed state.

Roughly (because this conflates several closely related senses of the debunker) '*x* is a pseudo-*F*' means '*x* is *F*' is associated with error. The nature of the association is the same as that between 'unhealthy' and disease. Under the primary reading, '*x* is unhealthy' is applied to a diseased individual. But there are secondary readings under which it applies to the causes of disease (unhealthy diet) or the signs of disease (unhealthy urine). Likewise, the primary reading of '*x* is a pseudo-*F*' is that belief in '*x* is *F*' would be a mistake. Suppose Allen passes himself off as a member of the Minudo singing group. Allen is a pseudo-Minudo because he encourages the error of believing he is a Minudo. We can illustrate a secondary reading by supposing that Bernardo got a position in the group through nepotism, despite his feeble singing and dancing. Bernardo is a pseudo-Minudo because the (albeit true) belief that 'Bernardo is a Minudo' causes error; we are apt to overestimate his Minudoid talents. Lastly, imagine Carlos is talented but got in because of a hiring mistake. Carlos is legally a Minudo, is quite up to Minudo standards, but 'Carlos is a Minudo' owes its truth to an error.

FACES OF DEBUNKERS

The basic thrust of calling *x* a pseudo-*F* is to deny something that people are inclined to say, i.e., that *x* is an *F*. But there are four ways to deny *x* is *F*. The first is a warning that *x* is apt to be *misclassified*, that it is a non-*F* with features that make it resemble an *F*. A second rebuff repudiates the assumption that *x exists*. In that case, you are cautioning against a referential error rather than a mis-chararacterization. A third form of denial draws attention to the *inappropriateness* of asserting that *x* is *F*. Now your principal worry is not about the truth of '*x* is *F*'. Instead, you are trying to prevent the audience from making a natural inference. These three paths of denial are incorporated into the first three senses of debunkers. (For extended illustrations of these three senses see Sorensen 1991b.) A fourth sense simply assigns the *truth-value* of falsehood to the thing in question.

Notice that in this truth-value sense, a pseudo-*F* is always an *F*. Thus it contrasts with the misclassifier and existential senses because they *preclude* *F*-ness. The truth-value sense also contrasts with the misleader sense because it entails *F*-ness rather than merely being compatible with *F*-ness. A further difference is that the other three senses are attributive; they are only meaningful when modifying another predicate. When a debunker is used to counter a misclassification, existential error, or misleadingness, we can always ask 'A pseudo what?' or 'A phony what?' or whatever. Contrary to Holden Caulfield's usage in *Catcher in the Rye*, people cannot be just phonies, they have to be phony somethings. The most charitable interpretation of such dangling debunkers assign 'phony' a syntactic role. Thus 'All salesmen are phonies' gets translated as '(*x*)(*F*) if *x* is a salesman who appears to be *F*, then he is not *F*' where *F* ranges over some suitably restricted class of properties. Likewise 'All saints are genuine' can be rendered '$(x)(F)$ if x is a saint who appears to be F, then he is F.' The search for the property of phoniness would be just as wrong-headed as G. E. Moore's (1953: 236–54) search for the property of reality. But in the truth-value sense, the 'x is an F G' construction does decompose into meaningful conjuncts. The wary detective's 'x is a false tip' entails 'x is false and x is a tip'.

Confusion between the truth-value sense and other senses is manifested when students turn to the topic of logical positivism: beginners frequently misconstrue 'pseudo-proposition' as ascribing a truth-value. They find it paradoxical that the falsity of a statement *ensures* that it is a genuine proposition. 'False analogy' almost always features the misleader sense of 'false' but is sometimes thought to be attributing a truth-value. Sometimes the equivocation is courted as with 'false consciousness'. In one sense, it means self-deceptive identification with the interests of a higher class. But the expression encourages the truth-value reading which implies a *mistaken* identification. Recognition of the multiple senses of 'false' is an asset to noncognitivist positions. For instance, ethical noncognitivism can explain away talk of false moral judgments as a non-truth-value usage. Responding 'False' to 'Suicide is always immoral' might be equivalent to shaking your finger.

A welcome check on the accuracy of this analysis is the parallel behavior of assurer words such as 'true', 'authentic', and 'genuine'. Debunkers warn us of trouble, assurers tell us not to worry. Hence, assurers have four kinds of (pragmatic) meaning. Either they assure us of the classification's accuracy or that the thing in question does in fact exist, or that it is appropriate to call the thing an F, or finally that the thing in question is a truth. Assurers are also instructive when their behavior interacts with that of debunkers. For negating one tends to activate the other. Thus, learning that a problem is not real leads us to infer it is a pseudo-problem and vice versa.

The epistemic relativity of debunkers

Since mistakes require mistakers, debunkers require relativization to a class of cognizers. Often the reference group is everyone in the speech community. But variations abound. Sometimes, the domain of thinkers covers only epistemic subnormals. For example, pseudo-isochromatic plates are plates that look alike to individuals with color vision deficiencies (and so are used to test for visual disorders). Paradoxically, debunkers are more commonly relativized to epistemic elites. Only specialists are in a position to make the sort of error 'pseudo' warns against in the following cases: pseudoconhydrine, pseudo-ceratitis, pseudo-perianth. A little knowledge is a dangerous thing because it makes you inferentially active.

On other occasions, we relativize to people with uncommon perspectives. Decoy airfields fool no one on the ground. They earn 'decoy' by their propensity for fooling enemy bombers. Nor should our anthropocentricism lead us to overlook animal perspectives. The world of perceiving organisms is a world of deception; human beings have no monopoly on camouflage, diversion, and mimicry. When an entomologist describes a butterfly's appendage as a false head, his universe of discourse only contains the butterfly's predators.

Syntactic ambiguities of debunkers

Thank the redundancy theory for tipping us off about the link between assurers and anaphora. But this deflationary account of truth also orients us toward structural insights about debunkers.

First scope. When an adjective is added to a noun phrase, there is an ambiguity as to what it modifies, e.g. 'big car salesman'. Since debunkers and assurers belong to this group of general adjectives, they often exhibit the same syntactic ambiguity, for instance, 'a fake silver toaster'. Many biological uses of debunkers intend the holistic reading. 'False vampire bat' must be read this way because it refers to bats that are easily mistaken for vampire bats. However, most debunkers only modify one word deep: decoy duck museum, pseudo random number generator, false claims statute, mock trial club.

Next consider ellipsis. When the Beech-Nut company was fined in 1987 for fraudulently selling a 'chemical cocktail' as apple juice, the independent supplier of the substitute was reviled as a bogus supplier. Here 'bogus supplier' is short for 'bogus apple juice supplier'. Counterfeit labeling spawns many elliptical debunkers: fake watch, phony jeans, specious document. The price of brevity is confusion over what the debunker modifies. The hazard is heightened by our practice of diluting the description of the debunker's target. If I know that the dyed grape sitting atop my pudding is a fake cherry, I may identify it with a less specific term – as fake fruit. Now there is the danger that my audience will think that the debunker is operating on 'fruit'. In fact, 'fruit' is only being used to identify (rather than to characterize) the object. People are especially likely to use general terms when a variety of things have been faked. The 1988 Blabscam scandal centered on 'phony guests' who faked various titillating occupations, views, and diseases in order to appear on talk shows. These imposters were guests but they were not sex surrogates and men-haters.

The operand/identifier ambiguity creates a false sense of unity. Consider Daniel Boorstin's use of 'pseudo-event' in *The Image: A Guide to Pseudo-Events in America*. The book appears to be about a kind of event like musical events and political events. But instead we find a hodgepodge of disparate kinds of happenings grappled together under the umbrella term 'pseudo-event'. Boorstin's first chapter features pseudo-news events. Unlike natural events such as earthquakes and floods, these affairs are contrived by boosters who profit their cause through publicity. Boorstin's second chapter examines 'the human pseudo-event', a deed that causes a wide but erroneous reputation. This is followed by a chapter concerning events that are staged to enhance tourism, a fourth on misleading distillations of original works, another on image-making, advertising stunts, and self-fulfilling prophecies, and a summarizing chapter on the 'American illusion'. The only way to understand these diverse things as pseudo-events is to assign 'event' an identifying role rather than the role of operand. In particular chapters, the operand role holds. But not throughout Boorstin's book. Only once we resign ourselves to interpreting the 'event' in 'pseudo-event' as merely identifying events that are pseudo-Fs, pseudo-Gs, and pseudo-Hs, does the absence of a unified subject matter come to light. Suppose Boorstin writes a sequel *The Truth: A Guide to Real Events in America* about events that are real Fs, real Gs, and real Hs. After we detect the operand/identifier equivocation, Boorstin's thesis of massive cultural illusion looks like a microcosm of what he laments.

Real vagueness

In some cases, the operand is difficult to specify. When viewers point out that the guy in the commercial is 'not a real person', they only have an amorphous idea of what they are debunking. He's an actor as opposed to what? A pedestrian? A consumer? You can also stump people by asking 'Is this a real F?' out of context. Austin opines that

> The wile of the metaphysician consists in asking 'Is it a real table?' (a kind of object which has no obvious way of being

phony) and not specifying or limiting what may be wrong with
it, so that I feel at a loss 'how to prove' it *is* a real one. It is the
use of the word 'real' in this manner that leads us on to the
supposition that 'real' has a single meaning ('the real world'
'material objects'), and that a highly profound and puzzling one.
Instead, we should insist always on specifying with what 'real' is
being contrasted – 'not what' I shall have to show it is, in order
to show it is 'real': and then usually we shall find some specific,
less fatal, word, appropriate to the particular case, to substitute
for 'real'.

(1961: 55–6)

Adding contextual cues rescues some reality questions from meaninglessness but others strike Austin as unsalvageable. His first recalcitrant case is hypothetical, featuring a fish that is vividly multi-
colored at its normal depth of a thousand feet but is a muddy sort
of grayish white when placed in normal sunlight. Which is its real
color? Austin (1962: 66) unbags further enigmata which I shall
variously quote and paraphrase into the following list:

1 What is the real taste of saccharine? (In tea, it tastes sweet; taken
   straight, it tastes bitter.)
2 What is the real color of a chameleon? The moon? The sky?
3 What is the real color of a *pointilliste* meadow composed of blue
   and yellow dots that look green from viewing at a distance?
4 What is the real color of an after-image?
5 What is the real shape of a cloud? Of a cat?

Austin toys with the cat question by asking whether the shape moves
when the cat does and whether the shape is smooth or serrated
(because of individual hairs): 'It is pretty obvious that there is *no*
answer to these questions – no rules according to which, no procedure by which, answers are to be determined' (1962: 67). Thus
Austin denies the exhaustivity of the appearance/reality distinction.
He thinks some things are neither real nor unreal.

Austin's ontological twilight zone is outlawed by my guiding principle that x is F if and only if x is a real F. For the conjunction of
this principle and excluded middle implies that each individual is a
real F or not a real F. My defense of the appearance/reality dichotomy begins with a distinction between the absence of rules or relata
and the absence of uniquely *salient* rules or relata. Austin's questions stump us because they involve ties between equally good
relativizations. With the fishy fish we are torn between loyalty to

a thing's natural environment and conditions optimal for detailed inspection by humans. We are tempted to say that saccharine is really sweet because it is intended to be tasted when mixed with a beverage. On the other hand, we also feel inclined to say it is bitter because we favor studies of things in their pure, 'unadulterated' condition. The pointillist picture also pits the intended observation condition against a clinical inspection: this time a 'close-up' view. Cats, clouds, and chameleons are puzzling because they lack a predominant color or shape.

What we are witnessing is the conflict vagueness of 'real', not a lapse into meaninglessness. A term is vague when it has borderline cases. Something is a borderline F when no inquiry could ever settle whether it is an F. As a redundancy theorist I hold that x is a borderline real F if and only if x is a borderline F. In the case of threshold vagueness, the borderline cases gradually arise as one reaches a certain quantity. Thus Eubulides presented the sorites paradox by supposing that grains of salt are added one by one until a heap forms. When did the heap first form? However, our discussion features *conflict* vagueness. This qualitative kind of vagueness arises from the clash of rival rules. Does the surface of this page weigh anything? We are apt to feel ambivalent because 'surface' might be defined as the outermost layer of the page or might be defined as an abstract boundary between the page and its surroundings. Or suppose we are waiting for an elevator on the fifth floor. You want to go up, I want to go down. It's going down. Is it going the wrong way? Here there is unclarity as to whose desires 'wrong' should be relativized. So we don't know whether the elevator is *really* going the wrong way – because we don't know whether it is going the wrong way.

One might object: how can 'real' be vague if it has no semantic meaning? The reply is that the vagueness of 'real' is completely parasitic on the vagueness of the substantive it modifies. Saccharine is a borderline case of 'really sweet' because it is a borderline case of 'sweet'. 'Really' is just going along for the ride.

Austin illustrates the relativity of 'real' with locutions that vary the modified substantive, that is, a decoy duck can be a real lure. His theme can be amplified with examples involving the selfsame substantive. Suppose Amy reunites her adopted son, Sid, with his birth mother Bertha. Since Sid resembles both Amy and Bertha, a confused observer could be clued in with 'Amy is Sid's real mother; Bertha gave him up for adoption.' But the observer could also be straightened out with 'Bertha is Sid's real mother; Amy only adopted him.'

Perhaps, when assurers grade something along a single scale they mark intensities. 'Some hot baths are not real hot baths' can be made consistent by supposing that 'real' jacks up the standard for 'hot'. (This would obviate the earlier inelegant postulation of a separate sense of 'real' equivalent to 'very'.) The mid-sentence shift can also occur from assurer to debunker as in 'Most real Rubens are fake Rubens.' This was an art historian's quip as he explained that Rubens' paintings are easily forged because he would simply touch up the work of apprentices and sign them.

In addition to privileging certain points on a single scale, 'real' can privilege one unrelated perspective over another. A metaphysician can seize the initiative by quietly elevating one such context. What does a woman really look like? As she appears when dressed up or when naked and without make-up? Rousseau presupposes that cosmetics conceal. A gentleman of Platonic sensibilities will view the feminine arts as idealizing correctives that bring out the true woman by smoothing away distracting imperfections. Substantive theories of 'real' can be thought of as insightful but confused perceptions of common vantage points from which it is relativized. Ideal-observer theories are impressed with relativizations to optimal examination conditions. Conventionalists are attached to the intended presentation. Naturalists are attracted to normal observation conditions.

Metaphysicians also use assurers to precisify along the great fault lines of language. Think of all the words that are indeterminate between an attempt reading and a stronger, result reading ('Did the impetus theory *explain* motion?'), between requiring at least n and requiring exactly n ('Is an equilateral triangle an isosceles triangle?'), between hole and filler interpretations ('If you remove the glass, do you remove the *window*?'). Assurers can be used to colonize these systematic indeterminacies: 'Is a sum in the head less real than a sum on paper? – Perhaps one is inclined to say some such thing; but one can get oneself to think the opposite as well by telling oneself: paper, ink, etc. are only logical constructions out of our sense data' (Wittgenstein 1953: §366). The precisification may transpire within a couple of paragraphs. In the Second Meditation, René Descartes begins using 'sensation' in a way that implies a body. But as soon as he needs to accommodate the skeptical possibility that he has no body Descartes avers that 'what is properly called my sensation' is an act of consciousness. From that point onward,

Descartes treats psychological terms as qualia markers – the interiorizing reading most conducive to dualism. In *World Hypotheses* Stephen Pepper argued that metaphysical systems are founded on root metaphors. A Nietzschean vagueness theorist could trace metaphysics to root precisifications.

Rules for relativization may also discombobulate by making the choice of relata so compulsory that we acquire the impression that no relativization is occurring. For example, 'move' looks absolute because there are ordinarily no rivals to relativizing to earth. The same mechanism makes 'Troy is real' appear to feature an absolute sense of 'real' – one in which it means exists. After all, 'Troy is real' does not arouse a curious 'Troy is a real what?' (This is the pattern of Don Locke's (1967: 95) attack on Austin's claim that 'real' is always substantive hungry.) However, we reality relativists insist that 'Troy is real' is short for 'Troy is a real existing thing.' Therefore, we agree that 'Troy is real' means 'Troy exists' but only because of ellipsis, not because of a *sense* in which 'real' is synonymous with 'exists'. The audience does not request specification of the relatum because the meaning is de-sensitizingly obvious. After all, detectives searching for counterfeit money do not ask 'Real what?' when one of them says 'These notes are real.' Normal discourse is about existing things, so 'real' has a role in assuring us that there is no reference failure. However, there are a few forms of discourse in which nonexistence is the normal state, so debunkers and assurers are capable of ontological role reversal. Imagine a psychologist who wishes to study hallucinations firsthand. He pays for a new kind of hallucinogen that is promised to cause especially vivid hallucinations. But it's all a big con job. The dope peddler makes the phony hallucinogen look effective by planting zebra-striped rats in the psychologist's laboratory. Once the psychologist learns of the trick, he complains that the zebra-striped rats weren't real. 'Real' can also be used to distinguish between two kinds of nonexistents. A teacher asks for two examples of mythical continents. When her student answers 'Atlantis and Glorpland', she replies 'Atlantis is a real case but you just made up Glorpland.' Or consider the movie critic who says that unlike the characters of *Hard to Kill*, those of *The Maltese Falcon* are real. It would certainly be a mistake to construe all usages of 'real' as *entailing* existence. For then 'Real tachyons do not exist' would be a contradiction rather than a contingent truth. So since we are committed to a nonexistential usage, parsimony instructs us to check whether that is enough.

Hidden relata can also create a bogus objection to the redundancy of 'real'. When people set their clocks ahead one hour for Daylight Savings Time, they make remarks like 'The reason why you are not yet hungry is that the time is really eleven o'clock.' Since the explainer knows that the time is noon, he seems to be using 'really *F*' in a way that does not imply *F*. But notice that same phenomenon holds for emphasis: 'The reason why you are not yet hungry is that the time is *eleven* o'clock.' The principle of charity will lead us to interpret the sentence as having a sensible relativization and so as expressing a truth (or at least a reasonable belief). Therefore, 'real' has no autonomous, *special* power to shift perspectives. 'Real' is the speaker's servant, not his master.

Pragmatic ambiguities

Thanks again to the deflationary account of 'true' for illuminating truth's emotive edge. We are now well positioned to probe the conversational ins and outs of debunkers.

Begin with emphasis. An accusation of false pretenses may be just an emphatic accusation of pretenses. The intensification pattern is also displayed by other double-debunkers such as 'phony baloney' and 'fake imitation cheese'. Here the adjectives modify something that is already deceptive by accentuating the deceptiveness. The natural analogy for this use is the double negative construction. 'I didn't do nothing to him' is an emphatic denial, not a circuitous confession. Since assurers are also used for emphasis, we can derive paradoxical synonymies such as 'Pseudo-hype is real hype' and 'False perjury is true perjury.' Repetition is another device of emphasis e.g. 'Dick is sick sick; it's a problem problem.' This explains the ambiguity of 'Free will is a pseudo-pseudo-problem.'

Turn now to the way 'real' falls in amongst words of praise. All commentators on 'real' claim to find a use that conveys approval. Austin says 'real' belongs, along with 'good', in the family of words that have the general function of commending:

> It is a curious point, of which Idealist philosophers used to make much at one time, that 'real' itself, in certain uses, may belong to this family. 'Now this is a *real* carving-knife!' may be one way of saying that this is a good carving-knife. And it is sometimes said of a bad poem, for instance, that it isn't really a poem at all; a certain standard must be reached, as it were, even to *qualify*.

(1962: 73)

One way of knocking a product is to deny that it's real. Thus we scoff 'Yugos are not real cars.'

One complication for this view is that 'real' is also used to deprecate as in 'Saddam Hussein is a real tyrant.' (Austin concedes this in a footnote: 'Colloquially at least, the converse is also found: "I gave him a good hiding" – "a real hiding" – "a proper hiding" ' (1962: 73).) So are we to attribute a denigratory sense to 'real' along with a commendatory sense? The redundancy theory provides a more testable and parsimonious explanation of the evaluative use. When Franklin Roosevelt conceded that the United States was in a real depression, he was not praising the economic decline. He was inviting his audience to treat the economic reversal as a clear case of 'depression'. In general, when 'real' modifies a word for something the speaker likes, it is a tool of praise. But when 'real' modifies a word for something disliked, it facilitates condemnation. Thus 'real' merely reflects antecedent value judgments. It is an axiological chameleon. Our vocabulary is poised for evaluative modulation by 'real' because words classify things of human interest. When 'real' modifies a word for an artifact, the upshot tends to be positive because artifacts are built to please. When 'real' modifies a word for a problem, the upshot tends to be negative because that semantic field taxonomizes trouble – thus the bad vibes emanating from 'real deficit' and 'real handicap'.

The reverse holds for debunkers. We condemn artifacts by calling them 'phony' and undermine dismay by applying 'phony' to ostensible evils. Nevertheless, pressures for simplicity ensure that debunkers are mostly used to denigrate and assurers are mostly used to praise. Debunked negatives are harder to digest than assured positives. The statistical association provides the foundation for many misleading (but true) advertisements: 'Our rings are mounted with genuine diamonelles', 'This establishment stocks only genuine K-mart apparel', etc.

Debunkers are most forceful when applied to status words. Indeed, it's hard not to project condemnation when deploying 'pseudo-genius', 'pseudo-sophistication', 'pseudo-heroism'. Although debunkers are used to condemn, accuse, and perform other speech acts, it would be an instance of the speech act fallacy to conclude that they therefore *entail* badness. 'Fake fur coats are better than real fur coats' is perfectly consistent. Compare debunkers with words that merely describe things that we find unpleasant: cholera, parasite, death. Although these words are mostly found in contexts of disfavor, they are purely descriptive.

The frequency with which fakes are judged inferior to originals provides statistical grounds for inferring that a fake *F* is not as good as a real *F*. However, as aestheticians have noted in their commentaries on forgery, the inference is not deductively valid. Some fake *F*s are as good as or better than authentic *F*s. The converse of this inference is also fallacious: '*x* is a bad *F*' does not entail '*x* is a fake *F*'. Philosophies that provide ethics with ontological touchstones, like Plato's forms, are prone to this fallacy (Thalberg 1962: 69).

PLATO'S FALSE BELIEF

Philosophy is wrapped up in the appearance/reality distinction, so one should expect debunkers and assurers to be in the thick of deep issues right from the beginning.

Sometimes a debunker that is used in a truth-value sense is misconstrued as having another sense. Plato's discussion of false belief in the *Theaetetus* and *Sophist* is worth reviewing because it is a parade of equivocations on 'false'. The paradox is instigated by the misleading resemblance between 'false belief' and phrases in which 'false' blocks a tempting classification: false saving, false mange, false labor (Angene 1978). In the classifier sense, 'false' obeys the exclusion principle so that false belief would not be belief. In other words, anything that was a belief would not be false – making error impossible!

Plato regroups with the observation that 'belief' is ambiguous between the psychological state and the object of belief. Perhaps 'false' applies to what the attitude is directed towards rather than the attitude itself. After all, the object of belief has content, says something, and so is sentence-like. To be false in the classifier sense, the object of belief must misclassify what it represents. Plato's predilection for viewing words as names leads him to interpret the misclassification as a misidentification. That is, mistakes are pictured as mental switches in which an ox is taken rather than a horse, Theodorus rather than Theaetetus, and so on. But this view is eventually rejected because it is implausible to attribute gross identity errors; when fog leads me to mistakenly judge Theaetetus as Theodorus, I do not believe 'Theaetetus is Theodorus.'

Plato's third pass at the problem yields the best-known version of the puzzle. If the object of belief is false, then the belief is about what is not. But what is not, does not exist. So the belief would be without an object, which is impossible. This fugitive object problem (resembling the problem of misnomers in *Cratylus*) is propelled by an equivocation between the truth-value sense of 'false' and its existential sense. On the existential reading, a false address is a nonexistent residence, a false crime is a hoax, and a false contribution is just conjured up for tax purposes. Just as it is impossible to reach a false address, it is impossible for our minds to grasp a false representation; you cannot grasp what fails to exist. (This equivocation is more tempting in Greek which only has one word to cover existence and predication.)

Plato eventually extricates himself with an insight about negation that lets him recognize an autonomous truth-value sense of 'false'. Rather than being a kind of misclassification or failure of reference, falsehood is treated as obverse affirmation. The denial 'Theaetetus is not a fish' is equivalent to the affirmation 'Theaetetus is a cow or man or . . .'

MONTAIGNE'S FALSE PLEASURE

Montaigne's essay 'How the soul discharges passions on false objects when the true are wanting' contains a precocious reference to transference:

> it seems that the soul, once stirred and set in motion, is lost in itself unless we give it something to grasp; and we must always give it an object to aim at and act on. Plutarch says of those who grow fond of monkeys and little dogs that the loving part that is in us, lacking a legitimate object, rather than remain idle, thus forges itself a false and frivolous one. And we see that the soul in its passions will sooner deceive itself by setting up a false and fantastical object, even contrary to its own belief, than not act against something.
>
> (1965: 14)

It is tempting to analyze the falsity of a false desire as a truth-value. This is how Plato proceeds in his discussion of 'false pleasure'. But then false pleasure becomes an impossibility. As commentators on *Philebus* point out, pleasure itself cannot be false. We can make sense of the pleasure's object being false: the misinformed can be pleased that p when p is actually false. Should we then say that pleasures are false in the way beliefs are false? No, again. Unlike 'belief', 'pleasure' is not ambiguous between attitude and object; it always denotes the attitude (Williams 1974). So the appearance of falsehood in pleasure cannot be explained away in terms of an equivocation between attitude and object.

To salvage the coherency of false pleasure, we must drop the truth-value reading in favor of the misleader sense. A false pleasure is a pleasure that would be inappropriate to describe as a pleasure. Some abnormality is being imputed. The anomaly could be an irregular origin. This possibility comes to life in discussions of the experience machine. Since this device doles out experiences that are as vivid as real-life experiences, hedonism implies that a life lived hooked up to this machine would be just as good as an experientially identical life in the real world. This consequence strikes most people as absurd, so they conclude that the veridicality of our experiences has value. But notice that we want more; we want the experiences to be caused in normal ways. Automated experiences strike us false if they only match the real world by coincidence or contrivance or connivance.

In the case described by Montaigne, the love normally directed at type A objects is directed at type B objects. The rarity of the redirection suffices for the attribution of 'false pleasure'. But the ground could also be normative. The mildest normative construal takes the agent's background desires as the standard. Perhaps, the love of monkeys and little dogs is discordant with the rest of your desires just as a false note fails to fit in with the rest of song. More vivid examples of inharmonious wants are those induced by circus hypnotists, brainwashers, and drugs. These false desires ensnare compatibilist definitions of 'free'. If freedom is just doing as you desire, then actions aimed at satisfying implanted desires would be free. Yet addicts appear enslaved by their desires.

The issue of false desire plugs into paternalism. It is permissible to infringe on a person's rights when he is not acting on his 'true desires'. Thus others may restrain a thirsty man who does not realize that his lemonade has been poisoned. At a superficial level, the man wants to drink the lemonade but at a deeper level, he does not. Our interference can be justified as deference to the deeper desire of self-preservation. Similarly, some people thwart suicide on the ground that the desire for death was not genuine – not emanating from the self-terminator's 'true self'. (Martin 1980)

Talk of genuine desires brings to mind the existentialists' call for authenticity. The meaning of their exhortation blurs out between the four readings of debunkers. The core idea is that one should face up to some hard, general truths and live accordingly. Thus an authentic person carefully works out the consequences of his own

mortality and contingency. He does not distract himself with superficial affairs or self-deceptive rationalizations of his existence. In
contrast, the inauthentic individual immerses himself in false beliefs
(truth-value sense), has contrived goals (misleader sense), fails to
be an individual (misclassifier sense), and obliterates himself by
absorption into the herd (existential sense).

STRAIGHT TALK ABOUT PERVERSION

The ambiguities of debunkers also worm their way into 'pervert'.
Commentators fall into a two-stage trap. First, they equivocate by
trying to assimilate all the senses of 'pervert' to one. Then after
slanting the data, they commit a naturalistic fallacy by identifying
perversion with a teleological property.

Like most of our sexual vocabulary (frigid, impotent, pet), 'perversion' has a sense specific to sex and another more general sense
as in 'perverted science' and 'a perverted sense of justice'. In the
sexual sense, 'perversion' means false sex. (In Sorensen 1991b I
defined 'perversion' too narrowly, as that which is only misleadingly
described as sex.) This definition is simple in formulation but complex in application. The first problem is that the sexual revolution
has undermined consensus about sex. This background controversy
leads to disagreements over what qualifies as false sex and doubt
about whether to apply it to anything. Thus social turbulence nar-
rows our stock of paradigm cases.

The second obstacle is that 'perversion' is a stronger pejorative
term than 'false sex', so there are kinds of false sex that we are
reluctant to describe as perverted. This creates a trap paralleling
the one that gets us to believe in degrees of reality. There, a
pragmatic scaling of weak to strong assurers is misinterpreted as a
semantic scale. In the case of perversion, we confront a scale of
debunkers. Although the debunkers are semantically homogenous,
people use some and avoid others. This discrimination amongst
synonyms is partly a matter of conversational style. Witness the
British fondness for understatement. More generally, moderate
speakers shy away from extreme language. This reticence is easily
mistaken as skepticism. But resistance to talk of krauts, chicks, and
cocks has no more ontological significance than abstention from
loud talk. People vary widely in their deployment of emphasis.
Scientists prefer low-key, explicit, highly specific commentary and
so make minimal use of highly context-sensitive debunkers and
assurers. They go to the trouble of specifying the implicit adjective.

Say dyed grass, not phony grass! Precise, objective scholars want the facts to speak for themselves and so find devices of emphasis intrusive and paternalistic. Thus the sociolinguistics of science makes talk of perversion faintly unprofessional.

The scholars who have analyzed perversion have almost all concentrated on the misleader reading of 'false sex'. In this sense, sexual perversion is an activity that can only be misleadingly described as sex because there is an irregularity in the origin, structure, target, means, or result. Sigmund Freud focused on origin. According to him, the pervert's desires issue from a psyche in a state of arrested development. Thomas Nagel (1979) suggests that perverted sex is structurally abnormal. Normal sex involves a Gricean iteration of sexual desire. In addition to being aroused by Juliet, Romeo is aroused by Juliet's being aroused, and Juliet's being aroused by Romeo's being aroused by Juliet's being aroused, and so on. The desires of the voyeur and the exhibitionist lack this iterated intentional structure. Simpler souls lock onto the sexual target: fetishism, bestiality, necrophilia, and homosexuality have inappropriate *objects*. A fourth group of commentators focuses on means: perversion is regarded as an abuse of the sexual organs. This view requires one to make sense of organs having purposes. The old theological account spelt out this goal by an appeal to divine design. God made sexual organs for reproduction, so sex that circumvents this aim is perverted. The secular explication of 'purpose' appeals to the natural design enforced by evolutionary processes. Just as nature designed teeth for chewing food, it designed the penis for impregnation. Thus Michael Levin (1984a) argues that homosexuality is perverted because sexual organs are used in a way that thwarts their natural function.

Other oversimplified analyses focus on senses of 'false sex' that have less currency. For example, Michael Slote (1980) assimilates talk of perversion to the existential sense. According to Slote, certain concepts (monster, uncanny, eerie, freak, obscene) play the role of psychological defense mechanisms. They let us deny the existence of a disturbing desire by characterizing it as unnatural, as literally outside of this world, and so not really existent in us. Psychologically sophisticated people have reconciled with these troubling desires and so have no need to resort to denial. Thus they will not apply the concepts to anything, correctly perceiving them as empty.

Many commentators complain that 'pervert' users jerk across Hume's is/ought gap by leaping from a purely factual description of false sex to the conclusion that it is wrong. For example, condemnations of homosexuality often begin by noting its irregularity and end with moral conclusions without justifying the hidden premise that the irregularity is bad. Some frustrated thinkers urge that we ban 'pervert' because it only does emotive mischief. However, unlike 'yuk', the term does cognitive work. When we speak of perverted sex, we hedge its status as sex. We cancel implicatures and put the audience on its toes. Granted, 'pervert' is vague. Granted, 'perverted' has a high potential for offense because the implicit debunker waves off favorable inferences drawn from 'sex' such as affection, consent, respect, etc. But many meaningful words are vague, thin, and offensive: bastard, bigot, redneck. Why pick on 'pervert'?

HOORAY FOR 'PSEUDO-SCIENCE'!

It is widely felt that some theories differ significantly from others in that they are *scientific*. This conviction is especially acute when one contrasts 'real sciences' such as physics, with pseudo-sciences such as astrology and numerology. However, the distinction has proved difficult to draw. This history of failure has prompted a growing school of thinkers to suspect that the demarcation problem is a pseudo-problem. These dissolutionists say there is no interesting distinction between science and pseudo-science. I shall argue that there are important differences but that they are obscured by the existence of five related readings of 'pseudo-science'.

The most natural and popular reading of 'pseudo-science' is as a nonscience that is apt to be mistaken as a science. This misclassification reading raises the classic demarcation problem of specifying criteria that will systematically separate science from pseudo-science. The dominance of the misclassifier reading is responsible for the consensus that no pseudo-science is a science.

In the existential sense, '*x* is a pseudo-science' denies the existence of *x*. For example, in the 1940s an inspired reader of Isaac Asimov's 'I, Robot' series might have asked his librarian for an introduction to robotics. The librarian would have had to disappoint him with 'Robotics is a pseudo-science; the field was just made up as science fiction.' The real science of robotics only came into existence in the 1960s though it was named after the fictional field. Happily, this sense of 'pseudo-science' is too rarely instantiated to sow confusion.

The opposite holds for the sadly neglected *misleader* interpretation. When '*x* is a pseudo-science' is used in the misleader sense, it means that the judgment that x is a science is apt to produce error even if true. That is, the classification encourages erroneous inferences about the field's origin, structure, target, means, or result.

Many denunciations of pseudo-science commit the 'genetic fallacy' of concluding that the product must be defective because the process giving rise to it is flawed. This is a mis-inference only when deductive; it's reliable as an inductive argument. The fact that chiropractics was founded by a shopkeeper rather than an anatomical expert increases the probability that it is a pseudo-science. However, this focus on peculiarities of origin does not logically commit one to saying that the pseudo-science is not a science. The critics might be using the term merely to point out the irregularity. Compare him to the art historian who describes Escher's *Waterfall* as utilizing pseudo-perspective; the debunker merely draws attention to the picture's departures from the standard rules of perspective.

'Pseudo-science' is also applied on structural grounds. Kuhn (1977) thinks pseudo-scientific fields are missing the framework of normal science. Creation science and Lysenkoist genetics are called pseudo-science because of the presence of extra parts (impurities): commitment to Christianity and Marxist ideology, respectively. This contamination theme conforms to Francis Bacon's conception of pseudo-science as adulterated science: pseudo-science mixes in extraneous elements such as metaphysics, politics, and religion.

The third misleader reading of 'pseudo-science' concerns peculiarities of function, goal, or object. Peculiarities of the object of study need not imply that the field is defective. A nice example is pseudoptics which is the study of optical illusions. Rather than debunking pseudoptics' status as optics, 'pseudo' marks the misperceptions that constitute the subject matter of the field.

The fourth misleader reading concentrates on illicit means: pseudo-science is a body of beliefs generated in an abnormal way. According to Karl Popper, pseudo-science fails to maximize falsifiability. Paul Thagard (1980) contrasts the correlational thinking of scientists (who infer causes from correlations) with the resemblance-thinking of pseudo-scientists (who infer causes from similarities).

Other commentators on pseudo-science are result-oriented. Thus the progress of science is contrasted with the stagnation of pseudo-science. Whereas genuine science produces knowledge and technology, pseudo-science yields only fads and confusion.

Art historians study forgery, illusions, and special effects. Biologists write books devoted to mimicry and deception amongst animals. Criminologists study fraud, counterfeiting, and hoaxes. An ambitious unifier might try to organize these disparate inquiries into a larger enterprise called 'pseudo-science'. The subject matter of pseudo-science would be pseudo-phenomena. The answer to 'Is pseudo-science is science?' would depend on how the field developed. The answer would be 'No' if 'pseudo-phenomena' only covers a mishmash of odds and ends. Recall that I criticized Boorstin's 'pseudo-events' on the grounds that it was a misleading umbrella term. Lack of progress would be evidence that 'pseudo-phenomena' was also a misleading umbrella term. On the other hand, it may turn out that there is the appropriate generality. A good test of this would be cross-fertilization. Late in the nineteenth century the American artist, Abbot Thayer, discovered the principle of countershading after a careful study of wildlife. In addition to the natural application to biology, Thayer applied the principle to military camouflage in World War I. A pattern of such positive transfers would confer unity on pseudo-phenomena. Results from other fields could provide further evidence that pseudo-science is a genuine science. For instance, the theory of kinship selection suggests a deep biological basis for fakery. 'Selfish genes' lead an organism to favor kin and help those who help it or its kin. Thus a sneaky creature who can pass as kin or who can fake reciprocity will be able to exploit this genetically programmed altruism. Since suckers die off, there is a corresponding evolutionary pressure to detect fakers. Fakers will in turn, develop more effective ruses to circumvent these unmaskings and so the cycle of measure and countermeasure spirals up into greater and greater sophistication. When we add the other sorts of fakery involved in sexual selection and predator-prey relations, we appreciate the biological centrality of pseudo-phenomena. Should sociobiology be vindicated, pseudo-science could acquire the kind of grand vision that has been so helpful in consolidating other fields.

The assumption that no pseudo-science is a science fails more dramatically when 'pseudo' is given the truth-value reading. For here 'x is a pseudo-science' is compatible with 'x is a science'. We may picture pseudo-science as science suffused with falsehoods just as pseudo-testimony is testimony loaded with falsehoods. Since science has no absolute guarantee against massive error, its product can be a cognitive disaster.

The history of microscopes provides many examples of pervasive error. One source of illusion was the unreliability of the instruments, especially before 1837 when Giovan Battista Amici constructed the first microscope with a hemispheric frontal lens. Another source of error was the effect of substances used to prepare slides. The prominent Dutch physician, Hermann Boerhaave, developed an entire theory of pathology based on microscopic observations suggesting that blood corpuscles could be divided into smaller corpuscles. He did not realize that the water used in the preparation of the slides was merely dissolving the blood into nonfunctional bits and pieces. Boerhaave's misfortune made his theory of pathology a tissue of untruths. So it was pseudo-science in one sense. Yet he did adhere to scientific scruples in the production of this theory, so it was science – albeit one smashed by bad luck.

Larger-scale error is imaginable. Clever Christians have attempted to reconcile creationism with the paleontological record by characterizing fossils as the devil's lure. That is, God created the universe to look like it conflicts with Genesis to test our faith. Suppose this hypothesis is true. Then paleontology is a corpus of justified false beliefs. Those who believe good methodology is sufficient for scientific status could say 'Paleontology is a pseudo-science' while still believing it to be a science.

Ordinary people are inclined to construe the 'pseudo' in 'pseudo-science' as attributing falsehood. This can be seen in their attempts to characterize the difference between regular science and pseudo-science in terms of the truth of the former and the falsehood of the latter. This explains the irony of Popper's falsifiability criterion. Inverting intuition, he counts theories as pseudo-scientific by virtue of their inability to be *falsified* and scientific by how boldly they risk refutation.

It is impossible to interpret all occurrences of 'pseudo-science' as having the truth-value reading. Sometimes the term is used as Popper describes, to mark positions that only appear to be empirical. On other occasions, the complaint is that the field is composed of obfuscated common sense (Andreski 1972). The pseudo-scientific claims are both true and empirical but old news.

The final and fifth reading of 'pseudo-science' is evaluative. No doubt 'pseudo-science' is disapprovingly used in objections to some experiments. Nazi hypothermia studies are described as pseudo-scientific because of their immoral use of human subjects. Animal rights activists label the Draize test as pseudo-science on the grounds that too little information is gained at the price of too much suffering. Defining 'pseudo-science' as evil science makes it a value-laden notion. Doubts about the objectivity of the value judgments behind 'evil' then infect the concept of pseudo-science. Those with strong doubts will come to view 'pseudo-science' as an ideological tool, more properly studied by sociologists than philosophers of science. For example, Roger Cooter (1980) argues that 'pseudo-science' has played 'an ideologically conservative and morally prescriptive social role in the interests of that order'.

Others shrug off subjectivity by construing pseudo-science as bad in a non-ethical sense. Usually, this amounts to grading the field in question by science criteria just as apples are graded by apple criteria. Evaluative terms function descriptively under this usage (Urmson 1950). Low scoring fields are then counted as pseudo-sciences. For example, Philip Kitcher applies the criteria of independent testability, unification, and fecundity: 'When does a doctrine fail to be a science? If a doctrine fails sufficiently abjectly as a science, then it fails to be a science. Where bad science becomes egregious enough, pseudoscience begins' (1984: 48). There are two versions of the appeal to scientific values. The first portrays the pseudo-scientist as accepting a certain set of standards and then scoring low against them, in the manner of a weak pupil who accepts the grading criteria. The second case portrays the pseudo-scientist as someone with a different set of cognitive values. (Some of these norms are specified in Merton 1973.) The deviant does not accept the standards and so attaches little cognitive significance to the low score. At least according to the conventional scientist, the deviant is a pseudo-scientist because he has 'false values'.

Part of the attraction of the normative conception of pseudo-science may lie in the honorific use of 'science'. Other words lead a similar double-life: art, culture, friend, religion. This laudative usage is often signaled with assurers. Substituting debunkers reverses the tone. This pejorative transformation raises the question of whether 'pseudo-science' merely conveys disapproval. But some uses of 'pseudo-science' are clearly value-neutral. For example, Kingsley Amis is not disapproving of science fiction when he defines it as 'prose narrative treating of a situation that could not arise in the world we know, but which is hypothesized on the basis of some innovation in science or technology, or pseudo-science or pseudo-technology' (1960: 18). Indeed, he cheerfully concedes that many of the best works of the genre are pseudo-scientific.

Under the classifier reading, 'Astrology is a pseudo-science' means that people commonly misclassify astrology as a science. Notice that although someone who says 'Astrology is a pseudo-science' is probably denigrating it, he need not be. The speaker can cancel the suggestion by explicitly saying that he only means to warn that scientific status is mistakenly ascribed to it. Compare him to a logicist who thinks that science has to be *a posteriori* and so declares 'Geometry is a pseudo-science.' It would be misleading to leave it at that. But suppose our blunt logicist adds that there is nothing lamentable about the cognitive status of geometry; it's as rigorous and well reasoned as you please. Geometry's only problem is the external one of so often being misclassified as a science. Someone greatly impressed with the distinction between science and technology might say 'Medicine is a pseudo-science' in a similar spirit.

The lessons learned about 'pseudo-science' hold for other bogus fields. For example, in the misclassifier sense, 'pseudo-philosophy' picks out non-philosophy that is apt to be mistaken as philosophy. A computer that generates arcane sentences by means of the sorts of tricks associated with computer poetry is generating pseudo-philosophy. A professor who passes off his personal brew of ideology and religion as philosophy has concocted pseudo-philosophy. The misleader sense is richly instantiated. Some philosophies arise from deception. For example, a huckster who invents a world view for fun and profit is a purveyor of pseudo-philosophy. Philosophy issuing from bad values is pseudo-philosophy (Count de Sade's system, for example). Pantheists such as Spinoza were accused of pseudo-philosophy on the grounds that their doctrines were deceptive: does a pantheist really believe in God? For God to be everywhere is for Him to be nowhere, so Spinoza is not using 'God' like plain folks! Atheistical philosophy was termed pseudo-philosophy because it was structurally abnormal: it was missing God. In the truth-value sense, pseudo-philosophy is philosophy stuffed with falsehoods. Hegelian philosophy is a good case. Hoax philosophies are pseudo-philosophies in the existential sense. Lastly, 'pseudo-philosophy' has an evaluative reading in which it expresses disapproval of the philosophy, viz. 'the pseudo-philosophy of the Khmer Rouge'.

AHEAD TO AN ELEPHANTINE TALE

The opening section showed that debunkers have the subtleties that have only been recently suspected of 'real'. The next section showed that these tricky features teach two lessons. One is that a set of apparently unrelated problems arises from the behavior (and misbehavior) of a single group of words. Complementing this theme of unity is a moral about hidden diversity. Debunkers don't work like most words. Moreover, each debunker has a number of senses which perform disparate tasks.

Past approaches to the problems have suffered from a curious mixture of narrowness and coarseness. By taking on each issue piecemeal, they overlooked the connections with other issues. Had they taken a synoptic approach, they would have acquired evidence against the univocality of the debunked expressions. Instead commentators on the debunker issues resemble the blind debaters in John G. Saxe's poem 'The Blind Men and the Elephant'. The sage who feels the trunk, reports that the elephant is like a snake. The sage who feels the ear, takes the elephant to be like a fan. The leg leads another to think it is like a tree. And so on, each generalizing from his own unrepresentative sample. Likewise, those who have debated the nature of pseudo-science, false pleasure, etc., have fastened on different aspects of our usage of debunkers. Yet only a wide, patient survey reveals the *true* nature of the beast.

3 Problems with 'pseudo-problems'

> There are no problems; only opportunities.
>
> (Oliver North)

This chapter applies the lessons learned about debunkers and assurers to 'pseudo-problem'. I impute much ambiguity to the word and much equivocation to the users of the term, especially to Wittgenstein. The first section shows how 'problem' piles on its own multiple meanings and logical hazards. 'Pseudo' is coupled with 'problem' in the second section. Emphasis is placed on how the interlocking traps set by the combined expression have mis-charted the course of analytic philosophy.

AN ANALYSIS OF 'PROBLEM'

Roughly speaking, problems are either situations or tasks. More precisely, 'x is a problem' is ambiguous between 'x is a bad state of affairs', as in 'The depletion of atmospheric ozone is a problem', and 'x is an imperative' as in 'Today's problem is "Determine the rate at which ozone is being depleted".' (Count interrogatives as a subclass of imperatives; they mean 'Tell me whether p' or 'Specify the value of y.') The situational sense has primacy because the imperative is usually issued to cope with a bad state of affairs. An evil need not be egocentric. Sympathy leads motorists to pull off the road to help strangers with car trouble. Human beings have a strong (though fickle) cooperative streak that leads them to pitch in when they happen upon others in need.

Although I will be chiefly concerned with the linguistic sense of 'problem', let me elaborate on my brief answer to the metaphysical question 'What is a problem?'. A state of affairs consists of objects being related in a certain way. (Properties, such as being dizzy, count as 'one-place relations'.) Thus a shirt being correctly buttoned is a different situation from a shirt mis-buttoned even though the objects are the same. The only way to *solve* a problem is to change the situation. The only way to change a situation is to add or delete objects or alter their relations. Alteration of an object's intrinsic properties (such as its size or shape) strikes us as a more genuine change than the alteration of its external relations (such as making the objects closer to each other). Thus the public sometimes feels that no work is being done by entrepreneurs who merely reorganize companies. No solution, no work. No work, no pay.

For the sake of brevity, we refer to problems by citing the objects constituting the situation (the leftover button) or just the relationship (the mismatch). Mixing the object-oriented descriptions with the relationship-oriented descriptions permits paradoxical observations: 'Recycling turns the problem into the solution', 'Matchmakers solve loneliness by putting two problems together', etc. States of affairs are causally related, perceivable, and analyzable. Hence problems can be felt, faced, and fingered.

It is tempting to say that *all* tasks are prompted by bad situations. However, illusory defects prompt tasks. Don't retreat to 'All tasks are prompted by *perceived* flaws.' For then whimsical tasks are the counterexamples: balancing an egg on a table, running backwards, eating a pie without hands. As Hans Vaihinger (1924) stressed in his 'Law of the preponderance of the means over the end', people eventually come to intrinsically value extrinsic goods. This explains the continued popularity of fishing and horseback riding. Vaihinger also placed thinking in the category of means that have come to be valued as ends in themselves. People try to solve some problems just because they like to puzzle things out. Thus there is a market for recreational problems such as jigsaw puzzles.

Scoring struggles

The pleasing aspects of problems create work for assurers. A connoisseur of conundrums *commends* 'Instant Insanity' by describing it as a real problem. Here 'real' assures us that the problem is challenging. Of course, our vocabulary for grading problems transcends assurers and debunkers. Logicians rank the 'deep' paradox of the liar over the 'superficial' Barber paradox. Problems are also valued because they improve skills. Thus a practical-minded father ranks the genuine problems of algebra homework over the phony interpretive problems of literary analysis. Lastly, some problems have diagnostic merit. Tasks that test for handicaps are praised for being valid and reliable measures. Thus the bogus ability tests fashioned by chiropractors are contrasted with the genuine ones designed by neurophysiologists. In sum, there are three ways in which assurers commend problems even though problems are principally negative entities.

Our intrinsic interest in intellectual tasks ensures that new ones can be created as idle transformations of other problems. For example, there is a military need for secret communication and thus a market for answers to 'How can messages be made hard to understand by outsiders?' However, cryptanalysts are a speculative sort and so became intrigued by the converse problem of making messages *easy* to understand by outsiders. Philip Morrison has studied the problem intensively and has even come up with a widely accepted solution to the problem of communicating with extra-terrestrials by radio.

Intellectual competition leads to the construction of tougher and tougher tasks. According to Vaihinger, many philosophical problems are the end products of this tendency of the mind to set itself increasingly difficult problems. For example, skeptical challenges become increasingly formidable as more and more potential premises are disallowed as 'question begging'. In the end, we find that we cannot justify belief in other minds or induction or the external world because the justificatory task has become artificially constrained into insolubility. The dialectical pattern of problem, solution, revised problem, may also arise from a drive toward flexibility and efficiency. Once a solution is found using a certain resource, we wonder whether it can be solved by a different means or with less of the same resource. Thus the accumulation of artificial hurdles and procedural restrictions eventually makes problems unsolvable even for super-minds.

The subjective face of 'problem'

From ethics we know that instrumental evil is relative to the purpose at hand and one's point of view. Since my purpose need not be your purpose, we should expect that what is a problem for me need not be a problem for you. A new video store increases competition and so is a problem for the old video vendors but it is not a problem for shoppers. The relativity of 'problem' to desires makes problems transferable. Thus the oil leak in a sold car used to be the seller's heartache but is now the buyer's.

The desire-dependence of 'problem' is masked by the pathetic fallacy. We project the feeling of difficulty and unease into the things that arouse those feelings. This illusion of externality is amplified by the fact that problems are usually *discovered*, not invented. Other psychological tendencies exaggerate this mild error into an outright irrationality. For example, our animistic tendencies take us into the scapegoat ritual. Here the sins of the villagers are transferred to a goat which is then driven out of the community.

One countermeasure against the pathetic fallacy is to picture a universe inhabited solely by indifferent observers. Since pure intellects lack desires, nothing frightens or frustrates them. But now suppose one of the watchers evolves preferences. Now we've got problems! But not because the external world changed.

The distinction between standard using and standard setting uses of 'good' and 'bad' is an omen that 'problem' will sometimes be used to legislate criteria and will sometimes reflect antecedently accepted criteria. By calling salary differences between male and female guards a problem, a feminist may secure acceptance of a standard of gender neutrality. But usually there are established criteria for what counts as a bad feature. Apple judges, car reviewers, and logicians have a checklist of agreed-upon defects.

The tricky usages of 'good' and 'bad' familiar to us from ethics should also dog 'problem'. Consider the ambiguity of 'bad in itself': (a) bad as an end (as opposed to bad as a means); (b) bad independently of human judgment; (c) ought to be judged bad; and (d) naturally bad (as opposed to being bad by convention). 'Bad' sometimes picks out things lying below an absolute threshold and is sometimes used comparatively. If I have won either $10 or $100, then news that I won $10 is bad in the comparative sense but is good in the absolute sense. Likewise, my car's fuel efficiency is a (relative) problem if it slips from excellent to good but is not an (absolute) problem. Lastly, we should also bear in mind old faithfuls such as the type/token distinction. By choosing a highly general problem description, one can make it seem as if we are always dealing with one big problem. For example, one of Kent Bach's (1984) pet themes is that we are always trying to solve the problem of what to do next. Other problem monists include Lenin ('What should be done?'), Camus ('Should I continue living'), and Hamlet ('To be or not to be').

Even those willing to grant the existence of more than one problem tend to be niggardly. For example, the pluralist Immanuel Kant asserted that all of our rational interests are combined into three questions: What can I know? What I ought I to do? What may I hope? (1781: A804–5/B832–3.) Historians of ideas ensure a continuity of problems by similar tricks with indexicals. William Charlton invites us to class philosophical problems with 'problems in the arts, which admit of good and bad solutions but which nevertheless present themselves over and over again to successive ages' (1991: 11). He denies that they are like problems in a mathematical examination that have uniquely correct answers. But this contrast is an artifice of how the askers frame the issues. Mathematicians and artists are equally free to formulate loose questions: What can be counted? How are numbers ordered? What is the relationship between arithmetic and geometry? These are as soft and interpretive as 'How is the human figure to be depicted?'. There may be strategic reasons for preferring tighter or looser formulations but the same logic lies behind all questions in all fields.

Manipulating standards

'Problem' stretches. We normally count something as a problem only if it is a *significant* difficulty. Significance depends on background standards. So ebbing standards 'reveal' many more matters that can be truly described as problems. Problem solving manuals exploit this indexicality to puff up their topic; just about everything we do, from scratching an itch to choosing a career, is hailed as problem solving. Compare 'problem' with 'bump'. Normally, protuberances must be of an appreciable size before we let them count as bumps. If we lower our standards, nearly all surfaces will have bumps, so nothing will count as flat (Unger 1984). Likewise, greatly lowering our standards for what counts as a defect will hatch out hoards of problems and all of our actions will seem dedicated to their eradication.

Standards are generally adjusted for wholesome reasons. *Raising* standards reduces clutter by submerging all but the most important problems into insignificance. Thus a neurologist will dismiss a rich array of disorders by concluding that the patient's real problem is a lithium deficiency. The word 'real' guides attention to the most easily changed cause of our woes. (In the mouth of a pessimist, however, 'real' beelines us to the most intractable obstacle.) Thus raised standards are often the first step to a comprehensible solution.

Unfortunately, problem consolidation tends to be an over-applied diagnostic strategy. Conspiracy theories flourish during troubled times because they unite a wide assortment of setbacks into an all too readily understood package. Many isms get their names from this grandiose reductionism. Messianism is the hope for one grand problem solver. Technophilism portrays all problems as want of technical know-how. And so on from extreme to extreme.

We should also bear in mind that standards are reconditioned to suit noncognitive concerns such as comfort and commiseration. Misery loves company, so the doomed grasp at the theme of universal mortality: 'Everyone is terminally ill – we just vary in how long we've got.' A common way of soothing a worrier is to put his concerns 'in perspective': 'You're not losing a daughter; you're gaining a son-in-law.' Setting current problems beside much bigger problems mutes their comparative severity. Things could be worse! Sometimes the comforter makes the current worry vanishingly small by raising the standard of what counts as a significant evil. The stratagem of successive standard hikes is exemplified by a World War I credo:

The Philosophy of an Airman

If you fly well there is nothing to worry about.
If you should spin, then one of two things may happen:
 Either you crash or you don't crash.
If you don't crash there is nothing to worry about.
If you do crash one of two things may happen:
 Either you are hurt or you are not hurt.
If you are not hurt there is nothing to worry about.
If you are badly hurt, then one of two things may happen:
 Either you recover or you don't recover.
If you do recover, then there is nothing to worry about.
If you don't recover you can't worry.

(Robinson 1924: 123)

When we begin the credo, we are willing to count the discomfort and delay caused by a spin as significant evils. But these are peccadillos compared to a crash. Destruction of the government's plane is also a big loss. But it pales in comparison to personal injury. Further steps down this slippery slope leave death as the only possible worry.

A cheekier way of minimizing the extension of 'problem' is to equivocate between the classifier and intensifier readings of 'real'.

A 'real problem' means something correctly classified as a problem, on the one hand, and an intense difficulty on the other. Since few of our problems are catastrophic, we are apt to concede that minor misfortunes are not real problems. We are then vulnerable to an equivocation in which the rebuker infers that the nonintense problem is not a problem at all. 'Blister on your foot? Oh, *too* bad. Nonose Ned should be so lucky! You're complaining about *nothing*.' The scolding is also abetted by distortions of the speech act behind the presentation of the problem. Troubles that are told to warn or amuse can be caustically misinterpreted as a whiny call for help or pleas for pity.

Local skepticism about philosophical problems

Wittgenstein selectively boosts standards so that nothing counts as a *philosophical* problem. There, it's out. I said it. I'm glad I said it.

But can I prove it? Probably not. Wittgenstein's aphoristic style makes him a hazy, moving target. So I will not undertake the thankless task of backing my overview of Wittgensteinian machinations with close exegesis. I'll settle for merely raising suspicions.

The first way to rig the context to support Wittgenstein's local skepticism is to characterize any apparently solvable philosophical problem as *misdelegated*; really a problem belonging to another field – a pseudo-philosophical problem. 'What is the nature of thought?' gets delegated to psychology, history of philosophy is assigned to plain old history, logic is dispatched to math, and any ethics that can't be translated as meta-ethics becomes a personal matter. To the extent that the problem looks *unsolvable*, discount it as no real problem at all. That is the fate of chestnuts such as the problem of other minds and induction. Although Wittgenstein does not brazenly appeal to the generalization 'All problems are solvable', he does make use of a patchwork of small scale disqualifiers that flesh out his faith in the generalization. He certainly strives for a clean sweep:

> For the clarity that we are aiming at is indeed *complete* clarity. But this simply means that the philosophical problems should *completely* disappear.

> The real discovery is the one that makes me capable of stopping doing philosophy when I want to. – The one that gives philosophy peace, so that it is no longer tormented by questions which bring *itself* in question . . .

There is not *a* philosophical method, though there are indeed methods, like different therapies.

(1953: §133)

Rudolph Carnap was blunter: 'We give no answer to philosophical questions and instead *reject all philosophical questions*, whether of Metaphysics, Ethics or Epistemology' (1934: 21). The way to understand Wittgenstein's metaphilosophy of dissolution is to regard him as a *local* skeptic about the expression 'philosophical problem'. Whereas the global skeptic denies extension to a wide variety of expressions, the local skeptic zeros in on just a few. Skeptics about parapsychology limit their attack to the essential vocabulary of that field: clairvoyance, psycho-kinesis, telepathy, etc. Hume's skepticism about miracles is directed toward a small cluster of terms in the semantic field of 'miracle'. Some positions that are not usually thought of as skeptical are profitably viewed as local skepticisms: pacifism is skepticism about 'self-defense', anarchism is skepticism about 'political authority', and psychological egoism is skepticism about 'altruistic deed'.

All local skepticisms share standard extermination devices engineered to hollow out the extension of the target term. Recall the first step: jack up standards for the term itself and any term implying or supporting it. The local skeptic's second step strives for an opposite effect: lower standards for contrary terms. A favorite ruse of hard determinists is to slacken standards for 'coerced' so that we seem compelled by basic biological drives and social sanctions. Also remember to question the *whole* area; reject as circular, any defense of a part in terms of another part. Fourth, dismiss apparent positive instances of the predicate as nonliteral (that is, explain it as ambiguity, linguistic error, humor, hyperbole, loose talk, metaphor, synecdoche). When all else fails, make a virtue out of necessity and advertise the apparently absurd consequence as an Amazing Truth easily overlooked were it not for the penetration and boldness of your theory.

Ordinary language philosophers were adept at exposing the shady operations of local skeptics. For instance, Peter Strawson blew the whistle on knowledge skeptics who tighten standards for 'certainty' and relax those for 'doubt'. Strawson (1951: 257) also resisted the skeptic's demands for the justification of entire institutions such as law, induction, and the attribution of responsibility. The ordinary language philosophers's most popular refutations of philosophical generalizations employed the paradigm case argument and excluded opposite argument. For a while, they were the weapons of choice against sweeping theses such as 'All statements are vague' and 'No history is objective'. Curiously, these arguments were never deployed against the omni-dissolution thesis that 'No problem is philosophical'. There is no mystery why the paradigm case and excluded opposite arguments have not been deployed against it within the past twenty years; articles appearing twenty years ago demonstrated they were fallacious (Passmore 1970). But why not before then? One suspicion is that the paradigm case argument and the appeal to excluded opposites were really being used as specialized weapons against *philosophical* generalizations, not as generic argument forms. 'No philosophical problem is genuine' could be freely propounded because it was not regarded as a philosophical generalization and hence did not constitute a target.

Most ordinary language philosophers did not embrace Wittgenstein's thesis that all philosophical problems are pseudo-problems. A few of them limited their dissolution thesis to a subfield. T. D. Weldon restrains his dissolution to political philosophy: 'the questions put by traditional political philosophy are wrongly posed. In the form in which they normally occur they cannot be answered but can be shown to be unprofitable' (1953: 14). Most ordinary language philosophers only claimed that a surprisingly large portion of 'philosophical problems' were pseudo-problems. They were committed to the claim that the ratio of pseudo-problems to genuine problems in philosophy is much higher than that found in other fields and that this ratio had been profoundly underestimated by past philosophers. This less ambitious thesis is more plausible than the Wittgensteinian panacea. But even 'Most philosophical problems are pseudo-problems' constitutes a substantial metaphilosophical generalization that will tempt its proponents to reach into the same bag of tricks.

Parity by pandemia

I deny that all philosophical problems are pseudo-problems but affirm that all fields have some pseudo-problems. Wherever we find problems solved, we find other problems dissolved. For a question is a tool under stress, deployed on uncertain information, buffeted by slapdash forethoughts and afterthoughts. Defects are not self-intimating; one can have a problem without believing so. After all, camouflage and censorship *mask* problems. Nor are problems incorrigible. Medievals believed that the Black Death was spread by cats. But the plague was actually due to rats hence the 'solution' of cat massacre just made the problem worse. The corrigibility of beliefs about problems makes pseudo-problems possible.

Although these observations seem trite, they refute most definitions of 'problem'. Most textbook definitions echo John Dewey's (1938) characterization of a problem as a felt difficulty. That is, they define 'problem' in a purely subjective manner, as an unsatisfied desire. Typical is Newell and Simon's definition: 'A person is confronted with a *problem* when he wants something and does not know immediately what series of actions he can perform to get it' (Newell and Simon, 1972: 72). Some definitions are more strenuous and require some initial failed attempts to achieve one's end. Still others are more lenient and define 'problem' as the gap between where you are and where you want to be. At the core of all the definitions is the notion that problems are frustrating situations that prompt ameliorative responses.

This frustration model neglects the distinction between the psychological satisfaction of desires and their objective fulfillment. I experience false frustration when things are as I wish but I believe otherwise; the desire is fulfilled but I am dissatisfied. I experience false contentment when I falsely believe things are as I wish.

The neglect of these two possibilities is enforced by the spatial metaphor of problem solving. The thinker is pictured as moving from an 'initial state' to a 'goal state' through a 'problem space'. The Artificial Intelligence community favored this model because it allows one to represent problem solving as the generic task of increasing the resemblance between the initial state and the goal state. However, the spatial model assumes that the components of a healthy problem are all in place. The assumption is natural because textbooks on problems are books on problem *solving* and so tend to presuppose that there is a real problem to be solved. That is, they presuppose that the person knows that there is a gap between how things are and how he wants them to be. And they assume, in the manner of political liberals and many economists, that no desires are 'illegitimate'. Moreover, they assume that the solutions are compatible with other problem solving enterprises.

But of course, a puzzled person can believe that there is a gap when there is none. For he could be mistaken as to how things are or how they should be. A miscalculation can lead me to believe that I do not have the funds to honor a check when I do. Factual errors lead me to think iodine should be poured on a scrape when the wound is better left undisturbed. Value myopia moves me to curtail my retirement savings so that I can have more fun as a young man.

'PSEUDO-PROBLEM' SENSES

All of the syntactic ambiguities noted in the analysis of 'pseudo' haunt 'pseudo-problem'. The most germane is posed by ellipsis. The expression 'pseudo psychological problem' could mean a psychological pseudo-problem or mean a problem that is pseudo-psychological. Eliding the middle term makes it seem as if the problem itself is defective when the actual complaint is the external one of being treated by the wrong group of thinkers. Perhaps some uses of 'pseudo-problem' in philosophy are elided versions of 'pseudo-philosophical problem' which is just a warning over *misdelegating* the problem to philosophers.

The *semantic* ambiguities of 'pseudo-problem' emerge when we superimpose the previous chapter's analysis of 'pseudo' on this chapter's account of 'problem'. Four senses of 'pseudo' (classifier, misleader, existential, truth-value) and two senses of 'problem' have been possible. So expect 'pseudo-problem' to have at most eight semantically induced readings. Two of these readings can be eliminated on the grounds that neither defects nor tasks have truth-values. The rest of the readings go through.

Classifier pseudo-problems

Given the defect and task senses of 'problem', nonproblems can be misclassified as problems in two ways. The first is by a misclassification of badness. A qualitative mistake occurs when a good or neutral thing is misclassified as bad. For example, low level brush fires were eventually discovered to serve the function of removing debris that fuels major forest fires. Examples of *neutrals* that merely look bad include the mites inhabiting your mattress and most unhealthy sounding food additives.

Quantitative mistakes occur when evil is overestimated. Experts on the insanity defense concede that it has occasionally led to further crimes by 'cured' maniacs. But they insist that these are rare eruptions whose frequency is greatly overestimated. For public opinion is fed by news services that only report sensational incidents, not the bulk of cases in which the insanity defense works out well.

Misidentifications create a third class of pseudo-problems. Here, one identifies x as the object of displeasure when y is the actual object. I may think I detest salad when it is actually the seasonings that revolt me. Often the error is motivated. A mother may think she is displeased with her son's fighting when her real ire is confined to the fact that he loses. The objects of displeasure need not closely coincide. A teenager's bad complexion rather than human greed may be the real object of his despair. Some people claim to find the secular vision of the world too depressing. They say they could not go on living if they believed that all life will eventually die out in the manner glumly prophesied by astronomers. Bertrand Russell dismisses this concern as bogus:

> Nobody really worries much about what is going to happen millions of years hence. Even if they think they are worrying much about that, they are really deceiving themselves. They are worried about something much more mundane, or it may merely be a bad digestion; but nobody is really seriously rendered unhappy by the thought of something that is going to happen to this world millions and millions of years hence.
>
> (1964: 11)

The notion that I can misidentify the object of my displeasure strikes some philosophers as contradictory. But what we have here is just a resurgence of Plato's problem of false pleasure.

In the task sense of 'problem', a misclassification would feature something that looks like a task but is not. For example, commercials with academic settings frequently have blackboards festooned with what purport to be complicated mathematical problems. But it's gibberish. Likewise, the insane pose 'questions' that seem eerily profound but which are just shards of verbal behavior.

We could put the early Wittgenstein's notion of a pseudo-problem into this mold. Suppose that a necessary condition of being a question is the presentation of a range of *propositions*. If this range contains only pseudo-propositions, then the question is a pseudo-question. In the *Tractatus*, Wittgenstein defended a 'picture theory' of meaning. This theory identifies the sense of a statement with the states of affairs that it includes and excludes. Consequently, all statements with sense are synthetic. A second group, senseless statements, express the rules of the language. Tautologies are in this set. The residual statements are nonsense; not genuine propositions. In *Notes on Logic* written for Russell in 1913, Wittgenstein wrote 'the word "philosophy" ought to designate something over or under, but not beside, the natural sciences. Philosophy gives no pictures of reality, and can neither confirm nor confute scientific investigations.'

The nonexistence of philosophical propositions is also the theme of *Tractatus* 4.112–4.115. All questions are selection tasks. But philosophical 'questions' bid us to select from a range of pseudo-propositions. Hence, they are not genuine questions; they are pseudo-problems.

Existential pseudo-problems

Sometimes what is taken for a problem does not exist. Illusory problems, in the defect sense, are common. Early in the twentieth century people bought pills as a precaution against poison gases emitted by Halley's comet. Superstitious people pay for counter-magic to ward off curses. Not all existential pseudo-problems are *foolish* phantoms. The Ford administration had ample evidence of an upcoming Swine Flu Epidemic for their failed inoculation program.

Nonexistent tasks are rare and not as philosophically interesting. Shakespeare scholars sometimes use 'pseudo-problem' to refer to the mythical debate over whether Francis Bacon actually wrote the works attributed to Shakespeare. Their point is that the scholarly controversy does not exist; no Shakespeare scholar argues that Bacon is the real author. Similarly, there was never any real religious debate on whether labor pains should be relieved with anesthesia: there was only preparation for a debate that never materialized (Farr 1983). Finally, pity the poor philosophers who are popularly pictured as perturbed by 'How many angels can dance on the head of a pin?' and 'If a tree falls in a forest, does it make a sound?'

Nonexistence is a dark concept. Are fictional problems nonexistent? Most seem so, but a mathematical problem posed in a work of fiction is treated as real. For example, Henry Longfellow's *Kavenaugh* introduced a novel geometrical conundrum: the stem of a water lily extends 10 cm above the water when vertical and the lily can be pulled 21 cm to the side; determine the depth of the water. There is a definite solution so there must be a genuine problem. What about hypothetical problems? An engineer will invent simplified problems and use their solutions as lemmas for his answer to the original, real-life problem. Although these hypothetical problems are about nonactual states of affairs, they exist as questions. *Latent* problems have a foot in the actual world and a foot in another possible world. That hairline fracture in a vase is real enough but the shattering of the vase exists only as a possibility.

Ontological skepticism about the past or future will confer an air of unreality on problems outside of the present. (Thus the tranquilizing effect of Here and Now philosophies.) Without sober metaphysics, we are apt to fall for actualism about problems – the view that only actual problems are worth considering.

The Amazon of pseudo-problems

Misleaders are the richest, most diverse, most neglected class of pseudo-problems. There are a Brazillion ways in which classifications of something as a problem can be a fertile source of error even if the classification is true. Desired defects produce our first group of misleader pseudo-problems. When 'bad' is used as part of a standardized grading vocabulary, its meaning is descriptive. This conventionality ensures that people with unusual preferences will desire bad things. A boy who relishes bruised apples prefers bad apples over good ones. A vasectomized swinger pays good money for the disorder of sterility. If we call his sterility a problem, we would be speaking the truth but would be misleading the audience into thinking that the man dislikes his sterility. Fear of miscommunication may even lead us to deny that his sterility is a problem. We must be careful here to distinguish between denials of truth and denials of appropriateness. If you describe my colleague as at least a minimally competent teacher, I may gainsay your remark with 'No, he is an excellent teacher' even though this entails the truth of what you said. My protest is against the implicature that nothing stronger can be asserted. Applying the distinction to the vasectomy case lets us view the man's sterility as a problem that should not be described as a problem.

Note that a defect can be desirable even though no one realizes it. A dented fender may lead a choosy thief to pass over your car. Indeed, sometimes both the defect and the fact that the defect is a pseudo-problem pass unnoticed. In *The Andromeda Strain* an isolated group of scientists send a message that a site containing killer microbes from outer space should be destroyed with an atom bomb. The message fails to be received because a sliver of paper becomes wedged in the bell used to signal the arrival of a message. Ironically, this problem saves Earthlings from cataclysm because the microbe thrives on all forms of energy.

A second kind of pseudo-problem occurs when we balk at necessary evils, that is, when we conduct an absolute appraisal when a comparative one is called for. Amputations are bad procedures in the absolute sense because they deprive you of a body part. But this does not mean the practice is in need of reform. For amputation is not bad relative to your other options. It's the best out of a bad lot. Only relative evils allow for the possibility of improvement. This makes the equivocation between absolute and comparative problems serious. A change from the least worst is a change for the worse! 'What cannot be cured must be endured.'

Infelicitous questions form a third group of pseudo-questions. These turn on violations of principles for performing speech acts. Rhetorical questions are sometimes described as pseudo-questions because the poser of rhetorical questions does not really ask; he indirectly asserts. Wittgenstein sometimes criticized philosophical questions on the grounds that the complacent askers were not sincerely trying to answer them. He felt that these collaborators had grown too fond of the Big Questions and were content to have them around forever.

In addition to violating the preconditions of *asking*, pseudo-problems often violate the preconditions of other speech acts such as assigning, ordering, commanding, etc. The problems constituting 'busy-work' and 'make-work' are called pseudo-problems because the tasks are not set for the sake of achieving their goals. The assignment serves an ulterior purpose such as mischief prevention, obedience training, or punishment.

Questions with abnormal origins are also called 'pseudo-problems' to ward off assumptions about their genesis. For example, questions planted by press-conference organizers are called pseudo-questions to smother the inference that the reporter asked out of curiosity. The issue of whether there was life on Mars intelligent enough to build canals was dismissed by many astronomers as a pseudo-problem on the grounds that it was based on a mistranslation of Schiaparelli's *'canali'*.

DEBUNKING MYTHOLOGY

Myths are widespread false beliefs. For example, it is an architectural myth that the arch and the vault began with the Romans. In the Near East these structures pre-date the Colosseum by 3,000 years. Roman civilization is so closely associated with the arch and the vault because the Romans made such common and monumental use of them – and because it is their bridges, aqueducts, and amphitheaters that still stand today. The myth that dissolution originated with analytic philosophy has a parallel foundation.

A fallacy, in contrast, is a widespread, bad *inference*. This section will focus on the mis-reasoning about dissolution that arises from the ambiguities of 'pseudo-problem'. These double-meanings have led philosophy's discontents into a catacomb of interlocking equivocations.

False unity

The most basic misconception about pseudo-problems is that there is just one sense of 'pseudo-problem'. This leads black-and-white dissolutionists to infer that there is a monolith of error when there is actually just a rock garden. Thus pseudo-problems invite the same error as Boorstin's pseudo-events. Wittgenstein writes as if he is studying a natural kind such as malaria. He is forever contrasting the wholesomeness of established patterns of inquiry with the pathology of philosophical investigation. Wittgenstein's analogy between philosophical questions and diseases has never been systematically explored even though philosophers of medicine have subsequently developed sophisticated, empirically disciplined analyses of diseases.

Many of the issues raised by pseudo-problems are indeed prefigured in the literature on disease. Naturalists say that 'disease' is a purely descriptive concept like 'shale'. Normativists assert that 'disease' is value-laden like 'weed'. They point to historical and cultural variation in what gets classed as a disease as well as the intimate connection between disease attribution and medical intervention. 'Disease' is action oriented. Naturalism, on the other hand, builds on the scientific aspects of medical evidence. Physicians claim to *discover* diseases and even seem to require diseases to be natural kinds. Your proctologist does not picture himself as in the context of *invention*.

There is parallel evidence for normativism and naturalism about pseudo-problems. A normativist will be suspicious of theories that assume that there is an essence to disease. For instance, the Germ Theory of diseases regards all diseases as infections. Before that the Hippocratic theory of disease said that all diseases are humoral imbalances. However, 'disease' may be a family resemblance concept lacking any interesting necessary and sufficient condition. The same issue arises for 'pseudo-problem'. Do all pseudo-problems result 'when language goes on a holiday'? Are they all forms of bastard mentation (such as the application of phenomenal categories to noumena)? Even a naturalist about pseudo-problems may doubt that 'pseudo-problem' has this kind of ontological backing. In short, the vexations of nosology (the taxonomy of disease) are likely to be visited upon any taxonomy of pseudo-problems.

Weasels and waffles

Stewart Chaplin defined weasel words as expressions 'that suck all the life out of the words next to them, just as a weasel sucks an egg and leaves the shell'. Assurers such as 'true' are busy weaselers. Any generalization can be 'saved' by exchanging the definiendum, *D*, for a look-alike, *true-D*. Champions of 'Art is the depiction of nature' stonewall against the counterexample of the Alhambra in Granada by insisting that an abstract geometric design is not *true* art. Statements couched in terms of weasel words have a trivial reading where the weasel word gerrymanders the generalization to avoid all counterexamples; and a substantive reading in which it is equivalent to the generalization that would result by deleting the weasel word.

The price of transit from 'All *F*s are *G*s' to 'All *true-F*s are *G*s' is relevance. If the task was to define *F*, then defining *true-F-ness* leaves the job undone. The further peril is that we will forget that the switch took place. In particular, we might agree that the problem is not a *true* problem (in the speaker's stipulated sense), and then be unmindful of the qualification, and finally come to believe there is no problem. Period.

Theorists rightly slap on assurers and debunkers in the course of sorting paradigms and foils. And a theory of problem solving will innocently retain some of its principles by denying that an apparent counterexample is a *genuine* problem. Weaseling only begins when this mobilization of assurers becomes irreparably vague. A robust theory of problem solving can plausibly substitute a more precise description for any use of assurers or debunkers. Assurers and debunkers are like checks; your credit stays good only as long as you stand ready to back your debts. When the system is run honorably, the theory of solution will mesh with the theory of dissolution. For a detailed justification of why recalcitrant data fall outside the domain of one theory will give a running start for the theory that does have jurisdiction over the data.

Assimilation to the existential reading

The only sense in which '*x* is a pseudo-problem' implies the nonexistence of *x* is the existential sense. Nevertheless, there is a tendency to slither from the other two senses of 'pseudo-problem' to this rarely instantiated existential sense and infer that the problem is a conceptual hallucination. For example, in his essay on 'Phantom problems', Max Planck first notes our satisfaction in solving a real problem. He then observes:

> it is an entirely different story, and an experience annoying as can be, to find after a long time spent in toil and effort, that the problem which has been preying on one's mind is totally incapable of any solution at all – either because there exists no indisputable method to unravel it, or because considered in the cold light of reason, it turns out to be absolutely void of all meaning – in other words, it is a *phantom problem*, and all that mental work and effort was expended on a mere nothing.
>
> (Planck 1949: 52–3)

Whoa! If you discover that a question is beyond our ken or lacks meaning, then you've given compelling grounds for halting research on it. But the pseudo-problem exists; it's just something that has been misclassified as a problem or is a problem that is not aptly characterized as a problem.

The fallacious assimilation to the existential sense need only result in a harmless hyperbole. However, the fumble is often tumbled into two further blunders. The first mistake is an instance of the illusion/delusion equivocation that Austin (1962) unscrews in his critique of the sense-datum theorist's argument from bent oars. Illusions are mild misperceptions experienced by normal perceivers and are of existing things. For example, the specious length inequality of the Müller-Lyer arrows and the apparent talk of a ventriloquist's dummy are appearances of existing things. Delusions are severe misperceptions that are not experienced by normal perceivers and concern nonexistent things. This quasi-psychiatric category brings to mind 'entities' such as the alcoholic's pink rats, the plots feared by the paranoid, and the giant rabbit in *Harvey*. Austin protests that the conflation of illusions with delusions tilts the playing field in favor of the sense-datum theorist. On the one hand, talk of illusion suggests that something is really being seen. On the other hand, passage to talk of delusions suggests

> something being conjured up, something unreal or at any rate 'immaterial'. These two implications together may then subtly insinuate that in the cases cited there really is something that we are perceiving, but that this is an immaterial something; and this

insinuation, even if not conclusive by itself, is certainly well calculated to edge us a little closer towards just the position where the sense-datum theorist wants to have us.

(1962: 25)

In the case of pseudo-problems, the insinuation is that the 'problem' is a hobgoblin of an imbalanced mind. As in the case of other delusional people, the poor devil needs therapy, not ingenuity. Combining this point with the thesis that traditional philosophy contains only pseudo-problems invites the conclusion that the field is an affliction of the mind. The enlightened philosopher is then viewed as akin to a psychoanalyst (Lazerowitz 1968, Wisdom 1969). He must cure the traditional philosopher of 'mental cramps'.

Although the analogy between philosophy departments and insane asylums has its charms, the reasoning behind it is fallacious. The first step down the garden path is to abridge the domain of 'philosophical problem' so that all or nearly all of philosophy is composed of pseudo-problems. Second, 'pseudo-problem' is assimilated to the existential sense which implies nonexistence. This makes philosophy's illusory problems look delusory. One then catches Sigmund Freud's wave of popularity and comes ashore with the conclusion that philosophers need counseling for their delusions.

Since philosophers live about as well as other academics and academics are actually less psychologically troubled than the rest of the population, the therapeutic thesis is literally false. Although mental illness has been romanticized in the twentieth century (just as tuberculosis was romanticized in the nineteenth), the thesis also fails to do justice to the sentiment that philosophical puzzlement is ennobling. The religious model of spiritual torment is superior in this respect. There is something 'wrong' with the seeker but it is a sign of something good. But the model is marred. Nearly all western religions require allegiance to doctrines that assume the legitimacy of traditional philosophical problems (free will, God's existence, immortality, the rationality of morality, the meaning of life).

Sophisticated forms of Buddhism offer spiritual salvation without endorsing traditional philosophical problems repudiated by the dissolutionist. Describing pseudo-problems as unreal, nonexistent, or 'mere nothings' ripens the analogy. Gautama Buddha thought life was suffering. He rejected attempts to achieve happiness through the satisfaction of desires. Indeed, Buddha portrayed desire itself as the root of suffering. Those with wants are doomed to frustration because the objects of desires are part of a grand illusion. The only way to escape suffering is to end the desires essential to frustration. Anyone who attains a desireless state achieves a freedom from problems because all problems imply desire. This flight from life into nonbeing proves surprisingly arduous. You can't worm your way out through suicide. For eastern thought embraces reincarnation. Nor can you strive to make yourself desireless because all striving implies desire. You must slip into the state spontaneously. Zen Buddhists lubricate the transition by posing *koans* such as 'What happens to your fist when you unclench your hand?' The absurdity of these questions is intended to plow apart mental ruts, so you can dumb-down into a blank receptivity.

The connection between pseudo-problems and Buddhism has been drawn by a number of commentators. In his biography of Ernst Mach, John Blackmore has a chapter entitled 'Mach and Buddhism'. After pointing out that Mach and the Buddhist reject the self, are anti-vivisectionists and pacifists, Blackmore cites Mach's comments on pseudo-problems to show the similarity between the Buddhist cure for unhappiness and Mach's theory of intellectual economy. For example, Mach warns of cognitive bankruptcies:

> Not all problems, which arise in the course of the development of science, can be solved; on the contrary, many will fall away because one recognizes them as *null* [*nichtig*]. By the *annihilation* [*Vernichtung*] of problems, which rest upon an inverted false manner of asking questions . . . science takes a fundamental step forward.
>
> (Blackmore 1972: 298)

Commentators on Wittgenstein have also regarded the preoccupation with pseudo-problems as a point of resemblance between therapeutic linguistic analysis and Buddhistic liberation. In *Wittgenstein and Buddhism*, Chris Gudmunsen first quotes a Buddhist: 'Foolish, untaught, common people have settled down in them [the dharmas]. Although they do not exist, they have constructed all the dharmas' (1977: 70). Gudmunsen compares this with George Pitcher's summary of the negative aspect of Wittgenstein's *Tractatus* and *Philosophical Investigations*:

> Yet in both works the problems are based on misunderstanding, and once this is removed, the problems disappear; they are revealed to have been really no problems at all. In the *Tractatus* Wittgenstein said:

4.003(3) And it is not surprising that the deepest problems are in fact *not* problems at all.

6.5(2) *The riddle* does not exist.

So, too, in the *Investigations*: the difficulties are unreal ones, which we have created for ourselves, and when we see things aright, the problems vanish as if by magic.

(Pitcher 1964: 327)

However, the big message percolates up from a conglomeration of verbal confusions over 'pseudo-problem'. Wittgenstein falls into a false unity by assuming that there is just one sense of 'pseudo-problem'. He then choreographs standards so that all philosophical problems fall under this heading. Finally, he assimilates the bogus monolith to the existential sense and so infers that philosophy is much ado about nothing, a delusion.

The ambiguities and vagaries of 'pseudo-problem' are major players in the metaphilosophy of dissolution. This serves as evidence of the practical difficulties of the concept. Yet we cannot abandon 'pseudo-problem' because it has had and will continue to have a lead role in our thinking about philosophy and problem solving in general. So given that we cannot get a unified account of pseudo-problems by the direct route, we must fashion an alternative. This indirect yet less labyrinthine approach will be mapped out in the next chapter.

4 The soft consensual underbelly of dispute

> To know what questions may reasonably be asked is already a great and necessary proof of sagacity and insight. For if a question is absurd in itself and calls for an answer where none is required, it not only brings shame on the propounder of the question of the question, but may betray an incautious listener into absurd answers, thus presenting, as the ancients said, the ludicrous spectacle of one man milking a he-goat and the other holding a sieve underneath.
>
> (Immanuel Kant)

The nay-saying chapters have shown that 'pseudo-problem' is too equivocal to serve as a basis for research nosology. Taxonomists need species rather than senses. The constructive phase of this book requires a more controlled, less jagged tool. Happily, 'dissolution' has what it takes to satisfy our craving for a general theory of defective disputes.

No doubt, 'dissolution' has its own ambiguities. But these are *standard* double-meanings, not the hyper-ambiguity of 'pseudo-problem'. I say that most dissolutions fail – like most solutions. 'Poppycock!', you say, 'a failed dissolution is no dissolution at all!' But there is no need to argue. 'Dissolution' has one sense implying success and another that merely requires an attempt. I say dissolution is an activity. You say it is an abstract entity like an argument. Time out; our assertions and counter-assertions have been tangled by the process/product ambiguity of 'dissolution'.

The process sense of 'dissolution' refers to the activity by which pseudo-problems are exposed; the dissolver refutes the assumption that the issue should be pursued. More specifically, he rebuts one of the preconditions of debating the issue. The terms used to define 'dissolution' suit it for the job of classifying pseudo-problems. For refutations are *arguments* and logicians have made 'argument' a well-understood term. Moreover, preconditions can be neatly detached from the body of dispute and probed with standard intellectual instruments in an orderly, hygienic setting. However, our anatomical ambition demands an understanding of the general nature of disputation.

BONES OF CONTENTION

Evolutionary anthropology reinforces Aristotle's theme that man is a social animal. Human beings flourish because they are capable of flexible coordination. Their adaptation for joint action demands a certain kind of psychology. And indeed, there is growing evidence that Mother Nature has favored the formation of a special human character.

On the one hand, cooperators need to be agreeable. An obstreperous species would have trouble arriving at a course of action and so be readily displaced by 'team players'. And indeed, we find that members of a human collective give each other the benefit of the doubt and drift toward central tendencies. There is strong tendency to believe what others say and to change your mind in the direction of the majority. We are a trusting species.

Human conformism goose-steps beyond the realm of *belief*. Preferences also bend to the group will. As we become better acquainted, I begin to want what you want. The primitive, biological grounding for this resonance is that those who are motivated to help their acquaintances retain and attract allies. However, there is also a cognitive dimension. Companions learn from each other and from their joint projects. Hence, their derivative desires tend to converge while their new desires awaken simultaneously. Moreover, the very act of discussion tends to change preferences toward the group's interests (Elster 1983: 33–7). An individual who only appeals to his own desires is less persuasive than one who appeals to the interests of his audience. So public discussion is dominated by reasoning that purports to further collective ends. Professing a proposition tends to make you believe it, so discussants wind up with desires that mesh with each other.

There are limits to the plasticity of our preferences and limits to the will to believe. If people were perfectly gullible and compliant, a mutant egoist could exploit their naivety. Lies and manipulation would ensure that the offspring of the selfish flourish at the expense of the pushovers' progeny. So stable cooperativeness requires safeguards against cheaters. Emotions such as outrage, resentment, and indignation can be seen as measures against the temptation to lie, steal, and cheat (Gibbard 1990). Guilt and shame can be viewed as emotions that heal interpersonal wounds and reassure others of our good faith. Thus the menace of social parasitism will produce mechanisms for detecting fraud. Metaphysics is just the most cerebral expression of a deep biological preoccupation with the appearance/reality distinction.

Human beings also need to spot the incompetent. Complete pliability would leave groups vulnerable to bad ideas. Thus there is further pressure toward circumspection. Instead of blindly accepting the first sincere proposal, we apply techniques of critical discussion. The give and take of dialogue leads to a pooling of information and control over what is inferred from the data. Often, this critical accumulation of reports and opinions is enough to crystallize a consensus (Lehrer and Wagner 1981). But on other occasions, more than one conclusion survives discussion. Like rival queen bees, they cannot co-exist.

SPLIT ENDS

The aim of a dispute is rational persuasion. One need not hope for an *immediate* conversion. Reasons often need a while to take root, so your adversary may only convert months later. This sleeper effect occurred in the controversy over anti-ballistic weapons. During an arms-control session with the Soviets in Glassboro, New Jersey in 1967, Secretary of State Robert McNamara argued that the security accruing from a policy of mutual assured destruction would be achieved less expensively by banning defensive weapons. If the Soviets deployed anti-ballistic missiles, the United States would not. Instead, the United States would follow the cheaper strategy of producing more offensive missiles, accepting that many would be shot down, but knowing enough would get through. So why not take the less wasteful option of having both sides ban anti-ballistic missiles? The Soviet Premier, Aleksei Kosygin, vociferously denounced the proposal on grounds that defensive weapons are moral and offensive ones are immoral. But eventually, the Soviets swung around to McNamara's theory of deterrence and signed the Anti-Ballistic Missile Treaty.

Contrast aims with motives. Motives for engaging in a dispute are multifarious: wonder, wealth, whim. The aim is a formal goal that renders the activity intelligible by means–ends reasoning. For example, the aim of soccer is to score more goals than the opposing team. But soccer players have all sorts of reasons for playing: exercise, winning a bet, kicks. Motives and aims are both reasons for engaging in the activity. But the activity only *commits* you to aims. For participation invites others to interpret your behavior as directed toward the fulfillment of the aim. Not having the aim makes your participation insincere, a sham.

And contrast rational persuasion with indoctrination. The indoctrinator only seeks to imbue others with a set of beliefs. Whether the beliefs are true or justified is extraneous. Indoctrination can be achieved by techniques such as reverse psychology, repetition, and peer pressure. Quite often, the conversion is effected by simply transferring the subject from an unbelieving group to a group of believers. Belief is contagious. But those who employ psychological tricks in disputes are insincere in the same way as those who do not try to win the dispute. For the aim of disputation is not the mere cultivation of belief. The goal is ambitious: knowledge.

Teaching also aims at rational persuasion. But much of the persuasion is by authority. Students are entitled to believe that the professor knows the answer and so gain knowledge just by taking his word for it. A student who asks for reasons is almost always seeking an *explanation* for the authority's fact not an *argument*. Explanation is a matter of giving reasons for a proposition that is not in contention. A student who asks why all sound arguments are valid already knows that the generalization is true; for he knows that the teacher said so and knows that the teacher would not have said so if it were not true. When the teacher responds by saying that 'sound argument' is defined as 'valid argument with true premises', the point is to provide knowledge of *why* the generalization is true; not to provide knowledge *that* the generalization is true. The student cannot learn something he already knows by authority.

OBSTACLES TO RATIONAL PERSUASION

Disputes are more egalitarian than lectures. At the outset, neither contender is entitled to believe that the other knows the correct answer to the question at issue. Knowledge of the answer has to be demonstrated. Furthermore, the demonstration is advanced in a competitive environment. For one's adversary is simultaneously arguing for the antithesis. Roughly speaking, a dispute is a 'teach-off'. Each side is trying to 'educate' the other. Each side believes he knows the answer. So each side takes the other to be in error and tries to right the wrong. Correcting error is easy enough when the mistake is committed by someone who believes that you know the truth of the matter. It is more difficult when they have no opinion as to whether you know the truth. Still more formidable is the person who believes you are as ignorant as he. In the most difficult case of all, the errant listener believes he knows and believes he must correct you. Hence disputes standardly involve the worst case persuasion scenario.

Debaters must also toil against the inertia of belief. Once a person believes something, he tends to continue believing it. If he does change his mind, he will minimize the change. Then there is adversary demotion. The very fact that you disagree with me tends to lower my opinion of your intellectual qualities. Processes are judged by their products. Once I learn that you harbor an opinion that I think I know to be false, I naturally form doubts about how well you reason, how well-informed you are, and how vulnerable you are to wishful thinking, self-deception, and so forth. Skilled debaters counter this effect by stressing points of agreement, displaying their command of the facts, sounding like the voice of reason, and localizing the zone of disagreement to the smallest area possible. Looking reasonable is important because appearances heavily influence how your claims are interpreted. You can't be persuasive unless your audience is willing to be charitable with you. Sadly, the inertia effect colludes with the process/product effect. That is, once I infer that you are intellectually deficient because I think you are in error on the issue, I begin to harden my heart and head. My low opinion of your judgment will lead me to interpret your remarks uncharitably. What goes for me, goes for you. You think that you know that I am in error on the issue. How could I make such a mistake? Probably because of a deficiency in reasoning, my feeble grasp of the facts, or my susceptibility to influence by irrelevant factors such as bias, carelessness, etc. So you interpret my remarks uncharitably, as the products of poor mental processes. Our uncharitable interpretations of each other begin to interact and reinforce each other. My lack of charity will prevent me from appreciating the strength of your arguments. This obtuse reception stokes your suspicions about my intellectual defects. And your lack of charity will lead you to underestimate the strength of my arguments and thereby fuel skepticism about each other's talents and character. Thus we are

sucked into a demonizing vortex of increasingly uncharitable interpretation. Misunderstanding breeds misunderstanding.

Ulterior motives form a fourth obstacle to rational persuasion by
debate. For irrelevant desires elbow out the aim of dispute. If my
motive is to win a court case or show off, I will be reluctant to
publicly concede that you are right. Indeed, when defeat looms,
self-interest is served by clouding the issue so that I do not appear
the loser. If my objectives can be achieved by *appearing* to be the
winner, I may abandon the aim of the dispute entirely and concentrate on deceiving people into thinking they know something they
don't. Even if my motives are not as nefarious as this, I may still
have a personal stake in not being shown wrong. The conflict
between the motives and the aim of the dispute is exacerbated by
the tendency to harmonize public behavior with private beliefs.
Happily, the aim of a dispute can be achieved without a public
concession of defeat. For the aim is to share knowledge, not to
publicly display shared knowledge. As long as you made me see
the light, the dispute has served its function, whether I admit
enlightenment or not. However, my need to reconcile my public
behavior with my private beliefs works against discreet enlightenment. I tend to believe what I publicly advocate. This makes me
hard to educate. If only people were better hypocrites!

STRUCTURAL AGREEMENT

Since the clash of claim and counterclaim dominates center stage
of a dispute, we underestimate the amount of background agreement. This context for controversy can be divided into a contingent
fringe and a necessary core.

The contingent portion is composed of beliefs that *happen* to be
shared by the debaters but need not be. Different debaters arguing
the same issue may differ where our pair agree. Two citizens debating capital punishment may coincidentally believe that the Amazon
river once emptied into the Pacific Ocean. In addition to irrelevant
points of agreement, they are also likely to agree on pertinent
propositions: contract murders are premeditated on a cost-benefit
basis, the framers of the US Constitution approved of particular
judicial executions, juries are fallible, death is irreversible, capital
punishment is outlawed in most countries, and so on. Members of
this relevant set can often be identified from their service as premises
in the debaters' arguments. Hope of victory rests on spreading
support from the stock of relevant shared beliefs to your thesis.

There is also an area of necessary agreement. Perhaps there are beliefs that every human being *must* have regardless of what else they believe. Belief in an external world, the reliability of memory, and a distinction between right and wrong may be examples. A logically pristine example would be a belief, p, such that *any* believer would have to believe: $(x)(\exists r)\Box(Bxr \supset Bxp)$. If there are such beliefs, they are incontestable. For the aim of dispute, rational persuasion, cannot be achieved without a change of mind. If I necessarily believe p, then you can do nothing to make me believe $\sim p$. Arguing in favor of p is equally unsuccessful. If I already believe p, you cannot *persuade* me that p. Persuasion marks a qualitative transition from a state of not having a property to having the property. So you can no more persuade someone who already believes you than you can slay the slain.

Extracting consequences from the mere fact that someone believes something is tough going. We have easier going once we use the fact that the parties, are disputing a particular question q: $\Box(x)(y)(Dxyq \supset Axyp)$. That is, anyone who debates question q must agree on proposition p. This formula is philosophically interesting because it locates, p, the soft consensual underbelly of disputes. (Note that p can be a conjunction of many points of agreement.) Every dispute depends on an area of agreement for its survival. If this agreement is punctured, the dispute dies.

My plan is to anatomize the points of agreement constituting this vulnerable region. The plan rests on a theory of dissolution which starts with the premise that each dispute necessitates a stock of shared beliefs. The conjunction of these beliefs is a necessary condition for there being a reason to engage in the dispute. So a successful challenge to an element of this common ground will lead the parties to abort their debate. No one wins the dispute, no one loses. Indeed, the dispute isn't even a draw. The verdict is akin to reneging at cards; the game cannot continue because a constitutive rule has been broken. The outsider's refutation *annuls* the dispute.

This powerful dialectical move wends its way in and out of the history of ideas. But in twentieth-century philosophy, it was made more frequently and ferociously. Only a minority of philosophers were willing to go all the way with Wittgenstein. But plenty were willing to go far enough to raise eyebrows. As they gained stature, they drew criticism. Under the pressure of detailed objections, the dissolvers refined their heuristics. Contemporary philosophers have thus inherited a battle-hardened corpus of programs, precedents, and principles.

The footwork of the problem scuttler resembles the movements of a complex peasant dance. The peasants learned the steps by watching other peasants. The dance began simply but grew more complex as each generation embellished. The dance may now be in a mature state. Maybe it is still growing. But no peasant is the choreographer. It is a collective invention. Peasants learn the dance by immersion because there is no manual recording the steps of the dance. Should the manual be written, it could be studied with a view to mastering the dance. Of course, dances require too much habituation to be entirely learned from the book. We all need our doses of osmosis.

On analogy with the dance theorist, I document the steps used to dissolve disputes. The account is intended to yield theoretical and practical benefits. Foremost is satisfaction of curiosity about the nature of dissolution. The second service consists of helping people to decide whether to choose sides. One of the least controversial claims about philosophy is that philosophers are experts on controversies. Besides being able to explain the issues and arguments, the philosopher is exceptionally sensitive to common defects of controversies. The philosopher gets savvy mostly through experience. Just as fire fighters get to know fires by dealing with lots and lots of them, philosophers get good at disputes by their daily dealings with the classic issues. Of course, their expertise is not entirely a function of the great number of issues they are exposed to. Even fire fighters learn to structure their experience of fires with the help of pyrotechnic lore and applied chemistry.

Philosophers have partially codified the lessons learned from the great and not so great debates. This codification is especially rich in analytic philosophy. But even analytics resort to coarse-grained diagnoses of defective disputes. Instead of specifying the exact flaw, they are content with vague and ambiguous dismissals. These hand wavers and forehead slappers tell us that the question is bad or pointless or empty. But we are not given the details or a systematic comparison with healthy issues. This vagueness breeds suspicion that the analytic is just hiding an unwillingness to face tough problems. He is all too reminiscent of an evasive bureaucrat who brushes off complaints by terming them ill formulated, irregular, or just not his responsibility. The imprecision also stunts one of analytic philosophy's key themes. From the beginning of this century, analytics have voiced the metaphilosophical conviction that earlier philosophers rashly overestimated the health of philosophical issues. Analytics have always urged that one enter philosophical waters warily and be prepared to withdraw promptly. Once the language of dissolution is precisified, we gain new opportunities to test this policy of circumspection.

Thus, the practical goal of quarrel quality control is yoked to two philosophical aspirations. The first is to consolidate gains made by the analytic movement in this century. The second is to differentiate sound dissolutions from bogus evasions. Success here would discourage dissolutions based on knee-jerk defeatism and laziness. More specifically, I hope to clarify the claims and standards of the dissolutionist so that his performance can be accurately assessed.

QUESTION LOGIC

Just as the history of television is aptly transmitted by television, the advances of analytic philosophy are nicely conveyed by analytic techniques. I have used and will continue to use a variety of methods along the way: semantic ascent, modal logic, speech act theory, and a dash of analytic distinctions, for example, entailment/implicature, use/mention, type/token. One tool, however, shall play a foundational role: erotetic logic (the logic of questions). This role is formed by the requirement that both disputants know what is at issue. Since the thing at issue is always a question, the structure of issues is influenced by the structure of questions. Although I will not need to delve deeply into the logic of questions, its basic outline will serve as the skeleton of my theory of dissolution.

First, all logicians studying questions have been heavily influenced by Hamblin's dictum: 'Knowing what counts as an answer is equivalent to knowing the question' (Aqvist 1975, Belnap and Steel 1976, Hintikka 1981). One might challenge the priority of answers with 'solutions looking for problems'. For example, medical researchers describe Interferon as a miracle cure in search of a disease because it has the marks of an extraordinarily useful antiviral agent. Unfortunately, they have yet to find an application that would vindicate the analogy with past cures. This reversal of the question–answer relation is at the core of the game show *Jeopardy*. Contestants try to infer the question from one of its true answers. The task is challenging because the 'answers' are often incomplete ('This US president nearly died on his expedition to the River of Doubt') and so function as questions. That's why *Jeopardy* is still a quiz show. The interrogative edge of answer fragments is also manifest in Douglas Adams' *The Hitchhiker's Guide to the Galaxy* in which the thinking machine Deep Thought computes the ultimate answer,

42 – but must defer the ultimate question to the next computer generation.

Hamblin's dictum can handle these inverted searches because 'knowing what counts as an answer' is interpreted as knowing the *range* of *complete* answers. Questions are *requests* for guidance either in the form of information or instruction. Nuel Belnap and Thomas Steel picture a question 'as presenting a range of alternatives as its subject, from among which the respondent is to make a selection as from a tray of hors d'oeuvres' (1978: 17). For instance, 'Do the planets ever line up straight?' has 'Sometimes the planets line up straight' and 'The planets never line up straight' as alternatives. The respondent's job is to pick the correct alternative. Other questions have larger ranges of alternatives. 'Are you an atheist, agnostic, or theist?' lists three possibilities, and 'How many prime numbers are there?' has infinitely many options. Questions also vary in the type of request they make. Although most request the selection of exactly one alternative, they can ask for more: 'Who are some of the signers of the Munich agreement?' It's the prerogative of the interrogative.

Each alternative is a 'direct answer' to the question. Here, 'direct answer' is being used in a somewhat technical way. For it is defined as a response that completely but just completely answers the question. It provides neither more nor less information than requested. In psychological terms, a direct answer is just the type of answer that the questioner intended to elicit. As such, direct answers are to be contrasted with *corrective answers*. A corrective answer claims that the question is flawed. To 'Are you grill treating your fife?' the unfluted reply 'I am fifeless.' Here, the question is flawed by a false presupposition; both direct answers require the existence of a fife. Since the respondent has no fife, none of the alternatives are true. In general, a question *presupposes* a statement S just in case the falsehood of S prevents any of the alternatives from being true.

Lastly, it will also be useful to follow the logicians in distinguishing between questions and interrogatives just as mathematicians distinguish between numbers and numerals. Interrogatives are sentences that are used to express questions. 'Was Bloody Mary decapitated?' and 'Did Bloody Mary get beheaded?' are different interrogatives but they express the same question. Questions are on par with propositions. Both are abstract entities that can be expressed by different sentences in the same language or even different languages. Both have fixed meanings. The sentence 'Is it clammy now?' expresses different questions depending on what 'it' and 'now' denote. Sentences can be ambiguous or meaningless; propositions – and questions – can be neither. Of course, we do ordinarily speak of ambiguous questions (and indeed I shall when there is little threat of confusion). But this can be paraphrased as really talk about the sentences expressing questions. If you like, questions cannot be *directly* ambiguous. They can only be *indirectly* ambiguous; that is, expressed by ambiguous *interrogatives*. Likewise, questions can only be *indirectly* meaningless, badly written, or pleasant sounding.

As the high profile for erotetic logic suggests, my theory of dispute dissolution is intended to explain the philosopher's use of terms like 'pseudo-question' and 'bogus issue'. Although questions and issues do not advertise their dialectical ties as openly as disputes, they are tied to the social world by the public nature of criteria for answers, solutions, and resolutions. So a proper analysis of the diagnostic 'pseudo-F' locution will spill over from an analysis of defective disputes.

NOSOLOGICAL PREVIEW: THE TREE OF DISSOLUTION

Debate coaches say that you should tell your audience what you are going to tell them, tell them, and then tell them what you told them. The maxim holds good for explanation in general, so let's preview the book's next nine chapters. Each is dedicated to a point of necessary agreement. Hence I shall analyze dissolution into nine species. (In the final chapter of *The Plato Cult and other Philosophical Follies*, David Stove argues that there are indefinitely many ways for thought to go wrong and so no definite taxonomy of pseudo-problems. But I take repair manuals and the nosology of physicians to be potent precedents.) The varieties of bad questions are presented in decreasing order of severity. Each new defect is presented with the understanding that the dispute has none of the preceding defects.

Chapter 5 tees off with meaninglessness. This is the gravest criticism and was the most popular in the rebellious stage of analytic philosophy. The rhetoric of dissolution is a corollary of the rhetoric of refutation: defects tend to be initially overstated and are then re-characterized into softer charges that stick better. (In time, the achievements of the surmounted are quietly co-opted; what was revolution grays into reform.) Hence, historical order tends to follow logical order. This makes the tree of dissolution a predictor of the evolutionary path of a dissolutional critique.

In a charge of meaninglessness, the disputants are said to be uttering disguised nonsense. Convincing the partisans implodes discussion. Given that we are debating whether God exists, we must agree that 'Does God exist?' expresses a question. In other words, atheists and theists must take the issue to have content. So, as long as we are willing to debate the issue, we ally against those who dismiss the issue as empty talk.

We dissenters must secondly agree that the same question is being addressed. If our schism is the effect of an ambiguity, then the dispute can be resolved by simply drawing a distinction: A: History changes. B: That's absurd; the past is fixed! A: But new discoveries are made about the past. A: Sure, but knowledge of the past leaves it the same. C: Time out! In one sense, 'history' means the past, in another it means the study of the past. There is no disagreement behind this debate.

The suggestion that the parties are tangled in a verbal dispute pleases the diplomat in us. Although it appears that one of the arguers has blundered, in reality the quarrel is the coalescence of two minor errors of interpretation. Disagreement is minimized. One sign of the value we attach to this verdict is the frequency with which it is fraudulently procured. Mediators regularly concoct 'miscommunications' as a face-saving means of ending a feud.

Our preference for interpreting people in a way that minimizes their disagreement is justified by charity. This principle instructs us to minimize the attribution of irrationalities. Since the interpreter can only play down *perceived* errors, charity winds up favoring interpretations that make the interpretee's beliefs resemble the interpreter's. Consequently, the principle has the effect of maximizing the interpreter's perceived agreement with his interpretee. When there are two interpretees, charity minimizes the depth of the disagreement. Hence a tactful preference for dissolution has methodological momentum.

The principle of charity is often portrayed as a misguided attempt to accentuate the positive, to give people the benefit of the doubt, or as a principle of scholarly sportsmanship. But bear in mind that we are only maximizing the rationality of people, not their nonrational virtues. Consider folks who believe themselves wicked. Charity gives extra momentum to the self-deprecator's hypothesis. Charity makes us reluctant to attribute 'virtues of ignorance' to others such as modesty and impulsive courage (Driver 1989). It encourages us to attribute vices of hidden knowledge such as insincerity, hypocrisy, and treachery. Thus when a taxpayer seems to have underpaid through stupidity, the charitable auditor suspects that he is 'playing dumb'. When leaders exhort us to work selflessly for the common weal, do not tarry over the hypothesis that their moral fervor has led them to overlook prudence. Rescue them from this blunder with an attribution of hypocrisy. Extend charity to people who defend incredible theses in debate. Don't conclude idiocy. Conclude insincerity.

Charity leaves us free to attribute slips and other minor errors that leave the interpreter innocent of inconsistency, circularity, or other inferential inefficiencies. Hence the charitable disagreer deflects blame away from his partner's logic and on to (what he perceives to be) nonrational sources of error such as perceptual deficits, memory lapses, and miscoded data. Since we should postulate the least cause to explain the effect, there is a corollary to charity, the principle of superficiality: explain foreground differences in terms of the most superficial background disagreements.

In addition to believing that our dispute addresses a question, and that we are addressing the *same* question, we also believe that one of us is correct. We just differ as to who is correct. So a third point of agreement is belief in all of the presuppositions of our issue. If a plane crashes on the border between Nicaragua and Panama, where are the survivors to be buried? Don't answer! Just point out that the question falsely presupposes that survivors get buried – and that Nicaragua and Panama have a border.

Since debaters also think each other to be mistaken, they exclude the possibility that both sides are championing correct answers. So in addition to agreeing that one of us is right, we agree on a fourth point; that one of us is wrong. Suppose a dispute breaks out over 'Who succeeded Grover Cleveland as president?' One party argues that Benjamin Harrison succeeded Cleveland while the other contends that William McKinley succeeded Cleveland. Here we can point out that both answers are correct. (Cleveland held two nonconsecutive terms.) In addition to questions having no correct answers, there are unambiguous questions that have more than one correct answer.

Since no debater can believe the rightness of his position is due to luck, both sides agree that it is possible to *know* the answer to the question at issue. As an example of a dissolution exploiting this fifth point of agreement, consider how agnostics attempt to break up the debate between theists and atheists.

A sixth point of agreement between proponent and opponent is that *reason* can lead *both* parties to the same position. The answer must be *co-knowable* by rational give and take. Belief that one of us has privileged access or that one of us is uneducable eliminates the prospect of persuasion. Hence disputes with the insane and the emotionally over-wrought are futile. The issue may be meaningful, unequivocal, and have a uniquely correct and knowable answer – and yet still not be fit for discussion. The other side may be beyond the long arm of the laws of thought.

Seventh, both parties must agree that debate can resolve the matter. For example, debate about ultimate values is frequently dismissed on the grounds that reason can only calculate means, not ends. Philosophers are particularly hostile to proposed limits on debate. The reason is that they are experts on argument and so like other professionals, tend to exaggerate the utility of their specialization. On the gloomier side, the philosophers' training keeps them ignorant or suspicious of alternatives. For example, compromise is often pictured as an effective but illicit means of securing agreement. This picture of compromise as a synthesis of opposed views is an outsider's misperception. Rather than being a convergence of belief, compromise is practical cooperation in light of disagreement (Benjamin 1990: 7). As familiarity with nonargumentative forms of conflict resolution grows, one becomes less insistent that all matters are resolvable by rational debate.

These first seven types of dissolution have an involuntary feel. Nothing counts as proceeding with an annulled dispute. However, a debate can also be criticized on normative grounds. In particular, the eighth point of agreement is that the question deserves discussion. Belittling the debaters' prize will therefore menace his issue. Observe how Peter Singer deflates debate about the nature of morality and the question of whether one can derive prescriptive conclusions from purely descriptive premises:

> I shall argue that the differences between the contending parties are terminological, and that there are various possible terminologies, none of which has, on balance, any great advantage over any other terminology. So instead of continuing to regard these issues as central, moral philosophers could, I believe, 'agree to disagree' about the 'is-ought' problem, and about the definition of morality, provided only that everyone was careful to stipulate how he was using the term 'moral' and was aware of the implications and limitations of the definition he was using. Moral philosophers could then move on to consider more important issues.

> (1973: 51)

Singer grants that definitions of key terms such as 'moral' and 'ought' are worthwhile as preliminaries to further investigation. But since he thinks that no great advantage accrues from choosing one definition over its rivals, Singer says that the pursuit of the definition should be cut short with designer stipulations.

A ninth and final point of agreement amongst adversaries is that the dispute is efficient. Many scientists complain that the medieval school men had an irrational loyalty to *a priori* methods such as conceptual analysis. Instead of *arguing* about whether women have fewer teeth than men, the armchair biologists should have simply counted!

A dispute is defective just in case one of the propositions in necessary agreement is false. A dispute is *dissolved* by demonstrating that it is defective. The demonstration is unspecific if it merely shows that some necessitated belief or other is false. However, typical criticisms of disputes pinpoint the defect. That is, they try to show that the dispute has one of the nine flaws just outlined, namely:

1 Meaninglessness: no question has been expressed.
2 Equivocality: different questions are being unwittingly addressed.
3 Presupposition Failure: none of the question's direct answers is true.
4 Compatibility: too many of the direct answers are true.
5 Insincerity: one side is being deceptive about his true position.
6 Inaccessibility: the answer is out of reach.
7 Powerlessness: debate cannot force both to the same answer.
8 Unworthiness: the question does not deserve discussion.
9 Inefficiency: the dispute should be modified to eliminate waste.

For the sake of modularity, each of the following nine chapters concentrates on disputes that exemplify just one defect. However, passing comments will be made on common combinations of flaws. The last chapter will change the topic from 'What is a dissolution?' to 'What is a good dissolution?' In particular, it will show how and why certain problems and pseudo-problems are *deep*.

5 #?'!+@me☺an$♪@ing~l∃ ss* ne$$^♪

> One of man's distinctive abilities is the privilege of absurdity to
> which no living creature is subject, but man only. And of men,
> those are of all most subject to it that profess philosophy.
>
> (Thomas Hobbes)

Absurdity equals meaninglessness – when severely interpreted.
Many early analytic philosophers were willing to take this hard line
against a much larger portion of philosophy than Hobbes envi-
sioned. To understand how the appeal to meaninglessness acquired
this following, one must understand the need it filled. To understand
this need, one must understand the classic debate between rationalists and empiricists.

COMING TO OUR SENSES: A TALE OF TWO TENETS

Although philosophers have always been ready to dismiss some
questions as meaningless, the appeal to meaninglessness acquired
its major methodological role within British Empiricism. Empiricism
is the view that all of what we learn about the world is derived
from experience. Granted, *nonsubstantial* propositions can be
learned without experience. Reason alone can establish that 'A
father is a male parent.' For this proposition does not pick out a fact
about the world; it merely states a relationship between concepts or
words. In the terminology bequeathed by Kant, propositions that
owe their truth-value solely to the meanings of the words expressing
them are *analytic*. Propositions that (at least partly) owe their truth-
values to the way the world happened to turn out are *synthetic*.

Thus 'The Atlantic Ocean is 165 million years old' is synthetic because it owes its truth to geological vicissitudes.

A second Kantian distinction encapsulates the classic controversy between the empiricists and the rationalists. A proposition is *a priori* just in case it is knowable without experience. It is *a posteriori* just in case it is knowable but only with the benefit of experience. The empiricist's thesis can be cast as the negative claim that there are no synthetic *a priori* propositions.

	A priori	A posteriori
Analytic	Some	None
Synthetic	?	Some

Rationalists contend that there are synthetic *a priori* propositions, that is, some knowledge of the world that does not depend on our experiences of it.

Picture the debate between the empiricists and the rationalists as a game. The rationalist wins if he can identify a proposition that is known to be true and yet manages to be neither analytic nor synthetic *a posteriori*. The empiricist wins if he can disqualify all of the candidates nominated by the rationalist. Over the past few hundred years, the empiricists have devised three basic strategies for disposing of the rationalist's synthetic *a priori*s. The third strategy is responsible for the rise of meaninglessness. But let's set up the discussion with an analysis of the others.

Perseverance is the first strategy. Insist that although the proposition is known and does not *seem* to be analytic or synthetic *a posteriori*, it really is. The appeal to hidden analyticity is illustrated by John Locke's insistence that the phraseology of 'Whatever is, is' obscures its analyticity. Once we carefully reflect upon its meaning, says the first great British empiricist, we see that the statement just boils down to the trivial logical truth that everything is identical to itself. Mathematical candidates for the title of synthetic *a priori* truth, such as 'Equals added to equals give equals' and 'Every cube has 12 edges' were also diagnosed as disguised tautologies. Logicism, the view that *all* of mathematics is reducible to logic, attained its zenith of popularity in the first half of the twentieth century after being launched by Bertrand Russell's and Alfred North Whitehead's *Principia Mathematica*. But the appeal to analyticity was never restricted to rebutting mathematical candidates. Empiricists have always given broad play to the insight that apparently synthetic propositions are sometimes covertly analytic. Three pedestrian examples: 'Tuesday comes after Monday', 'Three pawns cannot give mate', 'In monogamous societies, women comprise half of those married.' Empiricists compared these easy cases with apparent world-structuring synthetic *a priori* truths such as 'Everything that is extended in space has a shape', 'Nothing can be blue all over and red all over', and 'No cause follows its effect.'

Another variation of the perseverance strategy is to invent an explanation of how the candidate is really synthetic *a posteriori*. John Stuart Mill, for instance, held that arithmetic statements were just highly confirmed empirical generalizations; we believe $7 + 5 = 12$ for the same reason we believe all crows are black. Other empiricists note that many alleged synthetic *a priori* propositions are found along the border between (analytic) geometry and (synthetic *a posteriori*) physics. They suggest that the appearance of a synthetic *a priori* is sometimes the result of blurring together the synthetic aspect of physics with the *a priori* aspect of geometry. For example, Daniel Bernoulli claimed that the principle of the parallelogram of forces was a geometrical synthetic *a priori*: when two equal forces at right angles to each other act on a point, the direction of the resulting force is along the line bisecting the angle. Ernst Mach (1976) countered that it was a synthetic *a posteriori* proposition of physics. Mach complained that Bernoulli's 'geometrical proof' smuggled in physical assumptions.

This coterie of tactics deal with recalcitrant propositions with a more determined effort to pigeonhole them into the empiricist's two available categories for knowledge. The remaining strategies try to explain away the appearance of knowledge.

The gentlest version of this hidden ignorance strategy challenges the proposition's epistemic status without commenting on its truth. For instance, David Hume said that 'Every event has a cause' only appears to be known to us. The basis for the belief is custom, not experience or the analysis of concepts. So although there is a fact of the matter, it is impossible to know whether the proposition is true or false. Empiricists friendly to skepticism make especially heavy use of this move. They grant that we are confident in propositions such as 'The future will resemble the past', 'The world has existed for many years', and 'Everything did not double in size last night.' But they frostily deny that we know these things and deny we know anything that implies these facts. After Darwin, empiricism was supplemented with evolutionary arguments for our limited knowledge. For example, Herbert Spencer portrayed reasoning as just an advanced physical ability designed to help an organism adjust to its environment by analysis of empirical data. So when the mind is fed questions that go beyond experience, it malfunctions – like any abused machine.

The other variants of the epistemic strategy are bolder because they deny knowledge on grounds of falsity. The bluntest rebuff is to say that the alleged synthetic *a priori* proposition is flatly false. This was Hume's line against 'The actual world is the best of all possible worlds.' He would take the same position against Gottfried Leibniz's principle of sufficient reason and the propositions Leibniz claimed to derive from the supremacy of the actual world such as the principle of continuity ('Nature is gradual') and the principle of perfection.

The falsehood option is sometimes tempered with the concession that the proposition is *useful*. For example, taciturn atheists say that widespread belief in an afterlife increases adherence to moral codes, thereby enhancing the prospects of the social group subscribing to the myth. Classicists who study myths often claim that these catchy falsehoods organize experience and provide a general framework for discussion. Since the important point is to have *a* framework, not the correct one, there can be a plurality of serviceable myths.

False propositions can be useful even if not believed. This was the point behind Hans Vaihinger's (1924) 'fictions'. A fiction is a falsehood that we nevertheless act on because it works *as if* it were true. Contemporary philosophers of science try to capture a similar notion with their distinction between the context of justification and the context of pursuit. We normally realize that the fiction is false and only operate with it as long as it expedites inquiry. For example, Wolfgang Goethe realized that 'All animal species are modifications of a single archetype' was false and nearly all social contract theorists have explicitly denied that 'Many years ago people formed a society by drawing up an agreement.' But sometimes fictions go unrecognized by their beneficiaries. Vaihinger thought this to be the case with the economist's principle that 'Everyone pursues his own self-interest' and other propositions that look synthetic *a priori*: 'Everything is made of matter', 'Everything is made up of atoms', 'Living things differ from nonliving thing by virtue of their possession of a vital force.' (Notice that Vaihinger's sharp distinction between the truth of a proposition and its utility separates fictionalism from pragmatism.)

The third strategy is to say that the candidate synthetic *a priori* is neither true nor false. The diplomatic variation of this no-truth-value option is to say that the statement has a nondescriptive meaning. For example, Rudolph Carnap took 'Chemical weapons are evil' to be a hidden imperative of the form 'Don't use chemical weapons!' Since imperatives do not describe anything, they lack a truth-value. As George Berkeley first emphasized, language serves purposes beyond the exchange of factual reports:

> the communicating of ideas marked by words is not the chief and only end of language, as is commonly supposed. There are other ends, as the raising of some passion, the exciting to or deterring from an action, the putting the mind in some particular disposition; to which the former is in many cases barely subservient, and sometimes entirely omitted, when these can be obtained without it, as I think does not unfrequently happen in the familiar use of language.
>
> (1930: sect. 20)

Many of these nondescriptive functions of language can be categorized as prescriptive. The word-to-world fit has two directions. When describing, I try to make my words fit the world. When prescribing, I try to make the world fit my words. It is the difference between reporting 'The music stopped' and demanding 'Stop the music!' The prescriptive group contains orders, suggestions, rules, and questions (because questions are requests). Other nondescriptive functions are emotive, that is, they serve to express or evoke emotions. Optatives, cheers, and curses lie in this category.

The empiricist argues that some apparent cases of synthetic *a priori* knowledge can be traced to our predilection for treating utterances as descriptive. The rationalist Leibniz believed that principles of reasoning such as *modus ponens* must be known *a priori* because experience can teach us about the world only by applying the principles. We do not learn *of* the law of identity, we learn *by* the law of identity. Some empiricists reply that *modus ponens*, the law of identity, and the law of contradiction are *rules* of inference and so lack truth-values. Some empiricists are also willing to say that statements such as 'Everyone pursues his own self-interest' are only policy declarations or regulative principles. Inquiry goes well when we doggedly pursue causes. Compare these methodological imperatives to maxims such as 'Nothing is impossible' and 'Chance favors the prepared mind.' This noncognitivist line has been used to explain the apparent synthetic *a priori* nature of moral statements such as 'People should not be used as means.' Aesthetic remarks such as 'There must always be enigma in poetry' were also explained away on the grounds that they merely ventilate one's psyche.

The final possibility is to say that the utterance is devoid of any kind of meaning. This is stronger than merely denying that the utterance has descriptive meaning. The allegation is that there is no meaning at all. Berkeley noted 'We have learned from Mr. Locke that there may be and that there are several glib, coherent, methodical discourses which nevertheless amount to just nothing' (1930: 62). As an example he writes 'Say you the mind is not the perceptions but that thing which perceives. I answer you are abused by the words "that" and "thing"; these are vague, empty words without a meaning' (Berkeley 1930: 72). More famous is Berkeley's charge that 'substance' (in Locke's usage) is meaningless.

Hume sided with Berkeley and so extended the charge to 'Do perceptions inhere in a material or an immaterial substance?':

> In order to put a stop to these endless cavils on both sides, I know no better method, than to ask these philosophers in a few words, *What they mean by substance and inhesion?* And after they have answer'd this question, 'twill then be reasonable, and not till then, to enter seriously into the dispute.
>
> (1739: I.iv.232)

Hume then proceeded to show that 'substance' and 'inhesion' do not receive meaning by being ostensively defined as a kind of sense impression. Some suggest that 'substance' can be defined as 'something which can exist by itself'. But this is too broad because anything conceivable can exist by itself. Sometimes 'x inheres in y' is defined as 'x depends on y for its existence'. This scotches the possibility of perceptions inhering in a body because perceptions do not have locations. But to say that they inhere in an immaterial substance is incomprehensible. Why must perceptions inhere in anything? After further criticism, Hume concludes that all sources of meaning for the two expressions have been eliminated,

> which seems to me a sufficient reason for abandoning utterly that dispute concerning the materiality and immateriality of the soul, and makes me absolutely condemn even the question itself. We have no perfect idea of any thing but of perception . . . What possibility then of answering that question, *Whether perceptions inhere in a material or immaterial substance*, when we do not so much as understand the meaning of the question?
>
> (1739: I.iv.234)

Cries of 'Meaningless!' reached their crescendo in the first half of the twentieth century. Rudolph Carnap illustrates the charge against a fictitious thinker, who asserts that there is a levitational field as well as a gravitational field. The levitationist concedes that there is no observable effect of this newly postulated field. Carnap scolds his imaginary friend: 'Your assertion is no assertion at all; it does not speak about any thing; it is nothing but a series of empty words; it is simply without sense' (1935: 209).

'Meaningless' is a cinch to define: x is meaningless just in case it has no meaning. Nevertheless, it is tricky in a way typical of all privative expressions. Since the definition of 'meaningless' contains the quantifier 'no', the term is sensitive to the domain of discourse. This context sensitivity invites confusion over the breadth and depth of the accusation. In particular, those who only have grounds for denying an utterance descriptive meaning may say 'The statement is meaningless' and be understood as denying that the statement has any meaning at all. Often this stronger reading is misattributed to the speaker by an uncharitable or unsophisticated audience. Admittedly, the mongers of meaninglessness court misinterpretation by overstating their case for rhetorical effect. A famous passage from the final chapter of Hume's *Enquiry Concerning Human Understanding* exemplifies this positivistic panache:

> It seems to me, that the only objects of the abstract sciences or of demonstration, are quantity and number . . . All other enquiries of men regard only matter of fact and existence; and these are evidently incapable of demonstration . . . When we run over libraries, persuaded of this principle, what havoc must we make? If we take in our hand any volume, of divinity or school metaphysics, for instance; let us ask, Does it contain any abstract reasoning concerning quantity or number? No. Does it contain any experimental reasoning concerning matter of fact and existence? No. Commit it then to the flames: for it can contain nothing but sophistry and illusion.
>
> (1777: 164–5)

The verificationist criterion of meaningfulness enshrined this equivocation: 'A statement is meaningful if and only if it is either verifiable or analytic.' This check-or-chuck principle is concerned with an important kind of meaning but misleadingly suggests that this is the only sort of meaning. Statements such as 'B. F. Skinner died on 20 August 1990' and 'Copenhagen is a tropical city' count as meaningful because they can be established or overturned by observation and experiment. 'All pyromaniacs are fascinated by fire' counts as meaningful because it is made true by the meanings of its words.

When we move to metaphysical statements, we lose this friction with reality. 'Noumenal selves transcend causality' and 'The universe is governed by yin and yang' suggest no observations or experiments and are not true by definition. So although they look like they mean something, the verification principle unmasks them as nonsense.

FROM MUNCHIES TO METAPHYSICS

The verification principle counts all nondescriptive utterances as meaningless. This boldness lends a certain cold charm to the criterion. While in this sympathetic mood, we may be attracted to a slippery slope entwining nondescriptive statements with metaphysical ones. We begin by noting that verificationism accords with the common-sense prohibition against debating taste. If I greet roasted grasshoppers with 'Yum' and you with 'Yuk', we have diverging reactions. Period. Now suppose a wine connoisseur says that a particular type of wine is 'bold and forthright' while the other says it is 'timid and indirect'. Is debate over the wine any more appropriate than debate over roasted grasshoppers? One answer is that 'Yum' stands to 'bold and forthright' as 'fiddle' to 'violin' and as 'guess' to 'conjecture'. Linguists describe the difference between pairs such as (horse, steed), (woman, lady), and (eat, dine) as elevation. These examples concern words that are descriptively equivalent but differ along the parameters of politeness, style, and class. The cases of interest have no descriptive content and so are descriptively equivalent by default. Yet they nevertheless differ along the parameters of elevation. In short, the connoisseur might just have a classier way of saying 'yum'. The same nondescriptive difference is exhibited by (hurrah, bravo), (nifty, kudos), and (neato, jolly good). All of these merely toot approval but in ways that vary in elevation. They are nonetheless equally meaningless.

From the mumbo jumbo of wine-tasting voice-overs, we come to appreciate the poppycock of fashion narration. Since fashions change rapidly, usually within one's own recent memory, the arbitrariness of style is flagrant. And indeed the narration accompanying the model's exhibition is full of the obscurantist phraseology we hear at the wine table. But there is a higher degree of social pressure. The ill attired are more readily ridiculed and discouraged than those who have pedestrian taste in wine. So we react nimbly to signs of changing fashion just as traders respond quickly to signs of economic change. This creates bandwagon effects that further increase the illusion of objectivity by increasing uniformity of judgment.

The fashion world blends into the worlds of interior decoration, exterior design, architecture, and the art world in general. Paintings, sculptures, and plays seem more objectively good. Many more people are apt to view diverging reactions as betokening *ignorance*. A rube who prefers a Rockwell over a Renoir is thought unperceptive. Many more people are apt to believe that there are *experts* on the quality of art works who pick up on features most people miss. Consequently, many people are *apologetic* about their preferences: 'I do not know what is good but I know what I like.' And finally there is fear of *bias* which implies the existence of irrelevant and relevant factors in aesthetic judgment.

Etiquette shares fashion's increased degree of social pressure. Although the arbitrariness of how we eat and entertain is widely recognized, we are willing to suffer considerable inconvenience to abide by custom. Victorian women endured organ-crushing corsets for sake of a slim waistline. Etiquette eases us into morality. However, the amount of social pressure for morality exceeds the pressure for conformity to aesthetic judgments. Laugh at Art and you are jeered. Slash Art and you are jailed.

We can understand why societies take a hard line on acts gravely injurious to their members. Societies prosper when their members can confidently plan their futures. Plans require prediction and control of events and therefore a nondisruptive backdrop. Societies that do not furnish security are supplanted by those that do. So the prevalence of prohibitions against injury and theft comes as no mystery. But how do successful societies win conformity to moral norms that promote group self-interest but not individual self-interest?

Sanctions (such as fines for speeding) obviously play a large role by gnawing away areas of divergence between self-interest and group-interest. Habit helps by directing our attention away from the benefits accruing from selective adherence to rules. Mythical sanction is another device that introduces less plausible but more colorful sanctions (heaven and hell, karma, reincarnation). Mythical sanctions are cheap supplements to the terrestrial system of rewards and penalties. Logical myth may also help. Perhaps moral claims gain the appearance of objectivity by being cast as declaratives and mimicking descriptive statements. People instinctively seek truth and avoid error because accurate mappers of reality fare better than inaccurate ones. Of course, few people think about the psychobiological rationale. Our aversion to error is akin to the alarm triggered by falling backwards. This fear persists even when we realize that we are in a situation in which falling backwards is safe. So moralists tap into this anxiety by casting their utterances in declarative form, a form that suggests *description* of reality. So we come to fear moral *error* in the way we fear error about the edibility of a tomato. We obtain a full 'carrot and stick' account of logical myth by further noting that the descriptive mode appeals to our love of truth as well as our fear of error. So even if casuists do not *intend* to dupe their audience into thinking that their moral utterances have truth-values, the cognitivist illusion could slip in by an invisible hand process. Moralists who made their discourse seem like it had a truth-value would be more persuasive than those who did not, so discourse styles inviting a cognitivist attitude would supplant those that did not. A Gresham's law of logical form may operate for ethics: deceptively packaged utterances drive out perspicaciously packaged ones.

The objectification of taste also encompasses the *language* we use to describe the world. Communities develop privileged dialects that are defended as *the right way* to speak the language. Other dialects are treated as degenerate forms and their popularity as a widening corruption of the language as a whole. Since languages reflect conceptual schemes, and these schemes are connected to metaphysical systems, we come to suspect that metaphysical differences might be a matter of taste. In this spirit, Carnap compared metaphysical statements to poetry. Just as poetry expresses temporary feelings, philosophy expresses

> permanent emotional or volitional dispositions. Thus, for instance, a metaphysical system of monism may be an expression of an even and harmonious mode of life, a dualistic system may be an expression of the emotional state of someone who takes life as an eternal struggle; an ethical system of rigorism may be expressive of a strong sense of duty or perhaps of a desire to rule severely. Realism is often a symptom of the type of constitution called by psychologists extroverted, which is characterized by easily forming connections with men and things; idealism, of an opposite constitution, the so-called introverted type, which has a tendency to withdraw from the unfriendly world and to live within its own thoughts and fancies.
>
> (1935: 215)

Unlike a lyrical verse, however, a metaphysical statement is apt to be mistaken for a descriptive one. Indeed, the metaphysicians themselves are deceived by their own oratory. So metaphysics should be *rejected*.

INTERROGATIVELESS DISPUTES

Ernest Rutherford's favorite oral exam question was 'What is the self-inductance of a wedding ring?' One pupil replied '654.3, Sir.' 'Oh, and what units are you using?' asked Rutherford. 'Arbitrary units, of course, Sir.' Lesson: a meaningful question can meet with a meaningless 'answer'.

We now turn to 'questions' that *necessarily* lack meaningful answers. Here the issue itself is meaningless. For instance, some disputes are too amorphous to permit a statement of the issue. The debaters cannot tell us what question they are trying to answer because they cannot even agree on the interrogative sentence. Consider the play-acted argument of children. Like other make-believe activities, pretend-quarrel shades off into the real activity. This gives rise to borderline cases of disputes over issues that cannot be specified. Other defective disputes arise from imperfect mastery of the activity. When children omit essential parts of golf, cuisine, or explanation, we deny that they are really playing baseball, cooking, or explaining. When the component is inessential but nevertheless important, we assess the activity as genuine but still flawed. Since I take the ability to articulate an interrogative as an important but not essential component of a dispute, I grant that some interrogativeless disputes are disputes – just as toothless smiles are still smiles.

Play-time illuminates grown-up behavior. Normal adults have *competence* at disputation. Nevertheless, their *performance* is frequently flawed. Sometimes we confuse disputation with other joint speech acts. For example, a disputant who refuses to modify his position in response to a string of concessions from his opponent tends to be perceived as dogmatic. This impression of intransigence is triggered by the conflation of argument and negotiation. Another sign of this hybridization is the frequent posturing of disputants. Just as bargainers ask for more than they expect in order to get what they want, debaters advance stronger positions than they believe in order to arrive at a compromise position more in line with what they find credible. Defenders of 'creation science', for example, sometimes begin with the position that it is *better than* evolutionary theory in the hope of at least persuading others that creation science is *at least the equal* of evolutionary theory.

Separating interrogatives from non-interrogatives is a mechanical affair when they are part of a formal language. The existence of explicit, complete rules enables us to determine whether the interrogative is a well-formed formula. In natural language, the classification is thornier. The first prick is from the uncertainty surrounding the distinction between a bad sentence and an ungrammatical one. 'Bulldogs bulldogs fight fight' is difficult to parse and so is wrongly rejected as meaningless. (Try 'Bulldogs that bulldogs fight do fight.') Although logicians are feared as exposers of hidden nonsense, they also redeem statements by discovering hidden sense. A kindly modal logician can divide 'It is possible that it is possible that it is possible that dogs understand Russian' into digestible stages and thereby show that it is perfectly meaningful. But in other cases, it's hard to tell whether the problem is complexity or meaninglessness.

Our metalinguistic abilities also confound the recognition of meaningless interrogatives. An employer with many applications asks for your opinion of a friend. You try to be both loyal and truthful. So you carefully choose your words and struggle to reach an honorable end for your sentence. The employer interrupts with 'That tells me all I need to know.' Although you have not framed a complete thought, your hesitant utterance is a natural sign that your friend is not a good candidate. You might even tacitly invite the inference by making this unspontaneousness salient. We encounter this tendency to use conventional signs as natural signs as soon as we begin to learn a language. Mother does not wait for baby to form complete thoughts and baby quickly learns to depend on these interventions. So from the start, we rely on our interlocutors to fastforward conversation by picking through our proto-messages. Casual dialogue proceeds chop-chop. This mechanism for meaninglessness is not confined to the social sphere. An individual can also draw inferences from his own half-thoughts. Hence our ability to draw diagnostic inferences from incomplete thoughts ensures that we don't bother to give full meaning to our utterances. If it doesn't itch, don't scratch! Consequently, we have trouble telling the difference between elided utterances and communicationally useful but meaningless ones. The demarcation is further obscured by the practice of conveying meaningful propositions by uttering meaningless statements. For example, positivists try to expose nonsense by uttering similar nonsense as a logical analogy. Where do we draw the line between the directly and indirectly meaningful?

QUESTIONLESS DISPUTES

The more interesting kind of a meaningless dispute features two people who agree on an interrogative but who miss the fact that the interrogative fails to express a question. The mathematically naive may debate 'Is a zillion larger than a jillion?' But neither 'zillion' nor 'jillion' denote integers. A person can meaningfully use 'trillion' even if he does not know exactly which integer it denotes. For he is deferring the reference-fixing to mathematicians. We take advantage of this linguistic division of labor everyday. Only the experts know exactly what 'gold', 'black hole', and 'virus' mean. So even if the two of us are ignorant of the exact meaning of 'billion' and 'trillion' we can still use our rough grasp of the terms to dispute 'Is a trillion larger than a billion or the reverse?' I can know that a trillion is larger than a billion even if I do not know the exact integers they denote. Since we are successful in deferring reference to the experts, our interrogative has an exact meaning even if we do not know what it is. However, in the case of 'Is a zillion larger than a jillion?', linguistic delegation fails.

Sometimes philosophers dramatically declare a familiar word to be meaningless. Berkeley claimed that 'matter' was meaningless because it did not refer to anything observable. This is sometimes understood as a condemnation of any sentence that uses 'matter'. However, a meaningless word can be part of a meaningful utterance. This should be evident from my analysis of 'real'. However, I cannot forbear mentioning my favorite example. Each time William James emerged from the influence of nitrous oxide, he was frustrated by the impression that he had forgotten profound insights. So he finally resolved to write his thoughts down. Included in the corpus was this couplet: 'Higamus, hogamus, Women are monogamous; Hogamus, higamus, Men are polygamous.'

Syntactic meaninglessness

Some sentences manage to be meaningless even though each of the words in the sentence is meaningful. For example, 'Wobble in of stew and if then' is meaningless because it violates rules for sentence construction. 'Quadruplicity drinks procrastination' stays within the letter of ordinary grammatical law but philosophers and linguists extend 'syntactic meaninglessness' to these cases by maintaining that the sentences violate 'depth grammar'.

The flashiest accusation of syntactic meaninglessness was the one

Carnap leveled at Martin Heidegger's claim in *Was ist Metaphysik?* that 'The Nothing itself nothings.' Although Carnap grants that each word is meaningful, he says they have not been legitimately combined. So no question is expressed by 'Does the nothing itself nothing?' The vortex of nothingness also consumes Jean-Paul Sartre:

> The Being by which Nothingness arrives in the world must nihilate Nothingness in its Being, and even so it still runs the risk of establishing Nothingness as a transcendent in the very heart of immanence unless it nihilates Nothingness in its being *in connection with its own being*. The Being by which Nothingness arrives in the world is a being such that in its being, the Nothingness of its Being is in question. *The being by which Nothingness comes to the world must be its own Nothingness.*

> (1956: 23)

Intrigue with nothingness is international and trans-historical. Five hundred years before Christ, Buddha averred 'The no-mind not-thinks no-thoughts about nothings.' And recall that Plato was puzzled about how false beliefs were possible. Unlike Heidegger and Sartre, Plato made conspicuous progress. He fought his way from a meaningless question to a meaningful one. Gilbert Ryle recaps:

> The problem is not the unstatable problem, How can there be negative things? It is rather, How can things be truly or falsely denied to be so-and-so? In Aristotelian parlance, 'not' cannot be attached to the subject of a truth or falsehood; but it can be attached to what is predicated of that subject. We can say truly of Theaetetus that he is not flying or falsely of him that he is not sitting. What we cannot do is say anything at all about not-Theaetetus or un-Theaetetus. Statements can be negative, though their subject names cannot. So the authentic problem is, What is it to deny or affirm something, truly or falsely, of, say, Theaetetus?

> (1967: 329)

Ryle goes on to point out how Plato's insight about negation and ensuing investigation into the nature of propositions opened the road for Aristotle's inquiries into implication.

Heidegger's 'The Nothing itself nothings' is a popular illustration of meaninglessness because we immediately gag. But most appeals to syntactic meaninglessness concern sentences that cloak their unintelligibility. Ordinary language philosophers stress the role of a good ear for the language. For rather than being brazenly baffling, most of the troublesome cases only sound a bit discordant. So ordinary language philosophers would begin their analyses by stressing that it would be odd to say such-and-such or that no competent speaker of the language would say so-and-so. The point of such appeals was to provide reason to suspect rule violation. Since most philosophical sentences contain words that are individually meaningful, the meaninglessness of the sentence would have to be syntactic. And since most philosophical sentences clearly conformed to the sort of grammar familiar to all educated people, the critic would also agree that the sentence satisfied 'surface grammar'. The violation would have to be at a deeper, more theoretical level.

Study of this depth grammar was widely perceived as the neglected positive side to analytic philosophy. Just as explorers can produce interesting maps in their efforts to mark pitfalls, bogs, and false trails, philosophers can craft conceptual cartography of interest to linguists. Witness how linguists have elaborated topics introduced by twentieth-century analytic philosophers: presupposition, speech acts, modal logic, dialogue games, etc.

Pragmatic meaninglessness

There is a process/product ambiguity to 'meaningless utterance'. So far, we have concentrated on the product sense. That is, we have concentrated on how *what* is said can fail to express a proposition. But 'meaningless utterance' can also refer to the failure to perform a speech act. Utterances that would be meaningful in the mouth of a person are meaningless in the mouth of a parrot because the bird is psychologically deficient. Likewise, computers do not assert anything even though we find their utterances highly informative. (Or evocative as Racher's computer poetry in *The Policeman's Beard is Half Constructed*.)

People listening to crazy talk usually take the deranged individual to be incorrectly describing the actual world or to be correctly describing a private reality. But the notion of pragmatic meaninglessness introduces a third possibility; the lunatic is not describing anything. He is just spewing sentences. The same holds for people who talk in their sleep. Their utterances could be verbal twitches.

Wittgenstein saw an affinity between the out-of-context utterances of mad men and the remarks of philosophers: 'I am sitting with a philosopher in the garden; he says again and again "I know that that's a tree", pointing to a tree that is near us. Someone else arrives and hears this, and I tell him: "This fellow isn't insane.

We are only doing philosophy." ' (1969: §467) Norman Malcolm elaborates by criticizing G. E. Moore for uttering truisms such as: there exists at present a living human body, which is *my* body; the earth had existed for many years before my body was born; ever since it was born it has been either in contact with or not far from the surface of the earth; I am a human being; I have often perceived both my own body and other things which formed part of its environment, including other human bodies. Moore claimed to know these statements with certainty and so took them to be counterexamples to solipsism, idealism, and skepticism about time. Malcolm grants that the content of these statements is meaningful. However, he denies that they are in order when uttered in the circumstances Moore did. When Moore said 'This is a hand' to prove the existence of the external world, it was not to assuage antecedent doubts about him having a prosthetic hand, a malformed foot, or whatnot. Likewise, when Moore says 'I know I am seeing a tree' to prove that he can know he is not dreaming, the tree is in plain view. Moore was deliberately choosing utterances that did not answer any doubt. Malcolm insists that a genuine assertion must be intended to relieve a possible doubt and so he rejects Moore's utterance as a misusage. One might reply that Moore is trying to resolve a *philosophical* doubt. Malcolm denies that philosophical doubts are real doubts:

> Moore's opponent has a *philosophical* doubt as to whether he is dreaming, but this does not imply that he is *in doubt* whether he is dreaming. To call a philosophical doubt a *doubt* is as misleading as to call a rhetorical question a *question*. We should not say that a man was feeling a philosophical doubt as to whether he was having an hallucination if he was, *in the ordinary sense of the words*, in doubt as to whether he was having an hallucination. Nor should we say that was raising a philosophical question as to whether he might not be dreaming if the circumstances were such that there *was* some question as to whether he was dreaming.
>
> (1969: 207)

Malcolm says that a second point of difference is that Moore cannot give a *reason* to support his knowledge claim. For example, Moore says he knows that he is not dreaming but cannot say how he knows. There is no connection with an *investigation* that will settle the matter. Malcolm takes this to be a symptom of the fact that the question of proof does not arise; Moore neither knows nor fails to know the truisms. 'Moore's assertions do not belong to "common sense," i.e., to ordinary language at all. They involve a use of "know" which is a radical departure from ordinary usage' (1969: 218).

COMMON SOURCES OF MEANINGLESSNESS

Throughout his career, Wittgenstein operated under the conviction that many, if not all, philosophical disputes rest on disguised nonsense. In the *Tractatus* (4.003), he characterizes philosophy as abortive discourse:

> Most of the propositions and questions to be found in philosophical works are not false but nonsensical. Consequently we cannot give any answer to questions of this kind, but can only establish that they are nonsensical. Most of the propositions and questions of philosophers arise from our failure to understand the logic of our language.
>
> (They belong to the same class as the question whether the good is more or less identical than the beautiful.)
>
> And it is not surprising that the deepest problems are in fact *not* problems at all.
>
> (1922: 4.003)

According to Wittgenstein, correct philosophy is a matter of uncovering hidden nonsense. Thus much of his diagnostic effort consists of explaining how a sentence can *seem* to be meaningful when it actually violates the rules of language.

Misleading grammatical analogies

One of Wittgenstein's stock explanations of meaningless sentences is that they harken back to meaningful ones. If you have twenty odds and ends on a table and nineteen fall off, what is left, an odd or an end? This popular conundrum is puzzling because 'twenty odds and ends' resembles 'twenty quarters and dimes' and 'twenty men and women'. Specifically, we assume that 'and' is functioning in the logical role of conjunction and that 'odds' and 'ends' designate types of objects. In fact, 'odds and ends' is an idiom, that is, an expression whose meaning cannot be inferred from the meanings of its parts such as 'kick the bucket'. The 'and' in 'odds and ends' is as semantically inert as the 'and' in 'phil*and*ering'.

Beguiling likenesses become philosophically interesting when they figure into explanations of philosophical mistakes. For example, ordinary language philosophers have suggested that the misconception that infinity is a colossal number is encouraged by the expression 'going on to infinity'.

Some grammatical mis-clues are accidental, but others take shape systematically. For instance, the need to avoid refutation leads believers to evacuate the content of initially contradictory doctrines. For example, one can consistently say 'There is exactly one God but Jesus, his Father, and the Holy Ghost are distinct divinities' only if one bleeds off the statement's ordinary meaning so that it no longer entails 'There is exactly one god' and 'There are exactly three gods.' But if you do not infuse new meaning, you are only left with the exoskeleton of the old doctrine of the trinity.

Steer steer steer. The funny thing about wearing a hat is that when you put it on, you feel like it's off; and when you take it off, you feel like it's on. Nonsense is the same way. Repeating something meaningful makes it seem like nonsense. Repeating nonsense makes it seem meaningful. So I dub the doctrine of the trinity a xeroxymoron.

Misrelativization

Consider the continuum running from affixes such as 'pre- ' and ' -less' to complete words such as 'pincer' and on to phrases such as 'in the cell'. Before we reach complete sentences, we must pass through incomplete ones such as 'Ten miles distant' and 'Gandhi's religious views are irrelevant.' Incomplete sentences do not explicitly contain required variables. We try to elicit hidden variables with feelers such as 'Irrelevant to what?' When the variables are elided, the utterance is a meaningful abbreviation of a complete utterance. However, sometimes the speaker can provide no guidance as to what the missing variables are because he has tried to make a statement without their benefit. When this happens, the under-relativized utterance fails to express a proposition. Although people are not tempted to affirm or deny '____ ate ____ at the ____ ' they sometimes attempt to take a position on statements that are less conspicuously moth-eaten.

R. M. Hare (1981) once hosted a young Swiss gentleman who became morbidly depressed. He had become convinced that 'Nothing matters' after reading Camus' *L'Etranger*. Hare's remedy was to first get the young man to agree that saying that x matters is to express concern about x. Hare then urged that there must then be *someone* who has the concern about *x*; we may always ask 'Whose concern?' So we really do not understand 'Nothing matters' until we know the answer to 'Nothing matters to who?' The answer cannot be the author, Camus, because Camus was at least concerned about writing a good novel. The character in the novel who shouted 'Nothing matters' just before execution might pass for the non-carer because he is portrayed as indifferent to the things with which people are normally quite concerned. But so what? The object of the young man's depression was not that nothing matters to Camus' character. Well, what about the young man himself? Was the object of his depression 'Nothing matters to me'? This is closer but not quite right because upon Hare's probing, his Swiss guest did admit to caring about various things. Indeed, what bothered him was the incongruity of these concerns in light of his belief that nothing matters. At this point, it became evident that mattering had been misconstrued as a sort of activity rather like chattering; compare 'My wife matters to me' and 'My wife chatters to me.' The young man was expressing disappointment that things did not have the independent property of mattering. But Hare's discussion had exposed mattering as a chimerical concept born from our tendency to abbreviate expressions of concern.

Some existentialists have also been accused of making meaningless statements about responsibility. On the one hand they stress the importance of man's being responsible, but on the other hand they deny that our responsibility is *to* anyone and deny that the responsibility makes us subject to penalty. Since these are mandatory variables, the existentialist's utterance of 'Man is responsible' looks meaningful but is not.

Over-relativization is also possible. That is, *n*-place predicates are sometimes treated as if they had more than *n* places. For example, cultures heavily influenced by belief in sorcery, such as the Azande, tend to view disease on the model of attack. Just as attacks require attackers as well as victims, diseases require senders as well as sufferers. When ill, the Azande deem it always appropriate to ask 'Who made me ill?' Westerners who deny that anyone sent the disease are viewed as confused, as akin to someone who says a letter was addressed to him without any addresser.

Overextending a question pattern

Meaninglessness can result from innate but inappropriate drives such as the one de-voiced dogs manifest when they go through the motions of barking. Ludwig Boltzmann's tart appeal to cognitive instincts is in this spirit:

> babies have a sucking instinct, otherwise they could not stay alive, and this instinct became so habitual that later the child continues to suck empty rubber. Likewise the laws of thought often overshoot the mark and the philosopher seeks to suck a whole theory of the world out of the concept of nothingness. Likewise the old established and hereditary custom of asking for the cause (the child's eternal question 'Why?' already shows it to be hereditary) overshoots the mark if we ask for the cause why the law of cause and effect itself holds; likewise if we ask why the world exists at all, why it is as it is, why we exist at all and why precisely now and so on.
>
> (1974: 195)

Immanual Kant spoke similarly of regulative questions. According to Kant, we organize experience by means of categories such as cause, time, and space. We are programmed to ask questions in the mold of 'What caused that?', 'When did that happen?' and 'What are its parts?' This structured curiosity becomes enshrined in ideals that regulate inquiry such as 'Every event has a cause.' Philosophical problems arise when we construe these ideals as having more than a regulative function. For when 'Every event has a cause' is construed as a *description* of the reality behind appearances ('noumenal reality'), we are stricken with enigmata such as the Kantian antinomies.

In addition to the errors induced by nature, there are those induced by nurture. Useful actions become second nature. They acquire an inertia that carries adaptive behavior beyond the bounds of proper application (Boltzmann 1974: 166). For example, force of habit leads the clumsy man to apologize to a bumped stool. Mach (1986: 5–6) blamed the concept of the thing-in-itself on an over-application of our habit of designating complexes of ideas with single names. The naming habit spares us the labor of considering unwieldy components. Indeed, we can consider the conglomeration as the 'same thing' when components are mentally subtracted. Thus a cartographer simplifies his representation of a village by imaginatively subtracting irrelevant properties to form a map. However, metaphysicians try to abstract away all of the object's properties and so arrive at the pseudo-concept of pure substance.

Our susceptibility to habits of questioning should be no surprise since nearly all of our behavior flows through channels cut by repetition. When certain types of questions are rewarded, others of the same type follow. For instance, we prosper by following a policy of reciprocity. But we go too far when we reject appeals to posterity by demanding 'What has posterity ever done for us?' More general benefits flow from asking 'Why is x valuable?' This too leads to an overextension of the question pattern (Boltzmann 1974: 166). We ask what is the value of life itself. Our despair at the absence of a plausible answer pressures us into answers that are long on comfort but short on coherency.

Boltzmann's complaint point about excessive questioning is not epistemological or practical. He is not saying that the questions are just too hard to answer or merely lack sufficient pay-off. Their existence is an illusion. Just as an optical illusion can persist long after it is recognized as such, the 'spiritual migraine that is called metaphysics' can continue to issue false calls for explanation. The philosopher's job is to give a clear account of the tendency of mental habits to overreach. Furthermore, philosophy must

> aim only at the most appropriate expression of the given, irrespective of our inherited habits. Then, gradually, these tangles and contradictions must disappear. What is brick and what mortar in the intellectual edifice must be made to stand out clearly and we should soon be freed from the oppressive feeling that the simplest is the most inexplicable and most trivial the most puzzling.

> (Boltzmann 1974: 167)

Our (albeit slow and fitful) understanding of the antipodes and non-Euclidean geometry show that force of habit can be slowly surmounted. Hence Boltzmann anticipates Wittgenstein's view that philosophy has a modest, negative role in exposing the illusions that give rise to metaphysics and a prophylactic mission to frame truths in language that is less apt to trigger these durable illusions.

Going mental

The physicist Boltzmann would make philosophy a branch of applied psychology. However, most philosophers followed Wittgenstein in tracing meaninglessness to *linguistic* illusions. This has led to a neglect of the mental mechanisms behind meaninglessness.

What happens to the temperature of air as its volume decreases? One questionee mentally places a balloon in a refrigerator and so answers that the temperature decreases. Another thinks of air being pumped into a bicycle tire and so says the temperature increases. But actually the question is meaningless because temperature is a *joint* function of pressure and volume ($T \propto PV$). If the pressure stays the same, decreased volume will mean decreased temperature. But if the pressure decreases, then increased volume is compatible with any outcome for temperature. People tend to overlook the indeterminacy of the question because they tend to think *concretely*. This provides the sudden contrast needed for jokes that turn on generality rather than the more familiar ambiguity. A man spots his wife and mistress talking in a cafe (Paulos 1985: 47–8). He remarks 'Imagine a mistress spending the morning with her lover and having a friendly chat with his wife in the afternoon.' The adulterer's shocked companion asks 'How did you find out?' No ambiguity there. There are simply two ways for the statement to be true just as their are two ways of winking (with a left eye and with a right eye). Instead of following the narrator's instructions abstractly, the audience constructs mental models. Since the model has more detail than specified in the supposition, gaps are inadvertently filled in. This makes an underconstrained problem hard to recognize but easy to argue over.

Then there is vacuum activity. Konrad Lorenz (1966) believed that human beings have an innate aggressive drive. (He goes on to suggest that sport may sidetrack aggression into harmless channels. Meaningless debates could be assigned the same carthartic role.) Since Lorenz also had a 'psychohydraulic' model of drives, he pictured aggression as building up so that smaller and smaller stimuli were needed to release it. Eventually, the growing pressure bursts into behavior even in the absence of a stimulus. This vacuum aggression might take a variety of forms including a dispute over nothing. In any case, one would expect individuals to undergo 'stimulus generalization' so that less and less was needed to provoke verbal conflict.

Nowadays ethologists maintain that 'aggression' is a ragbag category covering disparate behaviors with a wide range of functions (hunting, defense of young, asserting rank, maintaining territory). So they doubt that a single drive undergirds them all. But even if there is no monolithic drive for aggression, it is evident that animals sometimes become so highly motivated that they will act out a complex 'response' without a relevant stimulus. During mating season, frogs clasp inappropriate objects such as rubber boots. House cats stalk and attack phantom prey. Perhaps amorphous curiosity accumulates in under-stimulated people so that the only outlet is vacuum inquiry. Here one goes through the motions of problem solving without any stimulus. This mechanism yields pseudo-problems in the existential sense. In *Rain Man*, the autistic Raymond fills notebooks with complex diagrams and calculations. But they do not tie into a real problem. Prisoners undergoing solitary confinement lapse into monologues that seem like responses to challenges. However, the problem solving only has a dream-like goal that beckons through a dank mental haze.

A third psychological source and sustainer of meaninglessness is opinionation pressure. Pollsters complain that interviewees give pseudo-opinions rather than admit ignorance. (Payne 1950–1). For instance, *Tide* magazine (14 March 1947) reported that 70 per cent of those polled on the (fictitious) Metallic Metals Act took a stand. The tendency to satisfy the social demand for an opinion can make a pseudo-issue look a real one. The very fact that many people take sides on the issue will make the issue look meaningful.

STUDENT UNREST AND THE DECLINE OF MEANINGLESSNESS

The 1960s inaugurated pluralism about bizarreness. Ordinary language philosophers such as Wittgenstein, Austin, and Ryle had assumed that the bizarreness of certain sentences was due to their violation of conceptual rules. For instance, Wittgenstein took the oddness of 'I remember my own name' to reveal that memory only applies where there is room for doubt. This explains why Wittgenstein saw a kinship between philosophical remarks and grammatical jokes. Their absurdity is a symptom of a conceptual error. Since the rules of language are brought to our attention by these violations, both philosophy and jokes can teach lessons about linguistic conventions.

However, some of the students of these philosophers protested that the peculiarity of a sentence could have a variety of sources. For example, John Searle (1969: 144) pointed out that the queerness of 'I remember my own name' might be restricted to the fact that asserting it would violate the prohibition against saying the obvious. Then the absurdity only illuminates general rules of conversation, not the particular concept of memory. (This result parallels the new quagmire in artificial intelligence. Researchers were able to program in some of the special common knowledge that undergirds practices (a.k.a. 'language games') such as ordering food at a restaurant but they have not been able to implant the *general* common knowledge that underlies the inference from 'The pen was released' to 'The pen dropped.')

General rules of conversation were studied in depth by H. P. Grice (1989). They are loosely organized around four maxims of cooperative conversation: Quantity (give exactly as much information as required), Quality (tell the truth), Relation (be relevant), and Manner (be brief but clear). Since conversationalists are tacitly aware of these rules, extra information can be conveyed 'in between the lines'. For example, if I say that the singer is either in the dressing room or the cake, you are entitled to infer that I don't know which (by the maxim of quantity). My ignorance is not *entailed* by the utterance; it is a conversational implicature. Unlike entailments, implicatures can be canceled 'The singer is either in the dressing room or the cake; I know which, I am just not telling'.

Although Grice's theory continues to suffer from chronic vagueness, it revolutionized the use of linguistic data. Now, anyone who wishes to draw a conceptual lesson from the bizarreness of an utterance must eliminate rival explanations based on conversational maxims. These deflationary counter-explanations have proved to be formidable competition. Gricean principles have had the effect of protecting bold theories from the 'counterexamples' deployed by ordinary language philosophers. Indeed, he originally invented the theory to defuse linguistic objections to the causal theory of perception.

As Grice's influence has waxed, the appeal to meaninglessness has waned. Of course, philosophers still use 'meaningless' as a diagnostic crutch, applying it to any flawed question. But this taxonomic laziness is not an endorsement of the old fashion appeal to meaninglessness.

Compare 'meaning' with 'number'. Both are vague notions that have given birth to a series of precisified sub-concepts. From 'number' comes negative numbers, irrational numbers, and imaginary numbers. From 'meaning' comes syncategorematic meaning, denotation, connotation, and emotive meaning. Just as there has been resistance to unfamiliar kinds of numbers, there has been resistance to unfamiliar kinds of meaning. As our models of meaning become updated and liberalized, there are fewer charges of meaninglessness. Hence, this historic dissolutional maneuver has a tendency to stimulate recognition of new kinds of meaning. Therefore, appeals to meaninglessness are self-limiting.

6 The devil's volleyball

I do not refute ideals, I merely put on gloves before them.
(Friedrich Nietzsche)

Whereas meaningless disputes are flawed by a bankruptcy of meaning, ambiguous disputes are embarrassed by too many meanings.

Not all quarrels over words are verbal disputes. In Matthew 16:13–20, Jesus notes that people have a variety of opinions about his identity and so asks his disciples 'But who do you say that I am?' Simon replied 'You are the Christ, the Son of the living God.' Jesus answers

> Blessed are you, Simon Bar-Jona! For flesh and blood has not revealed this to you, but my Father who is in heaven. And I tell you, you are Peter, and on this rock I will build my church, and the powers of death shall not prevail against it. I will give you the keys of the kingdom of heaven, and whatever you bind on earth shall be bound in heaven and whatever you loose on earth shall be loosed in heaven.

Papists interpret 'this rock' to refer to Peter. Protestants object that 'this rock' refers to the belief that Jesus is the Son of God. However, this dispute over an ambiguity is not an ambiguous dispute. For both sides are aware of each other's position.

An ambiguous dispute only arises when an ambiguity leads unwitting contenders to address different propositions. When their 'conflicting' remarks incite them to debate, they find each other's reasoning clumsy, checkered with *non sequiturs*, twisted evaluations, and symptoms of a poor grasp of commonplace truths. If the discussants are fortunate, they find each other's behavior bizarre enough to question whether they are talking about the same thing. This makes many ambiguous disputes self-correcting. Of course, the heat of a dispute temporarily lowers confidence in human rationality. Thus, detached third parties are often the first to suspect an ambiguity. In any case, most *grossly* ambiguous disputes are quickly detected.

The troublesome debates equivocate between nearly identical questions. For the resemblance will prevent the disputants from appearing bizarre enough to force recognition that they are addressing different questions. In general, the probability of self-correction varies inversely with the similarity of the questions.

PRE-PHILOSOPHICAL AMBIGUITY

The crudest ambiguity arises when the conversationalists are not coordinated about which sentence is under discussion. Thus garbled messages and homonyms cause verbal disputes. Near-homonyms formed the basis for the Gilda Radner's comedic character 'Emily Litella' on *Saturday Night Live*. Emily regularly editorialized about the attention lavished on 'endangered feces', 'conservation of race horses', 'violins on television', and 'Soviet jewelry'. When the anchorman corrected her mishearing, Emily Litella would end with her signature line 'Oh! That's different . . . Never mind'.

Not all ambiguity arises from *within* a language. A. J. Ayer and a Russian Marxist once debated whether philosophy is a science. In retrospect, Ayer suspected that the controversy arose from the fact that there is no straight translation of 'science' into Russian.

Mistranslation also slips in 'agreements' that are merely verbal. The short-term bliss of ignorance is sometime a prelude to long-term strife. Contemporary New Zealand has a problem with an indigenous Polynesian minority, the Maori, over its Treaty of Waitangi. The treaty was signed on 6 February 1840. In lieu of competent translators, Henry Williams and his son, Edward, agreed to prepare a quick Maori-language version of the document. The Maori chiefs happily signed because a mistranslation of 'possession' made the treaty appear to establish a protectorate relation rather than annexation. The different status significantly affects property rights and New Zealand courts have begun to take the Maori complaints seriously.

Although the above trouble-makers may be ambiguous disputes, they have been ignored by philosophers on the grounds that they are just technical glitches in communication. Competence at conceptual

analysis only comes into play once the sentences have been identified. Then the up-linked philosopher can take a professional interest
in figuring out what the sentence expresses.

CONTENT AMBIGUITY

There are two ways a word's route to the world can fork. The first
ambiguity occurs at the level of what individual words mean. The
second turns on differences in how groups of words are parsed.

Semantic ambiguity

On 3 July 1988 the US Navy warship *Vincennes* mistook an Iranian
airbus for an F–14 fighter jet and then shot it down, killing all 290
people aboard. Two days later, a moderator of the 'McNeill/Lehrer
News Hour' asked his panelists whether the United States should
apologize. Some said yes because of the tremendous harm the US
had inflicted. Others said no because the shooting was in self-
defense. The no-apology group stressed that the commander had
just finished a battle with two Iranian PT boats, that he had issued
seven unheeded warnings, and that the jet flew in a way uncharacter-
istic of civilian aircraft. The debaters eventually recognized the
ambiguity of 'apology'. The no-apology group had construed 'apologize' to mean an expression of remorse, that is, as a repudiation of
the deed as unjustified. The pro-apology group took 'apologize' to
mean an expression of regret; here one only laments the consequences of the act. Once their wires were uncrossed, all sides agreed
that the United States should express regret but not remorse.

Strident verbal disputes are generated by words that have a
narrow sense that entails a broad sense. For example, the narrow
sense of 'faith' means a conviction due to nonrational processes
while in the broad sense it just means conviction. 'Would a cogent
proof of God's existence give one faith in His existence?' will be
answered 'Obviously not!' by people who read the question in the
narrow sense of 'faith' and 'Certainly so!' by those who give 'faith'
the broad reading. Each side views its own position as a tautology
and so views the other as utterly contradictory.

In the case of polysemy, the possession of multiple senses as
above, the word is correctly identified but not its sense. Relativity
errors, in contrast, occur only after you have identified the right
sense of the word. The trouble concerns one's choice of relata. A
simple example of this miscoordination would be a debate over

whether the actress Marlee Matlin speaks well. Both disputants may agree that Marlee Matlin's speech is not fluent and that 'speaks well' must be relativized to language learning opportunities. Yet they may debate because one disputant is not aware that Matlin is deaf. Thus their different answers to 'Does Marlee Matlin speak well?' do not really disagree; one is really saying Matlin speaks well for a deaf woman, while the other is saying Matlin's speech is poor for a normal speaker. As a bonus, this example shows how factual errors can generate verbal disputes. For our conception of the facts guides our selection of standards.

The debate over whether each snowflake is unique has the same verbal character. Believers in unique snowflakes cleave to very precise standards of resemblance while their opponents use looser standards. Similarly, puzzlement over 'Is it now now?' arises from indexing 'now' to different time intervals. An affirmative answer follows when we relativize to the time of sentence utterance. A negative answer follows when we relativize to the exact time the word was uttered.

Questions usually involve tacit constraints. For instance, one physics problem asks how the height of a tall building can be measured with a barometer. A smart aleck once answered: tie the barometer to a rope, lower it to the ground, and record how much rope has been used. This 'solution' violates the tacit functional constraint that the measurement use the barometer as a gauge of air pressure.

Many of the illustrations of the 'creative problem solving' literature pass off this type of pseudo-solution as insights. For example, in the problem in Figure 6.1 one must connect the dots with four straight lines. The problem is impossible unless one gets over the 'mental block' of assuming that the lines cannot pass outside the

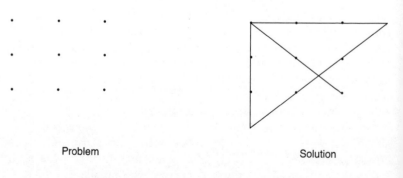

Problem   Solution

Figure 6.1

boundary set by the array of dots. However, it is more charitable to interpret stumped subjects as the victims of ambiguity. The problem can be interpreted with or without the constraint. Those who read in the extra constraint get stuck because that relativization yields an impossible problem. Those who do not read in the boundary constraint have a chance.

Why don't stymied subjects protest the unsporting ambiguity after the 'solution' is given? The most important reason is that the problem poser has authority over the problem definition. It's just a stipulation after all; the question means whatever the asker intended it to mean. A second consideration is the presumption of feasibility induced by the principle of charity. Interpretations that make a question answerable are preferable to those that make it unanswerable. For the latter forces us to uncharitably attribute an analytical error to the asker. Cooperativeness may also play a role. We want to satisfy the questioner, so we prefer interpretations that preserve the prospect of an answer or at least an answer to a similar question.

Cooperation is a double-edged sword. A charismatic listener can enchant the asker into making the question fit the charming answer. For example, in *Little Man Tate*, a school teacher asks a bored prodigy which of 0, 1, 2, 3, 4, 5, 6, 7, 8, 9 is divisible by 2. The kid answers 'All of them.' His answer slips off the constraint that quotient be a whole number. Similar deconstraint explains how visionaries domesticate questions that left the old guard in knots.

Syntactic ambiguity

Some verbal disputes are best registered with the help of logical notation. 'All problems are not mental' is structurally ambiguous between 'Not all problems are mental' $\sim (x)(Px \supset Mx)$, and 'No problems are mental'; $(x)(Px \supset \sim Mx)$. Since the different readings are not based on the multiple senses of a word, a dictionary cannot straighten out the matter. Likewise, ideal lexicographers who are in perfect consensus about the world might fall into a dispute over 'Is there a solution for every problem?' For Mr Lexicographer says yes because he believes that every problem has a solution, $(y)(\exists x)Sxy$, while Mrs Lexicographer answers no because she thinks no single solution works for every problem, $\sim(\exists x)(x)Sxy$.

By revealing alternative readings, the artificial language of logicians becomes an instrument for clear thinking. For it wards off two common fallacies: errors in reasoning due to overlooked alternatives and errors due to the conflation of alternatives. As an example of conflation, consider a coin conundrum. Two American coins add up to 30 cents. One of them is not a nickel. What coins are they? People become stumped by the question because of confusion over 'One of them is not a nickel.' If we let x range over the coins, there are two translations: $(\exists x)\sim Nx$ (At least one of the coins is not a nickel) and $\sim(\exists x)Nx$ (It is not the case that at least one of the coins is a nickel). The correct translation is $(\exists x)\sim Nx$ but people tend to mistranslate 'One of the coins is not a nickel' as $\sim(\exists x)Nx$. This misreading makes the problem impossible to solve. When correctly understood as $(\exists x)\sim Nx$ we are free to answer 'The two coins are a nickel and a quarter (which is the coin that is not a nickel).'

The principle of charity invites us to debunk many brain teasers as trick questions. Since intelligence tests make use of these equivocal conundrums, one might question their validity. However, a resilient defender of intelligence tests might insist that the ability to dissolve problems is as much a mark of intelligence as the ability to solve them. A smart test taker will ferret out the ambiguity and pick the answer that is perceived by the test constructor to be correct. We should not be sidetracked by the issue of whether the intended answer is really correct. Psychometricians are measuring intelligence, not knowledge. Note that the test-wise need not be aware of their own gamesmanship. If problems can be solved unconsciously, they can be dissolved unconsciously.

Like all thinkers, philosophers strive to put the minimum burden on our intelligence. Hence, they invent terminology that avoids syntactic ambiguities. Bertrand Russell introduced 'sensibilia' as a prophylactic against the amphiboles induced by 'unsensed sense data'. Sensibilia are defined as entities that have the same metaphysical and epistemological status as sense data but which need not be the object of anyone's attention. Being sensed is only a contingent property of a 'sensibile' just as being married is only a contingent property of being a man. Russell continues

> It is important to have both terms; for we wish to discuss whether an object which is at one time a sense-datum can still exist at a time when it is not a sense-datum. We cannot ask 'Can sense-data exist without being given?' for that is like asking 'Can husbands exist without being married?' We must ask 'Can *sensibilia* exist without being given?' and also 'Can a particular *sensibile* be at one time a sense-datum, and at another not?' Unless we

have the word *sensibile* as well as the word 'sense-datum,' such questions are apt to entangle us in trivial logical puzzles.

(1957: 143–4)

This passage illustrates the technique of dissolution by question analogy. The comparison shakes out the pseudo-question by exhibiting its resemblance to a clear pseudo-question. Such pairings have the advantage of brevity. But the audience is only convinced when the shared flaw is manifest. Otherwise, there is a lingering suspicion that a hidden point of difference will overturn the analogy and redeem the question. This is how it is with Russell's analogy. We need to be more specific as to why we cannot ask 'Can husbands exist without being married?' Fortunately, modal logic offers this detail. An affirmative answer to the question is ambiguous between $\Diamond(\exists x)(Hx \& \sim Mx)$ and $\Diamond(\exists x)(Hx \& \Diamond \sim Mx)$. Since the first reading says that it is possible for someone to be a husband and unmarried, it is obviously false. The second reading says that it is possible for there to be a husband who could have been unmarried. And that's obviously true because matrimony is not an essential state of any man.

Pragmatic ambiguity

In 1170, Archbishop Thomas Becket's quarrel with Henry II had reached a head. By some accounts, an advisor remarked to the king that 'While Thomas lives you will have neither peace nor quiet nor see good days' and the exasperated Henry responded 'Will no one rid me of this turbulent priest?' Four knights then slipped away and slew Becket. Henry explained the incident as miscommunication. Overzealous subordinates had misinterpreted his expression of frustration as a request for a hit. Notice that there is no semantic or syntactic ambiguity. The misunderstanding is over what the king was *doing* by uttering 'Will no one rid me of this turbulent priest?'

Pragmatic ambiguity arises when the hearer can't fathom how the speaker intends his utterance to be taken. As with other types of ambiguity, pragmatic ambiguity is most apt to derail conversationalists when the alternatives differ minutely. So expect the trouble to crop up between close cousins such as grading and recommending, suggesting and hinting, warning and threatening.

Emotivists contend that much of ethics rests on a confusion between reporting and expressing. They analyze 'Stealing is wrong' as an attempt to express or evoke disapproval of stealing, not a report of one of theft's properties. J. L. Austin (1961: 98–103) contends that when the man in the street says 'I know that water evaporates into outer space' he is not *reporting* knowledge. Instead, he is performing an act of assurance; guaranteeing a fact in the same way that we promise a deed. This serves as a precedent for those who wish to deflect the objection that prayer is pointless. According to this objection, the attempt to send a message to an omniscient God is silly because God will already know what you wanted to say. Praying is like trying to have a conversation with a perfect telepath. The rejoinder is to deny that prayer is a form of communication. The proponent will portray prayer as an expressive or evocative speech act rather than an assertive one.

The fact that a speaker is using an interrogative does not guarantee that he is asking anything. For instance, 'rhetorical questions' are really used to assert. The 'whimperative', 'Could you pass the saki?', is a request for action, and 'Do you remember your appointment?' serves as a reminder rather than a request for information. Function does not always follow form.

Perhaps some philosophical debates arise because emotive questions are misconstrued as information-seeking questions. The critics note that many philosophical questions have an emotional charge: 'What is the meaning of life?', 'Why should I be moral?', and 'How can I be sure of anything?' If the 'questioner' is just venting frustration, then there is nothing to answer. The philosopher, according to this diagnosis, creates a pseudo-issue by misclassifying the emotive interrogatives as requests for information. L. Jonathan Cohen suggests that some people may be led to the problem of universals through this misclassification:

> The question ['Why are things what they are?'] has a quite uncontroversial use to express the general spirit of human enquiry. But if a man has not yet learned to be satisfied with the fragmentary answers that gradually emerge from the detailed researches of scientists and historians, it is obvious that he may be tempted to propose a once-and-for-all answer like the theory of universals in Plato's *Phaedo*. He may be led by the grammar of 'Why are things what they are?' into thinking that, like any ordinary interrogative sentence, this is a question admitting of an immediate answer, whereas in fact it merely expresses the spirit in which a whole category of more detailed questions are asked.
>
> (1962: 109)

Philosophical ejaculations such as 'Everything changes' and 'We cannot change the past' may be verbal substitutes for sighs of resignation. This emotive usage is sometimes connected with overabstraction. According to Wittgenstein, a philosopher works himself into a state of astonishment about the mind/body problem by detaching his introspection from any purpose. The idled thinker then clutches his forehead and exclaims 'THIS is supposed to be produced by a process in the brain!' (1953: §412). Compare him to the giddy mountaineer who takes a break to watch the sunset and boggles 'THIS is how each day ends?!'

A related and more popular criticism is that some philosophical disputes rest on a confusion between questions seeking a declaration of choice and those seeking an assertion of fact. When a toy salesman asks 'Which water gun do you prefer?' he may be interested in a psychological report or he may be interested in eliciting a decision. A reply such as 'I prefer the Master Blaster but I have not made up my mind about buying it' furnishes a psychological report but no decision. 'We need not go into preferences; I choose the Master Blaster' provides a decision but no psychological report. In contrast with the clarity of these two answers, 'I want the Master Blaster' is pragmatically ambiguous. It could be an assertion of a psychological fact or a declaration of decision. The distinction is paramount for debating purposes. Mere declarations are not open to contradiction. Fiats are true as a matter of stipulation. We cannot debate whether a *decision* accurately portrays reality. Decisions don't depict.

Carnap blamed pragmatic ambiguity for ontological controversies. Ontology is the branch of metaphysics devoted to what ultimately exists – minds, bodies, properties, classes, numbers, propositions, etc. Debates over what exists tend to break out when a theory postulates certain entities to explain phenomena. For example, early biologists postulated vital forces to differentiate living organisms from dead ones. Mechanists contended that vitalists had no right to speak of vital forces because they don't exist. Vitalists defended their discourse by supplying evidence for the existence of these life-conferring forces. In such debates, it was agreed that the questions of existence were logically prior to the adequacy of the theoretical language which referred to the entities. Carnap challenges this assumption with a distinction:

> If someone wishes to speak in his language about a new kind of entity, he has to introduce a system of new ways of speaking, subject to new rules; we shall call this procedure the construction

of a linguistic *framework* for the new entities in question. And now we must distinguish two kinds of questions of existence: first, questions of the existence of certain entities of the new kind *within the framework* – we call them *internal questions*; and second, questions concerning the existence or reality *of the system of entities as a whole*, called *external questions*.

(1947: 206)

The reply to an internal question is an assertion. The reply to an external question is a fiat. Questions about the existence of particular things rarely cause confusion because they are plainly requests for descriptions rather than declarations. Hence philosophers are not tripped by plainly internal questions such as 'Is there a white piece of paper on my desk?', 'Did King Arthur actually live?', and 'Is there a tenth planet?' However, general existence questions can often be read internally or externally. If 'Do numbers exist?' is interpreted internally, then it has the trivial assertive answer 'Yes' (relative to a language that has number expressions). If 'Do numbers exist?' is interpreted externally, then the only response is an expression of decision. For the external question is a practical rather than a descriptive one. Like any practical question, we can consider the advisability of deciding one way or the other. Since we can make descriptive claims about the relative efficiency of linguistic frameworks, internal questions may enter into our deliberations over an external question. Nevertheless, says Carnap, the final answer is a choice, not a discovery. The resemblance between internal and external questions misleads philosophers into construing requests for decisions as requests for descriptions. This in turn misleads them into an attempt to answer existence questions prior to the acceptance of a linguistic framework.

Unfortunately, these philosophers have so far not given a formulation of their question in terms of the common scientific language. Therefore our judgment must be that they have not succeeded in giving to the external question and to the possible answers any cognitive content. Unless and until they supply a clear cognitive interpretation, we are justified in our suspicion that their question is a pseudo-question; that is, one disguised in the form of a theoretical question while in fact it is non-theoretical; in the present case it is the practical problem whether or not to incorporate into the language the new linguistic forms which constitute the framework of numbers.

(1947: 209)

Carnap's opinion of the dispute over the existence of numbers is intended to generalize to all ontological controversies. For, according to Carnap, the internal versions of these existence questions are either trivial or tasks for scientists rather than philosophers. And the external versions are not descriptive matters. Yet ontologists take themselves to be involved in nontrivial debates about the nature of reality that do not encroach on the domain of science.

Herbert Feigl's validation/vindication distinction parallels Carnap's internal/external distinction. Validations are justifications within a presupposed framework. Such frameworks contain basic principles, rules of evidence, criteria for terminology, and standards of reasonable doubt. When the disputants share such an infrastructure, rational persuasion can be transacted. Vindication concerns the *adoption* of frameworks. Since there is no framework for framework selection and all rational persuasion requires frameworks, vindication is arational. To recognize the validation/vindication distinction is to recognize that

> there are limits beyond which rational (i.e., logical and/or factual) argument cannot be extended. Intelligent reflection concerning means and ends, conditions and consequences operates within the frame of basic evaluations. Beyond those limits there could be only conversion by persuasion (rhetoric, propaganda, suggestions, promises, threats, re-education, psycho-therapy, etc.).
>
> (1952: 669)

Feigl uses the validation/vindication distinction to refine an emotivist view of ethics that makes room for the rational and arational aspects of morality. Pure value disputes are arational attempts to evoke and express emotions toward features of a framework of values. Ordinary grading procedures illustrate the validational aspect of morality which is rational because it takes place within an evaluative framework. For example, we can rationally discuss whether Margaret Thatcher was a good mother because we agree on the criteria for applying 'good mother'.

DYNAMIC VERBAL DISPUTES

For the sake of simplicity, we have focused on snapshots of debates. This freeze-frame approach gives the misleading impression that each side is *stable* even if confused. But once we look at the larger sequence of events constituting debates, patterns emerge.

The movement may be in a single direction. In the case of diverging disputes the gulf between how each side conceptualizes the matter may become too wide to count as a disagreement. We must instead suppose that each side has wandered into a different topic. For example, participants in the *vis viva* debate finally concluded that the proponents of $F = mv$ were speaking about momentum while the champions of $F = mv^2$ were talking about kinetic energy.

Since the modification of meaning sometimes produces a new and useful concept, diverging verbal disputes sometimes have fruitful side effects. These benefits are self-masking. For once we presuppose the concept, the process that generated it looks silly. The reason is that the conceptual legacy makes the original dispute easily diagnosable as verbal. The ease with which we do this makes our intellectual ancestors look dim-witted.

Other dynamic verbal disputes, do not change in any particular direction. This fickle oscillation is often precipitated by the chameleon-like quality of 'untruisms': 'An *untruism* is an ambiguous sentence which taken in one sense states a dull truism – an analytical or a platitudinous truth – and taken in another sense makes a statement that is interesting but either certainly or probably false or at least of uncertain truth-value' (Barnes and Robinson 1972: 189). For example, 'If you try hard enough, you will succeed' has a tautologous reading and a substantive but false reading. When an issue is stated by means of an untruism, the dispute is apt to evolve into an ambiguous one.

Untruisms are also hollowed out by the 'weasel words' discussed in chapter 3. Weasel phrases are also popular. Witness the deployment of 'in some sense', 'in the final analysis', 'could be thought as'. Paul Edwards pokes fun at F. C. S. Schiller's tendency to defend panpsychism by weaseling:

> Inanimate objects are 'responsive to each other,' but not the way in which human beings are – they are responsive in being gravitationally attracted by other inanimate objects. The stone is 'aware of us' but not, of course, in the sense in which human beings are aware – it is aware on '*its* plane'; the stone 'recognizes' other bodies and is 'interested' in operations like house building, but 'on the level of *its* understanding'; it 'plays its part,' but 'according to the measure of *its* capacity'; atoms and electrons know us no less than we know them, but 'after *their* fashion.'
>
> (1967: 30)

As Austin was fond of observing, 'There's the bit where you say it and the bit where you take it back' (1961: 2).

Central claims of theories are sometimes accused of being untruisms. The Darwinian slogan 'Survival of the fittest' has one reading in which it is a tautology. The behaviorist principle 'Reinforcing a behavior increases its frequency' also has a trivializing reading. Even laws of physics have subtle trivializations. Consider conservation laws such as 'The amount of energy in a closed physical system is constant.' Concepts such as 'potential energy' just seem to evince our determination to count energy as constant.

Untruisms and weasel words are associated with defensive oscillation between two theses. The defender replies to objections as if they were aimed at the much more modest look-alike position. Since the diluted position is easier to defend, a confusion between the positions makes his stronger position look like it has weathered a storm of objections.

The devices associated with defensive oscillation have militant counterparts. Let us say that an 'unfalsism' is a statement which is ambiguous between a patent falsehood and a statement that is not patently false. Sartre's 'To not act is to act' has a reading in which it is a contradiction and another in which it claims that omissions are just alternative acts. The hearer of the sentence (unfairly) castigates Sartre by fastening on the reading that makes his assertion a patent falsehood. Analogies also receive this brutal treatment. Suppose environmentalists are defended on the grounds that they are sincere. A critic responds that immoral people are sometimes sincere, for example, ardent Nazis. Then comes the rhetorical rejoinder 'Are you comparing environmentalists to Nazis?', insinuating that the analogy was intended to ascribe highly detailed points of resemblance.

'The whole is greater than the sum of its parts' is both an untruism and unfalsism. Holists defend the thesis by interpreting it as the claim that the properties of the whole are not determined by the nonrelational properties of its parts. One cannot understand the whole by understanding the isolated individuals composing that whole. Individualists assail 'The whole is greater than the sum of its parts' by construing it as reifying social wholes. So the individualists stress that the whole is determined by the interactions of the individuals. However, both sides are guilty of the strawman fallacy (misrepresenting your adversary to make him easily refutable) and the ironman fallacy (misrepresenting your own position to make it invincible). These matching fallacies are especially alluring in the heat of dispute because each party fixates on the reward of dramatically refuting an adversary. Like gamblers, they become enthralled by the possible outcomes offering the largest prizes and desensitized to the many other possible outcomes in which there is no triumph.

In addition to fomenting verbal disputes, untruisms conjure up verbal agreements. A charismatic speaker can capitalize on the latter to create a pseudo-solution to a difficult dilemma. Consider the New Testament story about how the Pharisees tried to trap Jesus with 'Is it lawful to give tribute to Caesar?' If Jesus answered yes, he would be accused of being a collaborator. If he answered no, the followers of Herod would report him to the Roman governor. So Jesus replied

> Why tempt ye me, ye hypocrites? Show me the tribute money. And they brought to him a penny. He saith to them, Whose is this image and superscription? They say to him, Caesar's. Then said he to them, Render therefore to Caesar the things that are Caesar's; and to God the things that are God's. And hearing it, they marvelled: and they left him, and went away.
>
> (Matthew 22:18–22)

Jesus' reply has a tautologous reading in which it only means that Caesar is entitled to whatever he is entitled. Christ's answer also has one substantive reading that says whatever is legally owed to Caesar is religiously owed and another which says that whatever is religiously owed is legally owed. This ambiguity lets Jesus straddle the dilemma while appearing to meet it head on.

QUASI-AMBIGUITY

If both parties agree on the meaning of the sentence framing the dispute and agree on the context, can they nevertheless have an ambiguous dispute? The question can be recast with the help of David Kaplan's character/content distinction. 'Content' covers that aspect of meaning that varies from context to context. 'Character' covers the context invariant meaning. For example, when Bill says 'I jog' and Hillary says 'I jog', the character of the two utterances is the same but they differ in content. Thus the formula of Kaplan's popularizers: 'Character + context = content' (Kaplan 1989: 506). Is the formula true?

Defining definiens

Suppose Charles and Diana disagree over whether $\triangle$ and $\vartriangle$ are congruent. They agree on the context because each perceives a big equilateral triangle and a small one. They also agree on the definition 'Triangles are congruent if and only if they have the same shape.' However, they disagree over how one of the definiens is to be defined. Diana defines 'shape' as 'a bodily contour' while Charles defines 'shape' as 'a bodily contour of a certain size'. So although they agree on the character and context of 'The big and little triangles on this page are congruent', they disagree on the content. (Indeed, Diana thinks the sentence expresses a contingent truth while Charles thinks it expresses a contradiction.)

One might try to save 'Character + context = content' by insisting that 'character' includes agreement on the definitions of the definiens. To avoid a counterexample at the next level of meaning, one must also require agreement on the definition of the definiens of those definiens, and then of their definiens, and so on. This holistic, slippery slope would make characters too hard to share between speakers.

Semantic solipsism and speaker meaning

One might try to bite the bullet. After all, intellectual historians have long emphasized how past mind-sets influenced the nature of issues. For instance, R. G. Collingwood defended a position that is now called 'meaning holism': the meaning of a belief depends on the meaning of other beliefs. Thus thinkers with diverging beliefs never mean the same thing even though the similarity of their utterances makes it seem like they are addressing the same question:

> If there were a permanent problem P, we could ask 'What did Kant, or Leibniz, or Berkeley, think about P?' and if that question could be answered, we could then go on to ask 'Was Kant, or Leibniz, or Berkeley, right in what he thought about P?'. But what is thought to be a permanent problem P is really a number of transitory problems, P_1, P_2, P_3, . . . whose individual peculiarities are blurred by the historical myopia of the person who lumps them together under the name P.
>
> (1939: 69)

Hidden diversity is also the theme of anthropologists when discussing the religious controversies of various groups. Similar sounding issues often belie differences in background beliefs that affect the meaning of what is said.

Paul Feyerabend (1965) is well known for his oily slide down the slippery slope to incommensurability. He has *reveled* in the paradox of meaning variance. Feyerabend argues that words only have meaning in a theoretical context. For instance, at the surface, the Aristotelian physicist and the Newtonian seem to agree that all bodies have inertia. Both define 'inertia' as resistance to change. But the Aristotelian regards change as deviation from the body's natural state: rest. The Newtonian regards change as deviation from prior velocity. So the Newtonian expects an undisturbed moving ball to continue moving while the Aristotelian expects it to slow down and eventually stop. Has belief in the same law and initial conditions given rise to *conflicting* predictions? Feyerabend responds that the appearance of consensus on the law of inertia is an illusion. Once we probe deeper, we find that the Aristotelian and the Newtonian really assent to different laws. In general, 'conflicting' scientific views have different theoretical contexts, so they are really talking at cross purposes. Thus Feyerabend infers the incommensurability thesis: theories cannot be compared against each other for greater accuracy, generality, simplicity, etc.

The relativistic consequences of this position are provocative only if the incommensurabilist is talking about an ordinary kind of meaning – not an artificial, highly idiolectical *invention*. Could this be speaker meaning? After all, the Kaplan crowd talks about this kind of meaning and it seems to have the sort of subjectivity needed to reflect individual conceptual differences. However, it should be noted that Kaplan draws his distinction within the realm of public, conventional meaning:

> The character of an expression is set by linguistic conventions and, in turn, determines the content of the expression in every context. Because character is what is set by linguistic conventions, it is natural to think of it as *meaning* in the sense of what is known by the competent language user.

> (1989: 505)

Indeed, Kaplan allows for cases in which the speaker is ignorant of the content of his utterance. In one illustration, Kaplan has us suppose that the wall behind him usually has a portrait of Rudolph Carnap. Kaplan points to that spot without looking and says 'That is a picture of one of the greatest philosophers in the twentieth century' (1990: 30). Unbeknownst to him, a portrait of Spiro Agnew has been substituted. So although Kaplan did not intend to say that the picture of Agnew was a picture of one the best philosophers, that's the proposition expressed by his utterance. Kaplan also invents cases to show that speakers may be aware of their ignorance.

Suppose a kidnapped heiress is locked in the trunk of a car and driven about (Kaplan 1989: 535–6). After the car finally parks she thinks 'It's quiet here now.' Although the heiress knows the character of her thought, she realizes her ignorance about its content.

Speaker meaning is surprisingly *objective*. 'Speaker meaning' owes its currency to H. P. Grice's distinction between what the speaker says (the proposition expressed by the utterance) and what he means (the proposition conveyed by the utterance). Grice illustrates by having you suppose you are writing a letter of recommendation for a student applying for a teaching position in another philosophy department. By writing 'Jones has beautiful handwriting and is always very punctual' you indirectly communicate your belief that Jones is no good at philosophy. Nevertheless, that is not the proposition expressed by your statement. It is a 'conversational implicature' that is inferred from the conjunction of the utterance and Grice's conversational maxims: Be true, Be relevant, Be simple, and Be informative.

Like Grice's maxims, the distinction between speaker meaning and utterance meaning has played a large role in efforts to rescue semantic theories by explaining away anomalies as pragmatic phenomena. For example, the referential usage of 'the' is an anomaly for Russell's theory of descriptions. Russell's theory implies that 'The murderer of Smith is insane' is true if and only if there is a exactly one murderer of Smith and that individual is insane. But suppose Jones is on trial for Smith's murder and we both believe he is guilty. We see him rant and rave, so you say 'The murderer of Smith is insane.' But it turns out that although Jones is insane, he did not murder Smith. Is your utterance false? Keith Donnellan (1966) says that the utterance is true as long as your use of 'the murderer of Smith' was only intended to refer to Jones and not to attribute the property of being a murderer. Thus Donnellan concludes that Russell's theory of descriptions should be explicitly restricted to attributive usages of descriptions. Saul Kripke (1977) replies that this referential usage does not constitute a separate *sense* of 'the'. It is instead an indirect use of the sentence. The speaker wants to convey the idea that Jones is insane but does the job with another sentence with a different meaning. So we merely have a case of people communicating truths with utterances that are literally false (as with metaphors).

Notice that the above usage of 'speaker meaning' is intended to be shared meaning. After all, the speaker intends to be communicating a proposition (albeit indirectly) to his audience. This other-directedness is also palpable in attempts to explain irony and meta-phor in terms of speaker meaning. Thus the verbal dispute between Charles and Diana over the triangles cannot be characterized in terms of speaker meaning.

Horizontal/vertical meaning

The horizontal meaning of a term is given by the definiens of the definition. The word's *vertical* meaning is the meaning it has once these definiens are themselves defined. Make enough vertical drops, and you get 'the full meaning' of the original term. These drops leave you at the bottom of a slippery slope but this time you didn't take every aspect of meaning along for the ride. Under this usage, Charles and Diana do have an ambiguous dispute even though they agree on the horizontal meaning of 'congruent'.

A vertical disagreement does not always require conflicting defi-nitions of definiens. The mere failure to agree on those definitions is enough. For instance, Henry Sidgwick and G. E. Moore were both utilitarians and so agreed that the right act is the one that maximizes good consequences. However, they disagreed over whether it was right to bring about harmless but sadistic pleasures. Moore brought out the difference with a thought experiment featur-ing a universe solely inhabited by a sadist who is under the delusion that he is torturing people. Moore insisted that an empty universe would be better. As a hedonist, Sidgwick defined goodness as pleasure and so was committed to approval of harmless sadism. A utilitarian who defined 'good' as self-development would disap-prove. This would be another example of a definitional clash over definiens. But recall that Moore insisted that 'good' was indefinable. So he was not opposing Sidgwick by proposing a rival definition.

A variety of reasons have been cited for the conclusion that a term is indefinable. Moore based his primitivism on the metaphysical thesis that 'good' refers to a simple and therefore unanalyzable property. (He compared 'good' to 'yellow'.) H. A. Prichard declared 'know' indefinable on epistemological scruples: the definiens need to be clearer than the definiendum but 'know' is already perfectly clear. Other philosophers cite methodological grounds – such as those who say 'definition' is indefinable because any definition assumes that the audience already understands what a definition is. Logicians stress the relational use of 'primitive' in which a term is part of the basic vocabulary of one formal system but a defined term relative to another. For instance, modal logicians are free to take possibility as primitive and define 'Necessarily p' as 'It is not possible that not p' and free to take necessity as primitive and define 'Possibly p' as 'It is not necessary that not p'.

Wittgenstein dismissed the bulk of classical definitional tasks as pseudo-problems. His rationale was that terms such as 'art' and 'know' are family resemblance terms. Let O_1, O_2, . . . stand for objects and A, B, . . . for properties:

O_1	O_2	O_3	O_4	O_5
A	B	C	D	E
B	C	D	E	F
C	D	E	F	A
D	E	F	A	B

All five objects resemble each other because each object shares at least two properties with every other object. However, no property is shared by all the objects. There do appear to be words that fit this description (whether or not we agree with Wittgenstein's particular examples). However, family resemblance terms don't fit Socrates' conception of words as having a meaning centered about a necessary and sufficient condition for use. The extension of a family resemblance term is instead determined by a network of overlapping similarities that reflect the word's opportunistic, haphazard etymology.

Primitivism about definiens keeps a vertical disagreement from running deep. This shallowness is more frequently caused by mere uncertainty about how the terms should be defined. Sometimes we are only sure of a necessary condition for the term. Thus a utilitarian may be confident that 'good' only applies to states of consciousness but plead ignorance on the question of whether hedonism is correct. Thus he restricts himself to a partial definition of his definiens.

Uncertainty can also be caused by a phenomenon that is intermediate between primitivism and partial definition. When a term is described as *vague*, one reports an impersonal, absolute, *limit* on its definability – not wholesale indefinability. Ideally, a definition of F partitions the universe into the F and non-F. However, most words have borderline cases which no (warranted) definition rules as F or as non-F. Of course, one can stipulate a new predicate F^* that does classify the borderline F as F^* or as non-F^*. But this does not answer the original question about whether the borderline F is an F.

Vertical indeterminacy is rampant in law. In *Peevyhouse* v. *Garland Coal and Mining Co.*, the key concept is 'damage'. The plaintiffs in the case sued for damages for breach of contract. Willie and Lucille Peevyhouse owned a farm containing coal deposits. They leased the premises to Garland Coal and Mining Co. with the agreement that the company would restore the land to its original condition after strip-mining. Expert witnesses testified that this would cost about $29,000. Garland conceded that it had not restored the land but insisted that it only owed $300 because the strip-mining only depreciated the land by that amount (as testified by experts). The issue then turned on the true measure of damages. On the one hand, Garland had broken its promise to do something that would cost $29,000. On the other hand, the devaluation resulting from the broken promise was only $300. (Garland prevailed in the Oklahoma Supreme Court by a 5–4 split decision.)

Semantic incompleteness is not always a flaw in law. Indeed, legislators often foresee the future semantic disputes. They know that when they use phrases such as 'appropriate authority' and 'reasonable effort', there will eventually be uncertainties of interpretation. Nevertheless, the legislators view this as a prudent delegation to better-informed subordinates and successors.

The relativity of the distinction

All differences in vertical meaning can be converted into horizontal differences. For instance, Diana and Charles have a horizontal disagreement relative to the following definition: two triangles are congruent if and only if they have the same contour and size. Diana rejects this definition, Charles accepts it. In general, one can derive a horizontal disagreement from a vertical one by plugging in the clauses of the controversial sub-definition. Doesn't this plasticity collapse vertical meaning into horizontal meaning?

It is true that the vertical/horizontal distinction must always be relativized to a system of definitions. But the same is true of 'postulate', 'derivable', etc. There is only a genuine collapse of the distinction if there is never any advantage to choosing the relata that create a contrast between vertical and horizontal meaning. However, there are at least three advantages to choosing definitional systems that distinguish horizontal meaning from vertical meaning.

The first advantage is brevity. A definition that contains nothing but primitive terms will nearly always be too long. Most of our predicates are so semantically lush that their primitivized definitions would be too long to remember and too cumbersome to work with. The point parallels Carl Hempel's (1965) solution to the problem

of theoretical terms. He granted that they were in principle eliminable in favor of a purely observational vocabulary but insisted they
were needed for 'deductive systematicity'. This systematicity is
offered by *networks* of interconnected definitions. This system of
definitions also has the advantages of modularity. We can replace
one part instead of starting all over again. Moreover, it tolerates
incompleteness. If the definer were confined to horizontal meaning,
he would not be able to postpone parts of his task. When the
vertical dimension is added, the definer can use definiens without
knowing their full meaning. He can delay the sub-definition or
delegate it to someone else or just leave the term forever undefined.
The definer can be an opportunist and a visionary instead of a rigid
planner and micro-manager.

Even those who grant that there is reason to draw the distinction
between vertical and horizontal meaning may nevertheless quake at
the arbitrariness of where the line is drawn. However, the arbitrariness is no greater than what is already accepted for other distinctions: near/far, cause/effect, language/dialect. The above rationale
plus general theoretical criteria tell us to draw the line between
vertical and horizontal meaning where it will do the most good in
terms of systematicity, opportunism, etc.

We can also appeal to the principle of charity. Since rationality
maximization has the effect of maximizing the truth of their beliefs
(from the interpreter's perspective), the principle winds up as agreement maximization. But if the interpreter maximizes his agreement
with his interpretees, he will also tend to maximize the agreement
between one interpretee and another. So charity is an engine for
consensus. Agreement maximization is not a purely quantitative
affair. The similarity between two belief systems has a qualitative
aspect. People are more like-minded as their agreement concerns
more and more universal propositions. Disagreement over details is
only important insofar as it reflects badly on one party's rationality.

A high quota for agreement will exclude the possibility of fundamental disagreement. Thus the highly charitable will frustrate their
'adversaries' by insisting that their apparent divergence in doctrine
is only a difference in behavior. Hans Hahn dismisses disputes over
logic for this reason:

> A person who refused to recognize logical deduction would not
> thereby manifest a different belief from mine about the behavior
> of things, but he would refuse to speak about things according
> to the same rules as I do. I could not convince him, but I would

have to refuse to speak with him any longer, just as I should refuse to play chess with a partner who insisted on moving the bishop orthogonally.

(1966: 231)

Quine gives deviant logicians the same brush off: they try to challenge the standard definitions of the logical connectives but only change the topic. They are paper radicals made of the same stuff as firebrands who clamor 'Make up down!'

Charity begins at home. The interpreter is using the principle to track the issue at hand, not all issues at once. So the pressure is on maximizing agreement for the beliefs relevant to this issue. The pressure diminishes as the line of relevance becomes longer. So when possible, blame disagreements on remote beliefs, not ones that are near at hand. Now notice that two people in a vertical disagreement at least manage to agree at the horizontal level – which is the level that contains the more closely related belief. Hence, interpreters maximize horizontal agreement by pushing disagreement down the vertical chutes. And indeed, disagreement over the definition of a term is regarded as cruder than disagreement over the definition of one of its definiens. People who agree at the horizontal level but not at the vertical are embraced as near-misses of consensus.

We have a cognitive stake in maximizing horizontal agreement because we make heavy use of belief–desire explanations. Just as my walk to the water fountain is explained by my thirst and my belief that the fountain is a source of water, bank runs are explained by the common love of money and the belief that leaving the money in the bank jeopardizes one's savings. Classifying people by their shared beliefs and shared desires helps to predict their behavior. But to count them as believing 'the same thing', one must formulate their doctrine in a way that avoids ambiguity (because then they really believe different propositions) and yet which does not exclude too many of them. Thus the horizontal/vertical distinction is needed for reference groups.

This also accounts for the intellectual's preoccupations with ' -isms'. When one hopes to prove a position, one must have an idea of how one's audience will react. Pigeonholing them confers the needed predictability. But once again, one needs broad categories. Thus it is useful to define 'behaviorism' as the position that behavior, not consciousness, is the subject matter of psychology – even though behaviorists differ on the meaning of 'behavior'.

Philosophers are just as appreciative of economical explanations of 'what the whole issue comes down to'. Thus in the last chapter I sided with the received view that the rationalism/empiricism debate comes down to the question of whether there are synthetic *a priori* propositions.

Many 'What is *F* ?' questions are really sub-questions that arose from the need to define key definiens of other questions. For example, philosophers of language ask 'What is a borderline case?' after agreeing that 'A predicate is vague if and only if it has a borderline case.' Knitting issues together as lemmas and sub-lemmas organizes inquiry by making issues in one area clearly relevant to its neighbors.

LIVING WITH AMBIGUITY

Very many disputes go bad because of ambiguity. Small wonder that proponents of ideal language philosophy always listed ambiguity as one of the flaws that would be expunged. What has actually happened is that philosophers have learned to live with ambiguity much as contemporary capitalist economists have learned live with 'market failures'. Piecemeal measures have developed which prevent, diagnose, and cure equivocation. But there is general resignation to a robust residue of superfluous factionalization.

But we can end on a lighter note. Ambiguity conceals both agreement and disagreement. Ethicists belittle the consensus over 'Happiness is our ultimate end' by harping on the conflicting definitions of 'happiness'. Generality can manufacture a similar kind of thin agreement. I remember a surprising nonconfrontation between a conservative legal scholar who advocated lighter penalties for rape and a feminist who espoused tougher penalties. My hope of keeping them amicably ignorant of their differences seemed dashed by his remark that rape law was polluted by deep irrationality about sex. To my relief, she simply concurred.

7 Popped presuppositions

Find out what cage you are in and climb out of it.

(John Cage)

Just as backwards reasoning and means–end reasoning are useful shortcuts for solving problems, challenging points of background consensus is a useful heuristic in dissolving a problem. Indeed, some philosophers have done the heuristic the honor of (mistakenly) *defining* 'pseudo-problem' as a question with a false presupposition.

EROTETIC PRESUPPOSITION AND ITS MIMICS

Presupposition. *Presupposition!* Presupposition? Philosophers and linguists used to speak freely about presuppositions of *statements*. 'The peasants sing of dance and balls' was said to presuppose 'There exist peasants.' The idea was that S_1 presupposes S_2 just in case the truth of S_2 is a necessary condition for S_1 having a truth-value. So if S_1 has a false presupposition, S_1 will be neither true nor false. Just as problems have their presuppositions, presupposition has its problems. First, there is the vexed question of how to distinguish presupposition from other notions such as entailment and sugges-tion. This has been especially worrisome with the growing accept-ance of Grice's theory of conversational implicature. Presupposition also forms fissures in logic. For starters, the 'truth-value gaps' cut by presupposition failure conflict with the principle that every propo-sition has exactly one truth-value and gums up inference rules such as *reductio ad absurdum*.

Happily, we can sidestep these sticky controversies. For our topic is the presuppositions of *questions* (erotetic presupposition) rather than presuppositions of statements. A proposition p is a presupposition of a question q just in case the falsity of p prevents q from having a true direct answer. For example, 'Is God male or female?' has {God is male, God is female} as its answer set. 'Who assassinated Zachary Taylor?' has as its set of direct answers propositions of the form 'x assassinated Zachary Taylor'. The falsity of 'Someone assassinated Zachary Taylor' prevents any member of this set from being true. Thus 'Someone assassinated Zachary Taylor' is a presupposition of 'Who assassinated Zachary Taylor?' Of course, the question also presupposes other propositions: 'Zachary Taylor was once alive', 'Assassination is possible', and their ilk. Indeed, questions typically have a series of nested presuppositions, some of which may be true and others false. Questions with false presuppositions have no direct true answers but do have corrective answers. Thus the coroners who autopsied President Taylor's 150-year-old corpse replied that no one had assassinated Zachary Taylor.

Questions with false presuppositions are deceptive because attention is on the direct answers. Presuppositions are part of the background, the stuff we take for granted. Trick questions exploit this passive trust: which weighs more, a pound of lead or a pound of feathers? Even clever people are fooled by a presupposition riddle as long as our tendency to fixate on the foreground goes unopposed. But once people suspect a bad presupposition, they are adept at ferreting it out. This indicates that the key is the direction of our intelligence rather than its magnitude. But until we smell something fishy, we are slow to recognize a corrective answer even when it is handed to us. One of Bertrand Russell's favorite anecdotes concerned his entry to prison for his anti-war writings during World War I. The warder of the gate had to take Russell's particulars and so asked him his religion. Russell replied 'Agnostic.' The warder asked how it was spelt and remarked with a sigh: 'Well, there are many religions, but I suppose they all worship the same God.' Russell said this kept him cheerful for a week.

Distinguish presuppositions from biases. A bias is simply an irrelevant influence – any kind of influence. Emphasis illustrates how the prejudicial element need not even bear content: did LEIF ERIKSSON discover America or Columbus? A bias works *within* the answer set by illicitly promoting or suppressing answers; it is not a precondition of there being a true answer in the set. Of course, loaded questions *sometimes* guide via their presuppositions.

But chapter 2's study of misleaders should lead us to predict a wide variety of leading questions.

Also distinguish presuppositions from diverters. A diverter is an assumption that directs attention away from a true answer. What is the second oldest city in the United States? Non-Hispanics pick a city along the East Coast because they assume that American cities were founded from east to west. But the correct answer is Sante Fe, New Mexico which was founded in 1610. The assumption of eastward settlement is not a presupposition because its falsehood is compatible with the existence of a true answer to the question. Many riddles exploit diverters and some are even regarded as enlightening tools for debunking myths. A parent has died in a car accident and the gravely injured son is rushed to the operating room. But then the surgeon declares: 'I cannot operate; this patient is my son.' How is this possible? Feminists take bafflement to be a sign of a sex stereotype.

When the diverter is a legitimate presumption, the problem is a trick question. However, the line between prejudice and rightful presumption can be controversial. Intelligence tests administered to English schoolchildren asked for the next three letters in the series O, T, T, F, F, S, S, . . . Since the children look for *letter* sequences, most of them don't get the answer, E, N, T. The sequence is derived from the first letters of the *numeric* series *O*ne, *T*wo, *T*hree, *F*our, . . . A critic might complain that the question is an 'Indian giver' that invites the assumption that only letter sequences are involved when setting up the problem and then takes back the assumption.

SEMANTIC PRESUPPOSITION

A presupposition can be classified in accordance with the type of a proposition it is. The Zachary Taylor question has an *existential* presupposition because 'Someone assassinated Zachary Taylor' asserts the existence of an assassin. 'What is the height of the Tower of London?' presupposes 'The Tower of London is in the category of things that have height' and so has a *categorial* presupposition. Since there are many ways to classify propositions, there are many ways to classify presuppositions. Mine is just one.

Phony facts

Proposition *p* is a *factive* presupposition when the question's answers merely state relationships with the fact that *p*. For instance, both answers to 'Did Stalin regret that France fell?' just state the absence or existence of an attitude toward the fall of France. On the other hand, 'Did Stalin believe that France fell' does not have 'France fell' as a factive presupposition because belief that *p* does not entail the truth of *p*.

'Why *p*?' has *p* as a factive presupposition because its answers are explanations of the fact that *p*. Thus why-questions can be dissolved by showing that *p* is false. This is brutally evident from the history of science. Medievals devised rival theories to answer 'Why does hot goat blood split diamonds?' Early nineteenth-century philosophers accepted spontaneous generation and so struggled to explain how meat transmutes into maggots and stomach juices into tapeworms. False factive presuppositions populate pseudo-scientific literature. For instance, 'Why are an unusually large number of planes and ships lost in the Bermuda Triangle?' falsely presupposes that the number of losses is unusually large.

Another genre encompasses amazing feats. They have the form 'How was *x* brought about?' where it turns out that *x* only looks like it was done. Consider the mystery of Archie's frog, a primitive species found on New Zealand. Since New Zealand is thousands of miles away from any continent, Charles Darwin wondered how the little frog migrated. It turns out that the frog never needed to make the trip. The islands of New Zealand just drifted away from the super-continent of Gondwana.

Mis-modeled modals

'Possible' is always short for 'possible relative to laws of type L'. Logical possibility is compatibility with logical laws. Physical possibility is compatibility with the laws of physics. Legal possibility is compatibility with legal laws. And so on. This variation in kinds of possibility enables specialists to provide *local* impossibility proofs. Quartz heaters were promoted as more efficient than other electric heaters. Physicists replied that all heaters must be equally efficient. An electric motor can waste energy as heat but the function of a heater is to make heat. The laws of thermodynamics guarantee that there is no place for 'wasted electricity' to go. So although a more efficient heater is logically possible it is physically impossible.

Since the logical possibility of states of affairs can be settled *a priori*, philosophers can resolve perplexities in a way that does not encroach on the sciences. For example, 'What is smaller than the smallest thing?' is easily dissolved on conceptual grounds. Inspection of the answer matrix '*x* is smaller than the smallest thing' reveals that every direct answer is a contradiction. The questioner is asking for the impossible.

The Zen *koan* 'What is the sound of one hand clapping?' has a true direct answer only if one-handed clapping is possible. But 'clapping' means 'applauding by striking one's hands together'. The definition explains why 'two-handed clapping' is a pleonasm and suggests a quick recipe for homemade *koans*. Take a redundant expression, negate one element, then embed this oxymoron in an interrogative that presupposes possibility: what does a lipless smile look like? How do you nod without a head? How do you wink without eyelids?

What happens when an irresistible force meets an immovable object? This presupposes 'It is possible for an irresistible force to meet an immovable object.' Without leaving his armchair, the philosopher can first note that 'irresistible force' means 'force that can move any object' and 'immovable object' means 'object that can resist any force'. He can then deduce the impossibility of an irresistible force co-existing with an immovable object and then infer the falsity of the alethic presupposition 'It is possible for an irresistible force to meet an immovable object.' Those ignorant of the false presupposition are apt to debate the question by *reductio ad absurdum* arguments that eliminate one alternative. We are then invited to accept the remaining alternative. When both alternatives are vulnerable to *reductio ad absurdum* and both disputants agree that one of the alternatives is correct, the disputants become preoccupied with the absurdity of each other's positions. By selectively attending to just some of the conditions of the puzzle, an impression arises that one is clearly right and the other side is clearly wrong. But since both alternatives are absurd, both sides are mistaken. Perhaps this danger of goose-stepping into antinomies lies behind the widespread preference for direct proof.

Deliberative questions of the form 'Should we bring about event *e*?' presuppose that *e* has not yet taken place. Showing that *e* has already occurred undermines the decision problem. Ecologists who wonder how the environment can be saved are greeted with the rejoinder that the old ecosystem is already lost. Don't buy oats for a dead horse!

Those who follow through on their affirmative answer to 'Should we bring about event *e*?' by bringing about *e* resolve the issue in a dynamic fashion. Given the *fait accompli*, we can no longer have a healthy debate because the question *has acquired* a false presupposition. The 1948 debate over whether the United States should be the first nation to recognize Israel was closed by the deed of first recognition. This example illustrates the importance of looking at a debate over time, not as static abstract object. Time systematically defuncts deliberative issues because most decisions are over whether to act within a deadline. So restraint can settle an issue as definitively as action. In 1975, war-weary congressmen stalled plans to save South Vietnam until all opportunities for intervention lapsed. As historical agents, we have control over what is possible and so can undermine issues through action and inaction.

A madman initiates a normal dialogue and then begins to overwhelm his interlocutor with questions. Instead of waiting for a reply, the madman asks another question and another. The disorienting dialogue is transformed into an interrogative monologue.

A philosophical investigation may also accumulate so much momentum that the questions run amuck. The query pattern gets pushed further and further until we arrive at a rogue question that presupposes an impossibility. For example, Voltaire opens his article 'Why?' by posing why-questions about specific phenomena: why do girls pray in a language they do not understand? Why didn't the ancients engage in theological quarrels? Why do we only do a tiny fraction of what we could do? Voltaire eventually warms to a second, more serious stage of questioning: 'Why, as we are so miserable, have we imagined that not to be is a great ill, when it is clear that it was not an ill not to be before we were born?' Then comes 'Why do we exist?' and finally Voltaire sizzles out with the ultimate why-question 'Why is there anything?' It is at this apparently profoundest point that hardheaded analytics raise their singed eyebrows. Their suspicion is that the investigative frenzy has gone too far. Early members of the sequence of why-questions are legitimate. But there is a critical difference between the less general why-questions and completely general ones. Once we reach universal proportions, there isn't any room left for explanation. A quantitative difference swells to a qualitative, logical change. Specifically, questions of the form 'Why does x exist?' can only have answers of the form 'The existence of x is due to the existence of z'. Almost any substitution for x allows a possible answer. But no consistent answer is possible if we let x be the universe, conceived as *everything* there is. For then the answer has to be of the form 'The existence of everything is due to the existence of everything.' Every substitution for z yields a contradiction. So every member of the answer set of 'Why does the universe exist?' is an impossibility. Hence, the question has a false alethic presupposition.

Should we be saddened by the lack of an answer? A. J. Ayer maintains that there is room for rational disappointment only if the desire is satisfiable (1986: 363). So he concludes that the dissolution of 'What does it all mean?' fails to justify cynicism, despair, or any emotional attitude at all. However, Ayer is mistaken about the irrationality of disappointment over logical impossibilities. Mathematicians have hopes and fears about the truth-value of their conjectures. They know from the outset that the conjecture is either logically necessary or logically impossible. When their beautiful conjecture is shown to be impossible, they have received bad news because the relevant type of possibility is epistemic, not alethic. A proposition is epistemically possible when it is not excluded by the available evidence. Since you can be rational without being deductively omniscient, what is possible need not coincide with what is possible given by the available evidence. So logical impossibilities can be bad news to rational people. And good news. Those who ask 'How do we prevent p?' are relieved to learn that p is impossible. Finally, the question of whether the news of an impossibility is good or bad sometimes varies with the hearer. Optimists are disappointed by arguments against the possibility of an after-life; pessimists draw a sigh of relief.

Quantitative presuppositions

A question has a false quantitative presupposition if each direct answer implies a miscount. Thus a false existential presupposition will be a special case in which the actual number of items is 0. For instance, all of the direct answers to Ponce de León's 'Where is the fountain of youth?' entail there is at least one fountain of youth.

One of J. L. Austin's pet peeves was the tendency of philosophers to create pseudo-entities by over-abstraction. According to him, philosophers fall into problems about meaning by overgeneralizing from particular questions such as 'What is the meaning of "rat"?' to the topic-neutral 'What is the meaning of a word?' Austin calls this 'the fallacy of asking about "Nothing-in-particular"' which is a practice decried by the plain man, but by the philosopher called "generalizing" and regarded with some complacency' (1961: 57–8).

Horror stories about quests for nonexistents are apt to jade us. We can balance the effect with examples of 'pseudo-pseudo-questions' that only look like they have false existential presuppositions. Try to give an example of a four-letter word ending in E, N, Y. Most people reject the task on the grounds that there is no such word. The victim of this riddle is led to this conclusion by an elimination argument. He runs through all 26 possibilities by saying them to himself. But since he assimilates the possibilities to familiar words, they sound like aeny, benny, cenny, denny, eeny, . . . leading him to pass over 'deny'.

So far we have dwelt on cases in which an existential presupposition is denied as definitely false. In other cases, the existential presupposition is rebuffed in a milder fashion. One merely denies that there are grounds for believing the existential presupposition. An eliminative reduction is essentially an alternative description or explanation that does not imply the existence of the thing targeted for elimination.

The technique of using redescriptions to avoid ontological commitments has been popular enough to merit distinctions between kinds of eliminative analyses. Adverbial analyses are among the most important. Although 'Bill drank with gusto' has the same surface grammar as 'Bill drank with Gus', 'gusto' is not a drinking buddy. Its role is to modify the type of drinking Bill did. Hence, the cause of clarity is advanced by reformulating the statement in a way that makes this adverbial role explicit: 'Bill drank gustily.' Likewise turning a key with dread is dreadfully turning a key and looking with lust is looking lustily. Couching these matters adverbially defuses the temptation to view 'gusto', 'dread', and 'lust' as designating *things*.

The adverbial approach promises to whisk away even those stubborn mental entities: sense data, pain, mental images. Philosophers will give it a go wherever they encounter ontological eyesores. And they are willing to yank around surface grammar to achieve this beautification. Consider how Nelson Goodman purges fictional entities. Negative existential statements deny the existence of an entity. The problem is that although some negative existentials are true, there is a pungent argument to the effect that they are contradictions: if 'Satan does not exist' is true, then it is meaningful. And it is meaningful only if the thing it is about exists. But since it is about Satan, 'Satan does not exist' is meaningful only if Satan exists. Hence, 'Satan does not exist' cannot be true. Parallel reasoning shows that the same holds for all negative existentials. Goodman's solution is to interpret 'about Satan' as a phrase in which 'Satan' modifies 'about' rather than as naming the referent for 'about'. Hyphenation of the expression to 'about-Satan' emphasizes this resemblance to adverbial expressions such as 'fall down' and 'stray far'.

Whereas questions with existential presuppositions assume that there is at least one F that is G, questions with universality presuppositions assume that all Fs are Gs or assume that no Fs are Gs. This boldness makes them the most common form of false presupposition.

A recent example in philosophy of science concerns the debate between realists and instrumentalists. Realists maintain that science aims at providing a true description of reality. Instrumentalists say that science only aims at the prediction and control of phenomena. Dissolvers say that global realism and global instrumentalism are both false. They insist that some theories are given instrumental interpretations while others are given realist interpretations. Indeed, many theories (such as early Copernican theory and atomic theory in the nineteenth century) are initially regarded as predictive devices. Suspicion about the instrumentalist/realist distinction harmonizes with a lesson Austin drew from the debate between the phenomenalists and materialists:

> The question, do we perceive material things or sense-data, no doubt looks very simple – too simple – but is entirely misleading (cp. Thales' similarly vast and oversimple question, what the world is made of). One of the most important points to grasp is that these two terms, 'sense-data' and 'material things', live by taking in each other's washing – what is spurious is not one term of the pair, but the antithesis itself. There is no *one* kind of thing that we 'perceive' but many *different* kinds, . . .
>
> (1962: 4)

Austin adds in a footnote that 'In philosophy it is often good policy, where one member of a putative pair falls under suspicion, to view the more innocent-seeming party suspiciously as well' (1962: 4 fn.).

Since universal statements imply so much, they court disconfirmation. Hence, a question that has only universal answers in its set of direct answers runs a high risk of false presupposition. So there is often an evolution away from all-or-nothing thinking and toward questions involving more qualifications. Primacy-recency issues are representative. For instance, early persuasion theorists asked 'For the greater persuasive impact, should the favored side be presented first or last?' Some researchers answered that getting the first word was always best while others answered that those with the last word had the advantage. As the debate matured, commentators concluded that there is no general law of primacy or recency. There is only an assortment of factors that tend to produce primacy effects and factors that tend to produce recency effects. The universality presupposition of the original dispute was rejected. Of course, the researchers do not wish to simply conclude that sometimes recency is best and sometimes primacy is best. They still want universal generalizations – but now over subclasses rather than the whole class of phenomena. Scientists rightly treasure universality. If they cannot get unrestricted universality, they settle for restricted universality.

In our discussion of existential presuppositions, we saw how questions of the form 'Which is the F?' can fail because of the nonexistence of Fs. The question has no true direct answer because 'the F' implies that there is at least one F and at most one F. We now turn to cases where the 'at most one F' condition is violated.

One of the first questions philosophers of science are apt to ask is 'What is the role of scientific laws?' Are they descriptions of contingencies, claims of natural or analytic necessity, or what? Many philosophers came to reject this question as resting on the false presupposition that laws have a lifetime role. They suggested that laws begin as empirical generalizations and then repeated confirmation and proven fertility transmutes them into statements that are 'functionally *a priori*'. For example, N. R. Hanson argues that the law of inertia is actually a 'family of statements, definitions and rules, all expressible via different uses of the first law sentence'. (1958: 98). He compares 'What is the role of law?' to 'What is *the* use of rope?'

Crossing categories

A category statement is a statement about the ultimate kind to which a thing belongs. For instance, 'Pain is a sensation' and 'Smoking is a process' sort pains and smoking into ontological kinds. Discourse that violates these boundaries is dismissed as deviant. Although the accusation of category mistake is associated with Gilbert Ryle's (1949) attack on 'the ghost in the machine', the dialectical move goes back to the days of yore. Martin Luther dismissed many questions by comparing them to 'How long is a pound?' and 'How heavy is an inch?' Aristotle was a highly self-conscious categorizer.

Questions with false categorial presuppositions about meaning bear a confusing resemblance to meaningless questions. These presuppositional errors arise because some things look like the *sorts* of things that bear meaning but are not. Consider disputes over the meaning of SOS. Some say it abbreviates 'Save Our Ship' others say it means 'Save Our Souls'. However, it is only a distress *signal* that does not stand for anything. The letters were adopted only because they were simple to remember and transmit.

Hyper-interpretive people are apt to hear the rhythmical sounds of wind and trains as obscure utterances. Unusual events are treated as omens to be deciphered. Dreams are thought to convey arcane warnings and suggestions. But flat-footed terrestrials doubt that train sounds, strange events, and dreams are the *types* of things that bear meaning. These skeptics respond to 'What does the sound of the train mean?' by denying the presupposition that the sound means something. This differs from dismissing the *interrogative* as meaningless. Questions with false presuppositions that something can have meaning merely lack a true direct answer.

One of the tasks of the philosopher is to account for the meaning of mysterious discourse. This obligation can be voided by showing that the 'discourse' in question is not the sort of thing that conveys a message. During W. V. Quine's nominalistic phase, he allied with Goodman in assimilating mathematical formulas to the beads of an abacus (Goodman and Quine 1947). Although commentary about these computational aids is meaningful, the mental crutches themselves are semantically inert. This instrumental strategy has scientific precedent. One nineteenth-century hypothesis about the marks on Mars was that they were a kind of Morse code. Later astronomers searching for extra-terrestrial intelligence first interpreted the regular energy bursts from pulsars as a code. Speculation about the meaning of the signal was cut short by the discovery that the energy bursts were due to a faint star regularly eclipsing a bright star.

Sometimes the presupposition of meaningfulness is mistakenly challenged. The meaning of Egyptian hieroglyphs was a long-standing mystery that some sought to dispel by denying them meaning. According to the skeptics, the hieroglyphs were just decorations, not language. Discovery of the Rosetta stone overturned this hypothesis of meaninglessness.

Pseudo-anomalies

'Why *p*?' can be a pseudo-question even if *p* is true. For sometimes proper reasoning would show that *p* should be expected or at least is no more puzzling than ~*p*. Hence, 'Why?' is sometimes smartly trumped by 'Why not?' By questioning the question, we challenge the need for explanation (Driver 1984).

Anomalies are relative to background belief systems. If the earth is in empty space, what holds it up? This question no longer arises. With changes in background beliefs come shifts in what calls for explanation. Aristotle thought it odd that a projectile continued in motion after it left the hand of the projector and therefore labored to explain it. But he did not think any causal factor was needed to account for the circular motions of heavenly bodies. The reverse held for Newton because he had become convinced that it was natural for objects to continue in a straight-line motion.

A fact should strike us as strange only if it is anomalous; that is, if it violates some plausible principle or theory. Teflon frying pans were puzzling because they are counterexamples to the principle that heated food sticks to its cooking surface. High-flying birds make us wonder because they go against the law of least effort; why spend the energy to reach a high altitude when a low one provides a clear flight path?

People reify strangeness because the relevant set of beliefs tend to be background assumptions. We tend to overlook what we take for granted, so a faceless crowd of convictions can exert subliminal influences. For instance, plain folk who profess to be untainted by theory are often shocked to learn that a decent person is an atheist. Their puzzlement illustrates the fact that the divine command theory of morality is never more influential than amongst those who do not realize that they believe it. The belief that you have no theory usually means you unwittingly accept a bad theory. This is a disagreeable thought to dissolutionists who strike atheoretical postures. If Wittgenstein really means to deny that he has a metaphilosophy (1953: §121), then he is all too reminiscent of businessmen who deny that they have economic theories.

But let's be wary of over-subjectivizing anomalies. They can exist without any one's awareness. Prior to Joseph Black's discovery of latent heat in 1757, the consensus was that as ice is heated, its temperature rises continuously. When the ice reaches the melting point, it was thought to immediately melt. However, Black pointed out that this grated against the fact that snow only *gradually* melts after it reaches the melting point. The quick-melt hypothesis predicts that springtime brings violent torrents as ice is suddenly turned to liquid. Thus the slow liquefaction of ice was an overlooked anomaly.

Some phenomena only appear to be counterexamples to plausible generalizations because of bad inferences rather than false beliefs. Sigmund Freud wondered why slips of the tongue occur frequently following a discussion of these speech errors. After he would present a paper on the topic at professional meetings, there would be a rash of such errors committed by subsequent speakers. Amused members of the audience would give Freud strange looks as if he were psychically manipulating them into dramatic confirmation of his thesis. Subsequent researchers have concluded that the 'contagious' slip of the tongue is only an artifact of an alerted mind. Normally, we edit away all but the most glaring speech errors just as we ignore all but the most unusual slips. When cued, however, we notice them and are often surprised by their frequency. Unless we take account of the increase in our search efforts, we are liable to conclude that the feature in question has become more prevalent in the observed population. Epidemiologists need to guard against this fallacy of projection when determining the spread of a disease. Most cases of new diseases are misdiagnosed as familiar diseases. Generally, only severe cases differ substantially enough to prompt an innovative classification. As diagnostic techniques for the disease improve, less severe cases are recognized. Thus increases in *reported* cases need not be due to an increase in the number of cases. Put your suspicion in remission!

A particularly fertile source of pseudo-anomalies is marked by Aristotle's unfalsism that the improbable is extremely probable. On one reading, the dictum is a contradiction: there is an improbable event that is extremely probable. Of course, the intended reading is that it is probable that some improbable event or other will occur. It is likely that someone will be electrocuted by a toaster in 1999. We tend to grossly underestimate the number of improbables. Hence when the improbable event comes to pass, it does not seem to be a matter of chance and we grope for an explanation. Moreover, since the events are so extraordinary, many people incline to correspondingly extravagant causes: God, ESP, UFOs, and their ilk.

Mistaken inductive principles also propagate pseudo-anomalies. The assumption that causes must resemble effects made Louis Pasteur's contemporaries marvel at how a tiny germ could overpower a huge horse. How could micro-organisms so like each other in shape and function cause such disparate diseases?

Other pseudo-anomalies well up from pre-reflective analogies. For example, many educators were surprised by psychological research indicating that there is little skill transference from training in one field to another. Mastery of a field seems to be a matter of amassing armies of domain-specific problem solving strategies rather than by an arduous ascent to a few high-level principles. Part of the puzzlement is due to the undercurrent of analogy between brains and brawn. Muscles undergo a general improvement when put to difficult tasks, so it was inferred that cerebral challenges (regardless of their topics) would strengthen the mind.

Since backstage analogies go unwatched, they can be potent even when silly. We tend to think of time as a river (raising questions about how fast it flows) and space as a container (raising the question of its size). Wittgenstein called these pre-reflective analogies 'pictures'. We picture memory as a storehouse, the mind as a theater, words as names. Sometimes Wittgenstein would weaken the hold of pictures by burlesquing their absurd consequences. But often it suffices to merely make the analogy explicit. Many pictures disintegrate in the spotlight of consciousness.

Distinguish anomaly from unfamiliarity. Contemporary commentators on the mind–body problem sometimes characterize the problem as partly due to impatient ignorance. Until we gain greater familiarity with neurophysiological processes, the strong intuitive contrast between mind and body leaves us dissatisfied with our initial introduction to neurophysiology. When the neurophysiologist gives his account of how pains are caused by processes in the thalamus and the sensory cortex, some of his audience will be puzzled. They ask 'How can such dissimilar things be causally related?' The neurophysiologist has little better recourse than the reply 'Why not?' John Searle (1984: 23) compares the issue to the old debate between vitalism and mechanism. Vitalists thought life could not be given a purely biological explanation because of the dramatic contrast between living and dead organisms. They maintained that our thirst for explanation could only be quenched with vital spirits. According to Searle, the problem just had to be educated out of us.

Some critics give an extra twist to the denial that p is anomalous by insisting that $\sim p$ would be fishy. Paleontologists are fond of responding to 'Why did the dinosaurs go extinct?' with a cold-blooded comparison between the short history of mankind and the

2000-million-year epoch of dinosaurs. Extinction is normal and long survival abnormal, so our curiosity should be directed to the extraordinary fitness of dinosaurs. (Some dissolvers like to leave a piece of the hook in your lip when they toss you back into the water.)

Attend to how the assurers in 'genuine enigma' and 'real problem' re-channel curiosity away from superficial 'wonders' and towards a closely related but deeper issue. Instead of stopping the investigation dead in its tracks, this comparative approach preserves the momentum of investigation by *redirecting* our curiosity. The maneuver illustrates how dissolution need not be a *brake* on inquiry. Dissolutions also *steer* inquiry.

Behind every great solved problem is a harem of dissolved problems. The harem has the structure of closer and closer approximations to the genuine problem. Near-misses provide feedback for the next try. These attempts are guided by contrary-to-adequacy imperatives such as 'If there is no exact answer, then ask whether there are approximate answers.' Patient application of these heuristics tunes in the real question. Merciless treatment of problems runs the risk of an unstable dissolution. They re-surface from shallow graves.

The re-anomalizer's ability to shift the burden of explanation can be abused to achieve an effect akin to equivocation. 'Why are you a vegetarian?' excites the snappy comeback 'Why are you a carnivore?' The best defense is a good offense! The truculent vegetarian maintains that universal norms governing the humane treatment of animals imply a prohibition against meat-eating. So the vegetarian reasons that since meat-eating is contrary to the questioner's principles, it is the questioner who should be doing the explaining. Maybe there is no ethical anomaly to vegetarianism. But this is compatible with there being a *psychological* anomaly to vegetarianism. Ethical vegetarianism is demographically rare, so people wonder how this rare conviction took root. Their question is about the *psychology* of morality, not morality. So the vegetarian is re-routing the conversation into his preferred issue. The baited carnivore only spots the switch if he has a long memory and a cool temperament.

The failure to perceive a problem is frequently caused by the converse error of confusing familiarity with the lack of anomaly. For example, many people are slow to wonder 'Why do we sleep?' because sleep is so common. Bio-psychologists build a constituency for the problem by imagining a planet 'Daynite' that rotates on its axis only once a year. Consequently, one side of the planet always faces the sun. So nearly all life is concentrated along the twilight zone. These uniformly illuminated creatures never sleep. Now picture the surprise of Daynitian astronauts when they visit earth. They marvel at how animals appear to drift off into a death-like state only to resurrect a few hours later. What purpose could be served by this intermittent dormancy? This thought experiment raises a question by making the contingency of the phenomenon salient. Uniform conditions don't seem to need a cause, so our curiosity is only piqued when we can picture them as absent. Variety is a stimulant. This explains why travel to exotic places makes home more intriguing and why outsiders are often the most astute observers. Thought experiments supply *artificial* variety (Sorensen 1992a).

'Never explain the obscure in terms of the more obscure.' This maxim will yield opposed verdicts when people have opposite rankings of familiarity. Consider Mach's strike on the question of whether feelings can be explained by the motion of atoms. Mach was a sensationalist; he believed all knowledge is reducible to sensations. The sensationalist grants that theoretical entities such as magnetic fields, cash flows, and centers of gravity can be useful devices for predicting and controlling the flow of sensations. However, he denies that this shows them to be real objects; they are to be explained away like we explain away the average man. Since Mach regarded atoms as theoretical entities, he thought them much more obscure than feelings:

> It would be equivalent, accordingly, to explaining the more simple and immediate by the more complicated and remote, if we were to attempt to derive sensations from the motions of masses, wholly aside from the consideration that notions of mechanics are economical implements or expedients perfected to represent *mechanical* and not physiological or *psychological* facts. If the *means* and *aims* of research were properly distinguished, and our expositions were restricted to the presentation of *actual facts*, false problems of this kind could not arise.
>
> (1942: 613)

After Mach's death, atoms became entrenched in physics and behaviorism dominated psychology. So subsequent thinkers regard atoms as clearer than sensations!

A qualification: reversing the order of clarity is not *always* a fatal blunder. Newton explained the more familiar phenomenon of a free falling body in terms of the law of gravitation. Mathematicians accept the reduction of numbers to sets. But in these cases there is a compensating advantage in simplicity, completeness, universality, etc.

PRAGMATIC PRESUPPOSITION: THE PRECONDITIONS OF ANSWER*ING*

Recall that a semantic presupposition of a question is a necessary condition for there being a *true* direct answer. Pragmatic presuppositions focus on assertability rather than truth. That is, a pragmatic presupposition of a question is a proposition that manages to be a necessary condition for *answering p* without being a necessary condition of there being a true direct answer. Thus no pragmatic presupposition of a question is also a semantic presupposition of that question.

The point of distinguishing between the two types of presuppositions is that true direct answers are sometimes misleading. True but misleading answers are bad because the questioner swallows too many false beliefs along with his true one. Recall the joke about the Vermonter who was asked what he gave his horse last year when it had the colic. 'Oats and molasses' was the Vermonter's answer. The advisee later complained that when he put his horse on this diet, it died. 'So did mine' was the Vermonter's reply. Although true, the oats and molasses answer fails to correct the pragmatic presupposition that the treatment was safe and effective. Questioners presuppose that they are receiving answers that will help them achieve their goals. Hence the answerer is expected to supply *all* the available information relevant to the project at hand.

Riddles that exploit pragmatic presupposition look more instructive than those that turn on an equivocation. For they seem to reveal a genuine weakness in our thought processes. Hence purveyors of creative thinking techniques 'prove' the need for their services by stumping their audience with presuppositional puzzles. In one such pseudo-demonstration, we are to picture ducks swimming beneath a bridge, two in front, two in the middle, and two in the rear. However, there are not six ducks. How many are there? The answer is four; the ducks are swimming in single file. This purports to exhibit the hazard of assuming that distinct ducks are involved in pairing statements. However, the riddle only demonstrates that reports can mislead us by violating Grice's principles of conversation. (Double-counting is ruled out by the maxim of manner.)

'When you *assume* you make an ASS out of U and ME.' People

take this saying to heart and concoct a number of antidotes to presupposition failure. One approach is to coax each background assumption into the foreground. Or one might try to ask questions that guarantee themselves a degree of presuppositional success. P. N. Johnson-Laird asks 'When you believe that a sentence make perfect sense, why don't you notice the grammatical error that occurs in it (as in this one)?' (1983: ix). By *exemplifying* the phenomenon in the question itself, Johnson-Laird guarantees the truth of the existential presupposition. Lawyers lessen presupposition failure by paring down the superfluous content of the question. Thus instead of asking 'Did you kill Manny Chips with a Sears chain saw at 10.33 p.m. on 22 September 1993?', the prosecutor opts for the vaguer 'Did you kill Manny Chips?' Foundational philosophers reacted to the skeptic's challenge with the same strategy of vaguification. Instead of asking whether there was an apple on the desk, the phenomenalist asks 'Does it now seem to me that there is an apple on the desk?' The phenomenalist's sense-data jargon just facilitates this highly cautious form of discourse. (Recall the story about Calvin Coolidge. Coming across a flock of sheep, a friend observed 'I see these sheep have just been shorn.' Coolidge replied: 'Looks like it from this side.') Phenomenologists have developed an even more arcane vocabulary dedicated to the ideal of presuppositionless inquiry.

Current analytic philosophers agree that heavy insurance against false presuppositions is pricey. Let's not be gun-shy. Slightly chancy background assumptions are indispensable for any learning at all. Even vigilance requires preconceptions: to watch out is to watch out for something. Besides making inquiry possible, presupposition makes it efficient. By eliminating alternatives we position our assets on the lucrative options.

When we make assumptions, we gamble. These risks have a pattern. We assume that the description of a routine problem is clear (no ambiguities, obscurities, gratuitous vagueness), relevant (none of the information is misleading – no red herrings), and stereotypical (the situation is normal, ripe for heuristics, not 'an exception to the rule'). Riddles, tricks, and illusions show that this bull-headedness is cognitively bruising. But these exploiters of our adaptive naivety do not show a need to curtail our presuppositional generosity.

Granted, we are at fault when the gambling gets *reckless*. Stephen Gould and Richard Lewontin (1984) complain that sociobiologists regularly assume that a trait has a function – that the characteristic is not a side effect or a coincidence. They are not alleging that the sociobiologists are ignorant of the nonfunctional alternatives. The accusation is that these *presumptuous* sociobiologists fail to take the alternatives seriously. The complaint is not that 'What is the function of *x*?' always has a false presupposition, only that it tends to be recklessly presupposed.

The proper degree of caution is partly determined by a variety of sub-issues. Under what conditions do we accept a false presupposition? How easily do we recover? Do we have valid and reliable screening measures? These are empirical questions that are unlikely to be resolved in favor of the timid. No guts, no glory!

COMPETING PROBLEMS AND PSEUDO-PROBLEMS

False assumptions can lead us to neglect problems by spawning spurious solutions. Their presence in the reasoning behind answers is illustrated by the Renaissance 'solution' to the problem of weighing smoke: subtract the weight of the ashes from the weight of the original wood. Had the Renaissance men actually executed this procedure they would have found the ashes were *heavier*. They had falsely assumed that burning merely releases something from the fuel.

In addition to generating pseudo-solutions, false assumptions generate pseudo-pseudo-problems. 'Why do organisms age?' seems a pseudo-anomaly. Doesn't death make room for new individuals thereby benefiting the species? No, evolution only applies directly to individuals not species. Here's a second wet blanket. Machines eventually wear out, so why not us too? Biologists warn us off this response by attacking the mechanical picture of living things. Organisms are self-repairing. Moreover, the hard part of life is growing up. So why can't an organism solve the apparently easier problem of merely maintaining itself? Senescence is not universal. Bacteria and many eukaryotic micro-organisms divide indefinitely. Many plants and some simple animals, such as coelenterates, have regenerative powers that enable them to live indefinitely. Thus we *should* be puzzled by aging.

The rescue of a problem from dissolution tends to revive analogous problems. For instance, the above line of reasoning resuscitates curiosity about the decline of civilizations. Civilizations resemble organisms, so their deaths, though common enough, are paradoxical by parity of reasoning.

STRATIFIED DISSOLUTIONS

A question usually has many presuppositions. Moreover, these pre-suppositions can be placed in logical order. For instance, 'How long has Eliot known that phoenixes fly' presupposes 'Eliot knows that phoenixes fly' which implies 'Phoenixes fly' which in turn implies 'Phoenixes exist.' Although refutation of any presupposition is enough to dissolve the question, deeper-level dissolutions are the most informative. For refutation of 'Phoenixes exist' is also refutation of all the higher-level presuppositions.

Nevertheless, it is sometimes instructive to dissolve a problem at a more superficial level. Consider the science-fiction fear about time travelers changing the future. David Lewis (1976) contends that this worry is doubly unfounded. At the most fundamental level, the issue falsely presupposes the physical possibility of time travel (though Lewis defends its *logical* possibility). However, the more interesting mistake concerns the time traveler's ability to alter the future. Consider the teenage hero of *Back to the Future*. Marty McFly leaves his wimpy father in 1986 and travels back to his home town in 1955. There he meets his mother (who has yet to conceive him). She develops a crush on the time traveler. So he struggles to divert her affection to his father. In the course of these romantic redirections, the hero improves his father's character. So when the hero returns to the future, his dad is no longer a wimp. But wait a minute! Was dad a wimp in 1986 or not a wimp in 1986? The story has fallen into contradiction. But that doesn't disprove time travel – only time travel in which future events are altered. The lesson is that the time traveler can no more change the future than we can change the past. Of course, any time traveler affects the future. But these deeds are not 'disruptions' of the future. The time traveler's contributions were, as it were, pre-embedded.

THE PLASTICITY OF PRESUPPOSITION ATTRIBUTION

In 1943, the British were anxious to prolong the success of their centimetric radar against U-boats. So they misled the Germans into thinking that an infrared detector was responsible. A German scientist, Carl Bosch, invented an ingenious anti-infrared paint in response to the misdiagnosis of the U-boat vulnerability. But since the infrared detector was fictitious, Bosch's countermeasure was ineffectual. Question: Was Bosch working on a pseudo-problem?

The answer depends on how we describe Bosch's research activity. If we say he was addressing the question 'How can the British infrared detector be countered?', then we conclude Bosch was working on a pseudo-problem since his question rests on a false existential presupposition. But if we describe him as addressing 'How can a submarine be made invisible to infrared detection?', then his problem is genuine (even though the *ground* for the problem is defective). Nearly any inquiry that rests on a false presupposition can be redescribed as one free of false presuppositions. All you need is the attribution of a vaguer question that tiptoes around the thinker's misconceptions. If you want to see an extreme illustration of this technique, start a discussion about whether computers fall for pseudo-problems. Most people hate to attribute a mistake to a machine and so will artfully redescribe any putative computer pseudo-problem as a programmer pseudo-problem.

The converse also holds: nearly any inquiry that can be described as free of false presuppositions can also be described as infested with them. Problem solvers almost always make a few errors in assessing the problem. Incorporating these mistakes into the thinker's problem definition ensures that his project is partially misframed. For example, thinkers generally start out with the assumption that things are simple and so can be described as searching for *the* cause, *the* effect, *the* pattern. Subsequent complications refute the uniqueness presupposition. *The* cause of cancer? There are many causes of cancer! *The* effects of nuclear radiation? Radiation has a *variety* of effects! *The* scientific method? There are many scientific methods! In general, pseudo-problems proliferate with the specificity of the question.

Charity and expedience determine whether we should describe the thinker as a victim of false presuppositions. The principle of charity tells us to maximize rationality and so militates against the attribution of false presuppositions. Expedience tells us to draw attention to only those errors that suit the goals at hand. Thus we resent the pesterings of hyper-corrective kibitzers who only point out irrelevant misformulations of the problem. We grant that their corrections are true but dismiss them as picky, petty, or pedantic. A dissolution should avert waste; it should not be a forum for academic niceties.

IMPLICATIONS FOR THEORY APPRAISAL

When asked to justify a preference for one theory over another, it is natural to frame the comparison in terms of questions. Better theories answer more questions, answer them more accurately and more quickly. The idea is that there is a neutral agenda of questions that serves as a performance test. Theories earn points for answering a question correctly, lose points for incorrect answers, but receive no direct penalty for not answering a question. So according to this view, there is an analogy between theory comparison and grading students with standardized examinations.

The analogy summons claustrophobic imagery. For it pictures epistemic space as fixed. As we answer more questions, less and less space is left for subsequent investigators. Hence scientific progress deprives future generations of the opportunity to make fresh discoveries. As the intellectual frontier turns into a tourist trap, our cognition and character go as flat as last night's beer. How can human beings forestall this de-carbonation? John Stuart Mill recommends artificial debates (1859: 55). Just as dogmatic Catholics preserve their wits by playing the role of devil's advocate, the scientifically sated thinkers of tomorrow could keep nimble by debating exercises. Happily, Mill's academic pseudo-issues are a response to a false need. For the original analogy between grading theories and grading students is fundamentally flawed by two points of difference.

Students who take standardized examinations do not skip questions on the grounds of failed presupposition. Proponents of rival scientific theories, on the other hand, do reject questions – and their rejections do not completely overlap. This creates a problem for the grader of scientific theories: how does he score a theory that answers a question which the other theory excludes as resting on a bad presupposition? Adolf Grünbaum (1976) illustrates his point with a comparison between Newton's physics and Einstein's. Newton's theory answers yes to 'Is *the* geometry of the three-dimensional spaces in which gravity acts in accord with the laws of motion and gravitation Euclidean?' But in Einsteinian physics, the question has a false uniqueness presupposition. Einsteinian physics also rules out questions about the time needed for a force to accelerate a particle beyond light speed. On the other hand, Newtonian theory rejects a question that Einsteinian physics answers: 'Why is the orbit of a planet of negligible mass which is subject solely to the sun's field a slowly rotating ellipse about the sun?'

A second difference has been stressed by Nicholas Rescher

(1984). In a standardized examination, students are not permitted to add new questions. But theories can add new questions through the factual discoveries they stimulate. The round-earth theory led to Aristarchus' measurement of the size of the earth. By showing that the earth was much larger than previously assumed, he raised the question of undiscovered continents. Theories also raise new questions through *conceptual* innovations. Newton could not have asked whether plutonium is radioactive because he lacked the cognitive framework presupposed by this question. Similarly, we cannot even entertain the questions that will be answered by future revolutionaries. Ineffable questions add dimension to Ralph Sockman's 'The larger the island of knowledge, the longer the shoreline of wonder.' They are also handsome counterweights to worries about assuming too much. If forced to choose, it seems better to be the kind of creature that asks too many questions than one which asks too few.

8 The unity of opposites

> That the 'that' and the 'this' cease to be opposites is the very
> essence of *Tao*. Only the essence, an axis as it were, is the center
> of the circle responding to the endless changes.
>
> (Chuang-tzu)

Disputes over questions with false presuppositions fail because none
of the direct answers is true. There aren't enough *right* answers.
This chapter addresses the converse shortage; not enough *wrong*
answers.

This genre of dissolution is fostered by wide metaphysical vistas.
The eastern varieties tend to be long on ritual and soothing imagery
while short on explanation and detail. The organicism of Hegel gave
rise to strains of idealism and romanticism that are more discursive.
They begin with skepticism about the fit between our representa-
tional scheme and reality. Reason is accused of imposing discrete,
rigid boundaries on a continuous, living, growing world. Neighboring things that happen to be separated by one of reason's arbitrary
lines will be artificially alienated from each other. A shade of green-
ish blue will be lumped in with blue while bluish green will be
lumped in with green. Distant things that happen to fall on the
same side of the line will have their resemblance overestimated.
Since reason can only work with fixed categories, it neglects borderline cases and fosters uncompromising, all-or-nothing extremism.
Dissatisfaction with reason's systematic distortion of reality motiv-
ates the search for more supple spans to the real world. Thus
high-minded romantics cultivated arational and irrational states of
consciousness: dreamy reverie, intoxication, passion. Others

promoted intuition, empathy, and mental passivity. Even those who renounced mystical epistemology tended to retain the skeptical side of idealism. For example, John Dewey had a nearly pathological hostility toward dichotomies.

There are two ways to attack a dichotomy. Presuppositional criticisms deny that the dichotomy's set of alternatives is exhaustive – these dissolutions alert us to extra options. The compatibilist criticism, which is the focus of this chapter, denies the *exclusiveness* of the alternatives. Maybe there are *two* true options. Maybe the alternatives are not vying *descriptions* at all. Maybe we should get down to cases.

EQUIVALENCE: FALSE FACES AND CONVERGENCE

If sincere people *recognize* the sameness of the choices, they won't argue for one over the other. So the equivalence must be masked. The simplest disguise is the unfamiliar synonym as in 'Was the sesquipedalian defenestrated or did the speaker who used the overly long words get tossed out the window?' Since questions of synonymy are *a priori*, philosophers have special expertise in defusing this kind of misexclusion. Of course, they do not confine themselves to timid synonymies. Should I be moral or prudent? The ethical egoist argues that 'moral' and 'prudent' pick out the same actions. He traces apparent counterexamples to an overly severe conception of morality or an overly slack conception of prudence.

A whole family of equivalence theses emphasize the malleable nature of the predicates used to state the dichotomy. For instance, Andrew Oldenquist has argued that the flexible line between action and consequence undermines the debate between formalists who believe that the rightness of an action is wholly determined by what kind of action it is and teleologists who think that the rightness is wholly determined by the consequences of the action. Each side handles counterexamples by artful redescription. Formalists use right-making consequences to classify actions ('life-saving'). Teleologists reclassify right-making act descriptions into result talk ('promoting justice'). Oldenquist concludes that formalism and teleologism are 'compatible, and because their importance for ethics has rested on their supposed incompatibility, each is trivial' (1967: 101–2).

A second mask is accentuation. Here, one alternative highlights an aspect of a situation. Thus the optimist describes the weather as partly sunny while the pessimist calls it partly cloudy. Grading by reference to the positive end of a scale gives an upbeat impression, and vice versa. The cup is half full, not half empty! *Logically* equivalent expressions need not be attitudinally equivalent. A failure to draw this distinction misleads people into thinking that attitudinally different descriptions must have different truth conditions. 'If you are not part of the solution, then you are part of the problem' is gloomier than its contrapositive 'If you are not part of the problem, then you are part of the solution.' Another technique of 'spin control' is to rise from a low baseline. Thus it is more pleasant to think that the lowly onion belongs to the noble lily family than to think that the lily belongs to the onion family.

Is the price of gold fluctuating or is it the value of the dollar? Gold bugs take the value of gold as the basis for comparison and so attribute instability to the dollar rather than gold. The debate is foolish if it is over the question of which description is *true*. However, the debate is sensible if it is over the question of which description is *expedient*. Likewise, the debate over conversion to the metric system should not be over whether a metric description is more accurate than the Imperial system. It should be over the efficiency of the respective systems and the transition costs from Imperial to metric. Ditto for all notational variants.

The last facade of bogus opposition is resemblance to problems that do have uniquely correct answers. Suppose a man buys a plot of land in the shape of a huge equilateral triangle. He wants to build a house within the plot that will have three straight roads running perpendicular to each side of his property. Where should he build the house if he wishes to minimize the total length of the roads? This question has an infinite number of answers. All are correct. For any three paths sum to a constant equal to the triangle's altitude.

The meaning of a key term may evolve under the pressure of objections. Thus initially incompatible positions sometimes blend into the same position in the end. In the 1960s, many liberals hoped that capitalism and communism would converge. For capitalism grows closer to communism with the introduction of more socialistic remedies for market failure and communism approaches capitalism as exceptions for incentives accumulate.

Convergence is also produced by shifting standards. The debate between the catastrophists and uniformitarians illustrates this creeping consensus. Geological phenomena were initially described as the product of cataclysms such as floods, volcanoes, and earthquakes.

In the eighteenth century James Hutton (and in the nineteenth, Charles Lyell) proposed a rival to catastrophism. According to uniformitarianism, geological changes were the effects of gradual processes such as erosion, sedimentation, disruption, and uplift. As evidence for drastic changes came to their attention, their notion of what constituted uniform change became more and more liberal. Likewise, catastrophists met objections by loosening the standards for what counted as a catastrophic change. As geologists became aware of the diminishing difference between the new uniformitarianism and the new catastrophism, interest in the dispute dwindled.

The current debate about the nature of problem solving may undergo a similar merge. The received view used to be that the thinker proceeds through a four-step process of frustration, exploration, incubation, and insight. This final 'Aha!' experience is characterized as a sudden, qualitative shift in thinking. A growing school of quantitatively oriented psychologists (Simonton 1988) and philosophers (Lamb 1991) reject the model as romanticized irrationalism. These mental uniformitarians contend that solutions are obtained chiefly by trial and error within a larger, structured search. Instead of innovative leaps of the imagination, the creator hoards facts and applies low-level heuristics. It is a long grind requiring energy, memory, and the compounding effects of an extended research investment. The uniformitarians support their claims with evolutionary epistemology and citation statistics that crunch differences of kind into matters of degree. Thomas Edison said that genius is 1 per cent inspiration, 99 per cent perspiration. According to the mental uniformitarians, Edison was 99 per cent correct.

The problem solving version of the catastrophism/uniformitarianism debate easily extends from solution to dissolution. For the dissolver can be equally well pictured as a revolutionary re-conceptualizer or as a local troubleshooter dependent on training, routine, and luck. Each side of the dispute will bend to accommodate the other's strong points, so there should be eventual convergence.

Artful blurring of the fact/value distinction creates apparent exceptions to dissolutional effect of compatibility. The British idealist, Bernard Bosanquet (1885: 7) brazenly conceded that 'a consistent materialist and a thorough idealist hold positions which are distinguishable only in name'. Nevertheless, he promoted idealism because of the greater comfort that accrues from describing reality as essentially spiritual. Thus the quasi-religious rhetoric of idealism is an essential part of the package. Bosanquet is able to keep this philosophy of framing-effects afloat by smearing together ethics, aesthetics, and metaphysics. For then attitudinal contrasts differentiate otherwise identical metaphysics.

FROM ILLUSION TO INCLUSION

The most aggressive compatibilist claims that the thesis and its putative antithesis are actually equivalent. But only marginally less feisty is the assertion that one thesis implies the other. Early critics of Darwin objected that evolution was incompatible with human rationality. The vigorous reply has been that evolution *entails* rationality. The reasoning is that natural selection favors organisms that form true rather than false beliefs and any organism that systematically gets truth and avoids error is *ipso facto* rational. Any other conception of rationality is rule worship!

A classic philosophical dilemma is framed by 'Are we free or are we determined?' Daring compatibilists dissolve the issue by arguing that freedom *entails* determinism. After all, we are certainly not responsible for random events. David Lyons (1965) attacks the choice between rule utilitarianism or act utilitarianism by showing how the rule utilitarianism 'collapses' into act utilitarianism. Act utilitarianism says that right actions are those with the best consequences. The standard objections appeal to situations in which it seems better to obey a rule even though its violation would produce better consequences. For instance, a bookkeeper may have a safe opportunity to embezzle from his employer. The amount will help the poor bookkeeper a great deal and will not noticeably hurt the rich employer. Nevertheless, the theft seems wicked. Rule utilitarians appease these intuitions by redefining 'right' as the action that falls under the rule with the best consequences. Since 'Be honest' leads to better consequences than 'Steal whenever the theft has better consequences', rule utilitarians seem to side with the angels. But Lyons objects that this apparent difference between act and rule utilitarianism overlooks the plasticity of rules. Whenever a rule supports an action that does not support the best consequences, there will be a similar rule that makes an exception for this type of situation.

Scientists convey the cumulative nature of scientific progress by casting supplanted theories as limiting cases of their successors. For instance, diplomatic physicists urge that Kepler's astronomy is implied by Newton's physics and that Einstein's theory of relativity implies the Newtonian theory (as long as we take the Newtonian theory to be restricted to the behavior of objects at slow speeds).

INDEPENDENCE

The modest claim for a critic to make about the two alternatives of a dispute is that they fail to preclude each other. The point can be that the alternatives are both actually true or they *might* both be true.

The fallacy of thinking in opposites consists of inferring mutual exclusivity from the mere fact that two terms are antonyms. Of course, many antonyms are mutually exclusive terms. Nothing can be both hot and cold. No one can be both tall and short. But a disease can be both psychological and organic. An idea can be of both practical and theoretical value. Token military presence in post-war Berlin was both symbolic and important.

Alternatives can be made to look incompatible by conferring extreme interpretations on each. During the nineteenth century, controversy percolated over whether the scientist's task is to merely describe nature or explain it; that is, whether scientists are only supposed to find out *how* natural phenomena occur, not *why*. Rudolph Carnap cheerfully summarizes

> Today we smile a bit about the great controversy over description versus explanation. We can see that there was something to be said for both sides, but that their way of debating the question was futile. There is no real opposition between explanation and description. Of course, if description is taken in the narrowest sense, as merely describing what a certain scientist did on a certain day with certain materials, then the opponents of mere description were quite right in asking for more, for a real explanation. But today we see that description in the broader sense, that of placing phenomena in the context of more general laws, provides the only type of explanation that can be given for phenomena. Similarly, if the proponents of explanation mean a metaphysical explanation not grounded in empirical procedures, then their opponents were correct in insisting that science should be concerned only with description. Each side had a valid point. But description and explanation, rightly understood, are essential aspects of science.
>
> (1966: 244)

Fallacious application of laws also foments pseudo-incompatibilities. Creationists still try to show that evolution conflicts with physics by appealing to the second law of thermodynamics. This law tells us that entropy always increases (or more cautiously, never decreases).

Yet evolutionary theory says that many life forms are getting more complex and orderly. The appearance of incompatibility is generated by the fallacy of division. Sure, the energy of the whole system is degrading but that does not mean all the parts of the system are degrading. Organisms can increase their orderliness by increasing the disorder of their surroundings (say, by eating a tomato and turning its chemical energy into kinetic energy which is in turn transformed into heat).

Ignorance of enabling mechanisms is another source of illusory limits. Lord Kelvin argued that we must choose between physics and evolutionary theory. His (correct) premise was that no known physical force could keep the earth warm for the amount of time required by Darwin. Kelvin then inferred *ad ignorantiam* that there was no such a force. Big mistake. Madame Curie soon discovered radiation.

Conflict is usually generated by perceived scarcity. Diplomats react with an array of maneuvers that are intended to dampen this impression. Dissolvers have parallel techniques of peace through plenty.

One scheme is to assign separate jurisdictions. Descartes' metaphysics ceded the physical world to science and the mental world to religion. Compatibilism is often invoked in the early stage of a conflict to give the new contender breathing space. Thus early behaviorism was promoted as a *complement* to introspection rather than a rival. An alternative to this ontological division is the one built on methodology. Arthur Eddington compared the scientist to an ichthyologist who uses only a net of two-inch mesh. The ichthyologist is not entitled to conclude that all the fish in the sea are larger than two inches. Nevertheless, he knows he will never catch any fish smaller than that. The scientific method is like the net. So according to Eddington, the scientific method is suited for the capture of scientific facts but not for religious facts. The game plan is to debunk the dispute as an imperialistic attempt to extend the domain of one side at the expense of the other. Once the lines of jurisdiction are properly drawn and respected, clashes become impossible. Good fences make good neighbors.

Projects are often managed by dividing tasks along a part–whole hierarchy. Thus high-level officials deal with the big picture while subordinates sort out the snapshots. Reminders about the division of labor can therefore set the stage for an honorable withdrawal. The conversational presumption in favor of specificity creates an avenue of abuse for this technique. If philosophical problems lack a solution, then they are equally resistant to solutions by nonphilosophers. Wittgensteinians must disagree with the Marxists, systems analysts, and interdisciplinarians (such as Glymour 1990) who have maintained that science succeeds where philosophy fails. So the global dissolutionist must take issue with scientists who describe themselves as having discovered what the world is made of, its origin, fate, and general nature. Thus ordinary language philosophers revive the same boundary securing moves as their anti-scientistic predecessors. For example, the isolationist Rush Rhees (1969: 6) assures us that science tells us nothing about the *world*; it only describes heat, light, and living organisms. The suspiciousness of this retreat to remote parts is made manifest by pushing it further. You say that biology at least answers 'What is life?' Nonsense! Biology only studies organic processes such as reproduction, nutrition, locomotion. You say it at least answers 'What is reproduction?' Sorry, it only studies the mechanical and genetic patterns by which organisms perpetuate themselves. Further back-descriptions ultimately lead to a guild-oriented instrumentalism that totally disconnects philosophy from science.

The supplementalist contends that the alternatives are not *rivals* to each other: one just adds to or reinforces the other. Thus the Evolutionary Synthesis of the 1930s was aimed at reconciling Darwin with Mendelian genetics. After initially appearing at odds with each other, biologists were able to show that the pair are mutually supportive. Christians ward off the question of whether the Old Testament or the New Testament has precedence by casting the New as the *completion* of the Old. The debate over holistic medicine is dominated by diplomatic missions of this nature. Although aggressive holists claim that standard medicine is inferior, prudent holists position their services as supplements to rather than replacements for conventional therapies.

Subsumptivism is a reductionist maneuver. F. Lee Werth (1978) tries to quell the quarrel between parapsychology and physics by proposing physical mechanisms for phenomena such as precognition, telepathy, and psychokinesis. Religious scientists have long tried to cast miracle stories, such as Moses parting the Red Sea, as garbled descriptions of scientifically respectable events.

RETREAT FROM TRUTH

Noncognitivists abate debate by denying truth-value to at least one of the alternatives. The move caught on in the twentieth century. Three genres of noncognitivism have evolved.

Imperativalism first! 'Stop reading!' conflicts with 'Keep reading!' in that they cannot be simultaneously followed. But it does not follow that one is true and the other is false. Deliberative questions such as 'Which verb shall we conjugate?' are requests for directives rather than information. 'Let's conjugate!' has no truth-value. Hence, the question's alternatives reflect resolve rather than truth. Directives do not imply anything false because they do not imply anything at all. Only propositions imply. Nevertheless, a deliberative question can look like an information question. Hence the disputants mistakenly debate the question as if there was a truth to be gained.

Logical positivists went imperatival to reconcile the verification principle with scientific laws. 'Every body is gravitationally attracted to every other body' is too broad to verify. Yet the positivists could not dismiss the law of gravitation as meaningless metaphysics. So the early Wittgenstein and then Moritz Schlick suggested that the law does not describe anything. It is instead a directive for forming predictions.

Archimedes' 'Eureka!' *expressed* the joy of discovery – it did not *describe* it. So it lacks truth-value. Emotivism about a field such as ethics or aesthetics is just the view that the utterances within that field are merely expressing or evoking emotions.

Emotivism is a boisterous peace-maker. Real conflicts require a clash between utterances having truth-values. If one field is emotive, then utterances within that field cannot contradict anything. This strategy has been used to grease away the friction between science and religion. Emotive theologians grant that science is right about the earth being billions of years old but add that this fails to imply that Genesis is mistaken. For the Genesis story of creation is neither true nor false. They say the creation myth only evinces attitudes such as awe of the universe, and familial concern with fellow human beings. Stories such as Noah and the Flood, the Resurrection of Christ, and the suffering of Job, are said to lie at the complex end of a continuum of emotive utterances. At the simple end lie grunts. In between, we pass from single-word expressions ('Amen', 'Hallelujah', 'Yea') to phrases ('Oh my God'), to sentences ('When the Lord shuts one door, He opens another') and then paragraphs. But never does the utterance function as a *description* of how things are.

Distinguish emotivism from subjectivism. Subjectivists assert that statements of the form '*x* is wrong' mean 'The speaker disapproves of *x*'. Consequently, when David Dinkins and Ed Koch appear to disagree about whether the death penalty is morally permissible, Dinkins is saying 'Dinkins disapproves of judicial execution' and Koch is saying 'Koch approves of judicial execution.' Since both of these psychological statements are true, the ethical subjectivist concludes the dispute is merely verbal.

Charles Stevenson argues that emotivism is superior to subjectivism precisely because it does not try to dissolve moral disputes. Emotivism presents Dinkins and Koch as

> respectively praising and disparaging the same thing. It thus represents their issue as a disagreement in attitude – one in which the men initially express opposed attitudes rather than opposed beliefs and thus prepare the way for a discussion in which one or the other of their attitudes may come to be altered or redirected. Such an issue is far from any that can be called 'pseudo' or 'verbal.' It is not a purely scientific issue, but it is nevertheless a genuine issue and of a sort whose importance is beyond question.
>
> (1963: 82)

So according to Stevenson, there are two senses of 'disagreement'. The first is 'disagreement in belief' which arises when one party believes p and the other believes $\sim p$. The neglected sense is 'disagreement in attitude' which arises when A has a favorable attitude to something toward which B has a less favorable attitude. For instance, two men who plan to dine together may disagree over which restaurant to patronize because they have different desires. They agree on the facts, they just have opposed preferences. Their ensuing argument is intended to change the other's preference, not to edify an adversary on a feature of the world.

My theory of dispute precludes disagreement in attitude. A mere clash of preferences does not suffice for *disagreement*. Polo players have opposed preferences about possession of the ball but they don't *disagree*. Suppose we add the requirement that A prefer that B's preference changes. Still not enough! When Lovejoy bids for an antique, he prefers that other members of the audience prefer that he get the antique. But Lovejoy still doesn't disagree with his rival bidders. Of course, we do many things to make preferences converge. But cajolery, bargaining, and begging are *contrasted* with reasoning. Not that this makes these practices irrational. Nor do these conflict-resolution methods need to be legitimated by assimilating them to argumentation. Of course, opposed preferences are apt to excite debate. But the *cause* of debate need not be its *object*.

I agree with Stevenson that emotivism has an advantage over subjectivism in that it accommodates the intuition that there is a genuine clash. However, I think the import of emotivism is still dissolutional. Learning that the real function of our utterances is emotive reveals that our positions are dialectically inert. For example, Wittgenstein seems close to confessing intellectual dishonesty when he muses

> If someone says: 'There is not a difference,' and I say: 'There is a difference' I am persuading, I am saying 'I don't want you to look at it like that.' . . . I am in a sense making propaganda for one style of thinking as opposed to another. I am honestly disgusted with the other. Also I'm trying to state what I think. Nevertheless I'm saying: 'For God's sake don't do this.'
>
> (1966: 27–8)

Fans of Wittgenstein may be willing to adopt a style of thinking merely on the strength of his brow-beating. But so what? Cheerleaders readily induce a glibly partisan style of spectating but at least they don't pretend to be peddling enlightenment.

Of course, recognition of the nonargumentative nature of a problem does not itself dissolve the problem. It can continue to intellectually engage civilized people. For there are remedies besides brute battle. Indeed, bargaining theorists, rhetoricians, and psychologists have made a proper study of these methods. Happily, many dissolutional techniques can apply *analogically* to conflicting desires. For instance, the techniques used to expose ambiguous disputes suggest ways to reconcile apparently opposed desires.

The third anti-realist gambit is to instrumentalize one of the contenders, to forge doctrines into calculative *tools*. Is an awl true or false? Neither! So by showing that a 'principle' belongs in a toolbox rather than a creed, one can divert curiosity away from its truth-value and towards questions about the principle's utility.

Cardinal Bellarmine tried to defuse the Copernican crisis by portraying astronomy as merely concerned with the prediction of phenomena. According to him, a Catholic astronomer can accept the proposition that the earth revolves around the sun as long as the acceptance only amounted to belief that the hypothesis was a useful computational fiction for organizing the data. Heresy only commences when the astronomer believes the heliocentric hypothesis is *true*. Pierre Duhem generalized this strategy to dissolve apparent conflicts between religion and physics. A principle of theoretical physics is just a mathematical form that can be used to summarize and classify experimental results: 'By itself this principle is neither true nor false; it merely gives a more or less satisfactory picture of the laws it intends to represent' (Duhem 1974: 285). Science is also instrumentalized by some defenders of common sense. They say that science is just a tool for predicting and controlling experience (or nature) and so lacks a truth-value. Recently, eliminative materialists have suggested the reverse: common sense is only a device for controlling everyday experience, and it is science that concerns truth.

VERISIMILITUDE AND DOUBLE-TRUTH

Belief in degrees of truth is fostered by philosophies that make truth highly elusive. The nineteenth-century idealists, for instance, insisted that the only real truth is the whole truth. We mortals only have limited information, so our beliefs inevitably distort reality. However, beliefs that are based on more information encompass more of reality. This greater proximity to the whole truth gives them a degree of truth. Hegel amplified this consolation into metaphysical optimism by maintaining that our views become closer to the truth throughout history. When an historical figure advances a thesis, an important qualification is inevitably omitted. Thus it attracts an antithesis that tries to fill the gap – but at the cost of leaving out other elements. A more synoptic, third view overcomes these shortcomings by synthesizing the insights of each and eliminating their errors. However, this synthesis is itself a thesis that emerges from a limited perspective and so will elicit its own antithesis. From this conflict emerges a higher synthesis. And so on. This dialectical process is not aimless; contending views are getting closer and closer to Absolute Reality.

Verisimilitude is also alluring when one theory 'parasitizes' another. The parasite 'derives its explanations of data by modifying the explanations provided by the second theory' (Harman 1988: 40). Thus the parasite implies that things will appear *as if* the host is true even though it is not fully true. Recall how sophisticated creationists sought to reconcile *Genesis* with paleogeology by assuming that God made the earth to look *as if* it had been around for billions of years. Skeptical hypotheses are pretty parasites. The hypothesis that you are dreaming, the hypothesis that others are mindless machines, or that the universe popped into existence five minutes ago, are all designed to 'save appearances' so that common sense looks *as if* it is correct. The parasite theory characterizes its host as a working hypothesis but reserves the title of full truth for itself.

Distinguish the semantically daring notion of degrees of truth from the tamer position that both sides of the issue contain some truth. There is some truth to 'Water contracts as it cools' because the generalization holds for water cooling down from 100°C to 4°C. However, water begins to expand from 4°C to 0°C. So is the generalization 96 per cent true and 4 per cent false? According to the classical logician, the generalization is completely false even though it has lots of true consequences. So the classicist will say that talk of verisimilitude is only coherent if it is construed as a gentle diagnosis of a failed presupposition.

Medieval philosophers frequently accused each other of trying to resolve faith/reason conflicts by invoking two spheres of truth. However, no one counts as a clear subscriber to this doctrine. Nevertheless, some thinkers flirt with the view. In *Disputation on the Proposition, 'The Word became flesh'*, Martin Luther says 'the same thing is not true in different disciplines'. This has been widely interpreted as acceptance of the thesis that there are many truths that need not harmonize with each other. Thus Luther describes the thesis that a fallen man can do no good as true in theology but not in ethics. However, Luther is more charitably interpreted as making a semantic point about how topic alters meaning. Under this reading, Luther only contends that 'good' means one thing in a religious context and another in an ethical context.

Hermeneutics aside, one can appreciate the basic way the double-truth doctrine is supposed to work. Instead of partitioning off reality, one invokes two kinds of truth that cannot be reduced to each other or subsumed under a larger concept of truth. The doctrine will come naturally to anyone who subscribes to a double-reality. For under the correspondence theory, there would be two realms of facts and thus two ways for a proposition to match the facts in a 'pluri-verse'. The basic problem with this double-truth gambit is incoherence. For example, what are we to say about 'There are two realms of truth.' To be true, it must be true in at least one realm. But if it is true in at least one realm, the truths from the other realm muscle in.

Compatibilist dissolutions score well on the criteria of charity and diplomacy. Instead of having one side substantially in error, we have both sides guilty of a mild error. With neither victory nor defeat possible, each side exits gracefully. Moreover, both parties can correctly claim to be in the right – or at least not in the wrong.

One mark of the value attached to this pleasant resolution is the overapplication of compatibilism. The 'dissolution' is commonly co-opted by covert partisans of the debate. Thus we are assured that quotas for hiring disabled workers do not force us to choose between efficiency and justice; hiring the disabled will tap hidden reserves of productivity! We need not choose between kindness to animals and scientific progress; a ban on animal testing will stimulate the development of better experimental techniques!

The desire to reconcile rivals often blinds us to the real differences that ought not to be wished away. Thus the charms of compatibilism often sparkle us into self-deception. This is the thrust of C. S. Lewis' criticism of William Blake:

> Blake wrote the Marriage of Heaven and Hell. If I have written of their Divorce, this is [because] the attempt to make that marriage is perennial. The attempt is based on the belief that reality never presents us with an absolutely unavoidable 'either-or'; that, granted skill and patience and (above all) time enough some way of embracing both alternatives can always be found; that mere development or adjustment or refinement will somehow turn evil into good without being called on for a final and total rejection of anything we should like to retain. This belief I take to be a disastrous error.
>
> (Lewis 1946: v)

This marvelous rant against compatibilist dissolutions illustrates the possibility of metadissolution. A dissolution of a dispute is the refutation of one of the dispute's preconditions. It is an argument against arguing. Since a refutation can itself be refuted, dissolutions can themselves be dissolved.

9 Forging the stream of consciousness

> That philosophy begins in wonder is a stupid remark which has
> been repeated for 2500 years, although anyone might easily have
> observed that at any time philosophers are often the most incurious
> of men. No, philosophy typically begins in *pseudo*-wonder,
> expressed by asking 'questions' which are really no questions at all.
> (David Stove)

A variety of speech acts convey problems. Hence the presentation of a problem entrains diverse sincerity conditions. *Asking* is insincere (as is any subsequent investigative activity) when one already knows the answer. *Negotiating* is insincere when one does not hope to reach an agreement. *Complaining* is insincere when you're unbothered by the defect. Given the dialectical emphasis of this book, however, I shall concentrate on the sincerity condition imposed by the joint speech act of disputation.

The point of a dispute is to make the other side know your position is right. This goal should strike you as unattainable if you think you don't really subscribe to the thesis or if you regard your reasons as bogus or if you believe you are in no better position to know than your adversary. So to argue even though you believe (whether correctly or incorrectly) that one of these defeating conditions hold is to commit yourself to an enterprise that you do not intend to carry out. You cannot try to do something you believe to be impossible. Disclosing this dishonesty dissolves the dispute.

The immorality of duplicity puts an ethical edge on this instrument of dissolution. Lies are resented and condemned because the deceived tend to be disadvantaged by false beliefs. Lies become more tolerable when told to people who are unlikely to be discommoded by the deception: children, the senile, the insane.

SURFACE BELIEF, SURFACE DESIRE

The most straightforward argumentative insincerity is to espouse what you do not believe. This is permissible when done openly as part of advocacy or a debating exercise. These roles mute the maxim of quality.

The dishonest reputations of lawyers, salesmen, and politicians, are partly earned by their tendency to exceed their role of advocate. They try to get you to think that they really believe their spiels, that they are not merely serving as effective spokesmen. It's this overkill that constitutes the lie. Some lawyers defend the hokum on the grounds that they are obliged to make the most persuasive case possible. But this ideal of representation is constrained by a code that forbids fraud.

Deception is often motivated by the penalties incurred for bad intentions. Corporations are prosecuted for selling injurious products – especially when they foresee the harm. So unscrupulous sellers feign ignorance of the damage. Deadpan executives of the cigarette industry promote an insincere debate over the deadliness of tobacco. It's safer to look ignorantly destructive than wittingly so.

An interesting borderline case of 'insincere dispute' arises when one side is composed of a mixture of believers and disbelievers. After the Vietnam War, there were persistent rumors that American prisoners continued to be held by the Hanoi government. Since Vietnam has no discernible motive for secretly incarcerating American soldiers and since long, careful investigation revealed no substantial evidence of imprisoned soldiers, American officials knew that the allegation was false. Nevertheless, hopeful kin pressured their congressmen into repeated investigations. The issue flared again when Boris Yeltsin speculated that there may be American prisoners of war in the former Soviet Union. Vietnamese negotiators said that their counterparts in the re-normalization talks should drop the issue because these US representatives knew very well that the post-war prisoners are mythical. And indeed, if one counts only the American officials as their adversaries, then the charge of insincerity is accurate. However, if one includes the constituents of the American representatives, then the charge is less convincing. A moral of this example is that we cannot always treat each side as opposed monoliths. A side can be composed of an epistemically and motivationally diverse *collective*. Indeed, those fond of homunculi will caution against viewing even a single intact person as a monolith. They view the self as a collective of specialized sub-agents with distinct beliefs and desires.

Further distinguish between insincerity on behalf of the *participants* of the debate and insincerity on behalf of the *sponsors*. Businesses fund conservative think tanks to create countervailing intellectual pressures. They care little about the foundational issues that lie behind particular pro-business judgments.

An insincere dispute need not involve the witting defense of an unbelief. It is enough to advocate a beguilingly diluted version of the position one really holds. By 1981, for instance, segregationism could no longer be publicly defended in the United States. This led closet segregationists to instead advocate 'State's Rights', that is, greater autonomy for states. Hence integrationists were alarmed when Ronald Reagan stumped for States Rights as part of his presidential campaign. Their ire was not aroused by Reagan's federalism *per se*. They objected to his flirtation with segregationism. Although he explicitly disavowed segregationism, critics contended that his coy use of the code word 'State's Rights' was calculated to garner support by association.

Self-deception is common because it is often the most practical method of other-deception. Lies are cognitively expensive. They must be prepared, executed, protected. The liar's memory must be good enough to retain the lie but not so good as to betray his knowledge of the truth. Even a careful liar has trouble imitating the involuntary nuances of the true believer (such as smiling with eye muscles as well as the muscles controlling lip corners). So rather than shouldering the burden of fully conscious self-censorship, liars find it easier to use Stanislavkian acting techniques. This thespian double-think is a dramatic shortcut to achieving the complex behavior needed to sustain the deception. Over time, however, the half-belief may grow until the liar even fools himself. But he can also linger in a borderline state betwixt believing and disbelieving. This indeterminacy yields borderline cases of 'pseudo-problem'.

More puzzle cases are bred by other shadowy states of belief. John Stuart Mill's salute to free speech contains an astute observation about 'dead beliefs' (1859: 51). Once a belief stops receiving challenges, its roots into other beliefs wither. True, the understimulated partisan readily assents to the catechism framing the belief. But the belief's influence over action wanes.

Just as one can dissimulate belief, one can dissimulate desire. Some of this is innocent enough. A polite acquaintance inquires after your mother's health. The politically astute organization man affects concern for the hobbies of his coalition partners. Such gestures are the fertilizer of friendship.

Feigned desires only acquire a moral dimension when they lead others into wasteful efforts to satisfy them. But even here, there is an extra-wide gray area because deception about a bargainer's desires is a widely tolerated exception to 'Honesty is the best policy.' Nevertheless, there is danger in dissimulating desire: faking a problem sometimes makes it real. This is the rationale given by mothers who discourage children from imitating cross-eyed people. Martial tells the story of Coelius, who evaded obligations to the great of Rome by pretending to have gout. He swathed and anointed his leg. He affected the limp and general demeanor of a gout sufferer. But the sham was too successful: 'So much can skill and effort bring about: Coelius no longer feigns, but has, the gout.' Although this particular etiology is dubious, there is evidence that pretending to want something may spawn a genuine desire for it. Cognitive dissonance theorists have conducted experiments in which subjects are given a token payment to encourage a course of action. After a while, the paid spokesman becomes a true believer. Chagrined administrators discover that appointment to a post in which one must play the role of caring often leads to internalization of the goals. Thus many an opportunist has been converted into a dedicated civil servant by organizational osmosis.

Sham inferences

The baldest bogus reason is the supportive falsehood. For example, when Hitler invaded Poland, he fabricated an attack on a German radio station as his justification for going to war. More subtle is the irrelevant truth. Here you feign a connection. This is a favorite tactic of smear campaigns in which genuine facts are selectively reported to conjure an appearance of corruption or incompetence. So now we turn from cases of faked belief to cases of faked inference.

Irrelevancies look germane when they are part of an attractive standard of reasoning. For example, Descartes' standard of absolute certainty makes every proposition cry out for justification. One form of resistance consists in showing that the standard leads to incredible verdicts, thereby forcing a choice between something we can reject (the standard) and something we cannot (our concrete convictions). Thus G. E. Moore sternly denied that Cartesian skeptical worries constituted real doubts. He rebuked those who denied the truth or knowability of 'This is an inkstand' or 'This is a finger':

> It seems to me a sufficient refutation of such views as these, simply to point to cases in which we do know such things. This, after all, you know, really is a finger: there is no doubt about it: I know it and you all know it.
>
> (1922: 228)

Those who complain that a doubt is artificial are under an obligation to specify what would be a natural doubt. The American pragmatists tried to meet this challenge with a biological grounding of inquiry. The general idea is to subsume inquiry under the principles of homeostasis. Inquiry begins as an adaptive response to a disturbance. It aims at returning the organism to equilibrium. Thus, inquiry is successful to the degree that it terminates in behavior suited to survival.

In Charles Peirce's version of the homeostatic model, beliefs are defined as dispositions to action (1931–5: 5.373). Lack of belief, or doubt, prevents action and hence is irritating. This mental itch leads to inquiry. However, it can also prompt illegitimate ways of fixing belief. The method of tenacity deals with doubt by holding on to current beliefs and disregarding counterevidence. Our tendency to socialize undercuts this ostrich strategy. The method of authority is more robust in this respect and has proven more popular. Here one defers to a single institution such as the papacy. Unfortunately, no authority is sufficiently reliable over a wide range of issues. Unreliability is also the undoing of the *a priori* method in which one adopts whatever opinion one is naturally inclined to hold. Only the method of science removes doubt in a stable way. Testing hypotheses against an impersonal reality makes our beliefs self-corrective and hence more likely to weather the vicissitudes of future experience.

Peirce emphasizes that inquiry can only be prompted by *genuine* doubt. All doubt arises from a frustrated expectation, a loss of confidence, hence, every doubt is preceded by a belief. Since one cannot surprise oneself (with respect to a specific fact), all doubt has an external, involuntary origin (1931–5: 5.443). Therefore, Cartesian doubt is completely fictive. One cannot *decide* to doubt everything and there is no way that Descartes could have been surprised by everything.

But before the questionable questioner scurries home, skeptical tale between his legs, he should review the triumphs of artificial inquisitiveness. After all, the requirement that one put down foppish doubts is partly responsible for geometry. This holds for both the geometry developed in ancient Greece and the non-Euclidean geometries of the nineteenth century. Attention to unnatural doubts sometimes pays off!

Peirce backs off the Draconian implications of his theory of doubt by licensing general reviews of the causes of our beliefs. These reflections may awaken a genuine doubt and hence inaugurate legitimate inquiry (Peirce 1931–5: 5.373). Unfortunately, this is a large loophole that seems to permit Cartesian meditations under the guise of 'general reviews'.

Peirce's contrast between the calm, satisfactory state of belief and the nervous irritation of doubt only holds for selected cases. Belief that your taxes will double is a distressing mental state that promotes lassitude. Doubts about whether salt is really so bad increase serenity and prompt a junket to the snack counter. Doubt is not nearly as stimulating as Peirce suggests. Indeed, most doubtful cases are 'don't cares' that fail to prompt any inquiry. I doubt whether I own a prime number of shirts but am not moved to count them. The bulk of my ignorance concerns trivia and so is completely acceptable to me. Moreover, it is simply false that such doubts were preceded by belief. I have never been that opinionated! The general problem is that Peirce overlooks the role of desire in action. Roommates might both believe that their air conditioner is off but only the hot one bothers to turn it on.

Ernst Mach's misgivings about unnatural doubts are of more statistical bent. Occasional successes of the method have to be evaluated within a wider audit. In particular, Mach grumbles about how hypervigilant guidelines twist minds:

> Through this endeavor to support every notion by another, and to leave to direct knowledge the least possible scope, geometry was gradually detached from the empirical soil out of which it had sprung. People accustomed themselves to regard the derived truths more highly than the directly perceived truths, and ultimately came to demand proofs for propositions which no one ever seriously doubted. Thus arose – as tradition would have it, to check the onslaughts of the Sophists – the system of Euclid with its logical perfection and finish. Yet not only were the ways of research concealed by this artificial method of stringing

propositions on an arbitrarily chosen thread of deduction, but the varied organic connection between the principles of geometry was quite lost sight of. This system was more fitted to produce narrow-minded and sterile pedants than fruitful, productive investigators.

(1976: 309)

A fellow traveler, Pierre Duhem (1974: 200–5), complained that the Newtonian insistence on experiment had generated a great deal of trivial experimentation. Propositions that received ample support from common sense and theory were treated as doubtful just because they had not been certified by an experiment. So experiment sometimes degenerates into an empty ritual, completely unmotivated by pre-existing doubt. The Socratic demand that every assertion be backed by argument leads cajolery to be packaged as proof. For example, Frege deduces that zero is a number from the premise that 'None' answers 'How many?' Wittgenstein characterizes such 'puffed up proofs' as patter that brow-beats people into following a set of conventions. Just as the question begger passes off assertion as argument, the covert reformer passes off stipulation as argument.

There is ample anthropological and psychological evidence that human beings have evolved cognitive predilections for structures that are linear, spatial, discrete, hierarchical, balanced, componential, and shareable (Shepherd 1987: 252). These predilections provide helpful guidance in the formation and confirmation of hypotheses. However, these predilections can careen out of control just like grooming predilections that tumble into compulsive hand-washing. Some of this is transitory, such as the rule-mania of children. But other obsessions are manifest in (and perhaps constitutive of) some of the best minds. Consider Kant's architectonic reasoning. A moth-like fascination with symmetry leads him to postulate categories and relationships without any doctrinal necessity and to invent an ethical system that suffuses morality with universal principles that must be obeyed regardless of the consequences.

The straight rationalizer gives good reasons for a belief held independently on bad grounds. The reverse rationalizer gives bad reasons for a belief held independently on good grounds. For example, wise but theoretically incompetent judges arrive at correct conclusions but give inept legal rationales. Governors of British colonies were often obliged to preside at courts despite a lack of legal experience. Lord Mansfield advised one such prospective judge to give his decision boldly because it would probably be right – but to never give reasons because they were almost sure to be wrong.

Mach speculated that many early scientists clothed their important results in theological terms because they felt that a subject as important as theology had to be relevant to whatever was important. T. D. Weldon argues that much political theory has this status-hungry, epiphenomenal character:

> my political prejudices are very much the same as those of J. S. Mill and the British liberals of the nineteenth century. What is wrong with Mill is usually not his moral or political judgment but his attempt to support or fortify that judgment by means of a pseudo-scientific piece of reasoning.

(1953: 16)

Both disputants may engage in reverse rationalization and so come to resemble boxers who fight each other's shadows. For example, spokesmen for workers who feel underpaid sometimes appeal to Marx's theory of surplus value while employers' advocates counter with Ricardo's Iron Law of Wages. Stanislav Andreski comments on the effect of this double dose of reverse rationalization:

> The essential ethical point about whether people are treated justly was replaced by two pseudo-scientific proofs: while Ricardo's conceptual system ruled out exploitation by definition, Marx proved its ubiquity by a long chain of obscure and muddled arguments, employing the classical economists' labor theory of value to show that profit and rent were stolen fruits of labor.

(1972: 35–6)

Reverse rationalization should make us wary of a scientist's own description of his reasoning. Even good verbalizers have trouble articulating their reasons. Indeed, the reasoning is sometimes completely unavailable to introspection (Lewicki *et al.* 1988). But rather than disappoint us with the admission that the reasoner cannot describe how he arrived at his conclusion, he confabulates.

There can also be insincerity about whether one is in a position to give the other side knowledge. College professors complain about book salesmen on this basis. The publisher's representative tries to persuade the professor to adopt the book even though the representative has never taught and is ignorant of the field. This requirement of epistemic competence explains why emotivists cannot argue with each other. If it is common knowledge between them that they regard their utterances as merely expressive, then they cannot be trying to prove anything.

CAUSES OF INSINCERE DISPUTES

Defending a belief that you do not hold may persuade people other than those with whom you argue. In the 1987 presidential campaign, George Bush stirred up an insincere debate over Michael Dukakis' patriotism. Dukakis had vetoed a law making it mandatory for teachers to lead the pledge of allegiance because the law had been ruled unconstitutional. Bush presented the veto as if it expressed opposition to the pledge of allegiance. Although Bush was too well informed to have believed this, the strawman debate garnered votes from knee-jerk patriots. So one familiar cause of sham debates is the desire to persuade outsiders.

More subtle are format driven convolutions. People are not free to advocate any position they please in any way they please. So if they hold a forbidden position, they may champion a surrogate position in the hope of gaining oblique support for the one they really hold. For example, southerners who opposed negro enfranchisement campaigned for strict 'literacy tests'. Since these voter-qualification tests amounted to formidable civics examinations, few southerners of any race could pass. So there was no sincere support for the thesis that only well-informed people should vote. The literacy test was popular only because it was selectively enforced against negroes as part of the larger effort to suppress the negro vote.

If the coded language of the two parties becomes common knowledge, then the deceptive intent vanishes and the dispute becomes sincere. For instance, intellectuals evade bans on the promotion of certain viewpoints by anthropologizing the discussion. Instead of directly arguing for p, they *report* a foreigner's argument for p. At first, the author expresses personal disagreement with the stranger's scandalous viewpoint. If the authorities tolerate this, the author becomes bolder and lets the anthropological device lapse into a mere literary affectation. The *philosophes* of the French Enlightenment were adept at this circumvention.

In addition to creating insincerity about one's thesis, laws stimulate insincerity about one's grounds. In 1989, AIDS sufferers of one community passed legislation requiring that they be served at restaurants. The law was suspended by community activists who argued that the discrimination was on too small a scale to deserve a law. The mere fact that the repealers went through the effort of mounting a massive petition drive shows that they were not alarmed by the triviality of the law. Clearly, fear of infection was the real reason for their contorted opposition. But they could not cite this as a reason in court because medical testimony would have sunk them.

The goal of persuading your audience creates a number of practical necessities. For example, naked appeals to self-interest fizzle when the audience is not included amongst the beneficiaries. Thus self-interest must be pursued under the banner of the general welfare of those involved in the issue. This ensures that prudence will often be promoted with moral reasons. For example, farmers oppose food embargoes because they lower the price of their product. But the public has little interest in agricultural profit margins. So the farmers instead argue that it is immoral to starve enemy nations into submission. Likewise, the American Medical Association uses paternalistic reasons to defend the physicians' monopolistic access to therapeutic drugs. The organization does not argue that the monopoly should be enforced because it enriches physicians.

There is nothing illogical or immoral about furthering your self-interest by drawing attention to its convenient convergence with morality. Indeed, history demonstrates that the most cogent moral appeals are crafted by those who stand the most to gain from their acceptance. However, there is insincerity in presenting oneself as principally motivated by the moral reasons rather than prudential reasons. A person who coolly recognizes his accidental alliance with morality has no license to *press* his view on a reluctant audience. However, a person acting on moral conviction is permitted to use high pressure tactics. So a person who wants to maximize his repertoire of persuasion techniques will be tempted to present his moral reasons as his *effective* motivation.

Many people crave necessary connections between prudence and morality. Thus they subscribe to the kind of self-serving ideologies that Karl Marx was so fond of exposing. The joy of debunking particular social myths pointed Marx to the conclusion that all political and economic theories are just surface manifestations of class interests. All social controversy was discounted as fundamentally fraudulent. Issues in religion were dismissed as escapist fantasies and abstract philosophy was ridiculed as intellectual onanism.

Psychologies that characterize self-deception as a large-scale phenomenon provide statistical momentum for dissolutions appealing to insincerity. Friedrich Nietzsche maintained that our knowledge claims issue from a need for biological accommodation and comfort. He inferred that this ignoble motive makes many of the big questions exercises in evasion. Sigmund Freud likewise asserted that our assertions are the spider-like workings of uncontrolled, subconscious processes which cope with internal conflicts by spinning elaborate illusions.

The fruits of debate go beyond persuasion. Unscrupulous lawyers collude to churn up spurious disputes because they get paid by the case. Participants in rigged elections go through the motions of competitive campaigning to reap the benefits of a democratic cachet. Standing up for an ideal can promote a reputation even if it is not for debating acumen. Politicians treasure this external benefit and so often pick a fight just to show off their courage, sensitivity, fairness, or whatever. For example, the Nixon–Khrushchev kitchen debate over the utility or superfluousness of electric can-openers was designed to showcase Nixon's patriotism. A public figure's virtues can be made more conspicuous with stark themes.

Leaders profit from a reputation for rationality and morality, and so sedulously trump up rationalizations and justifications. Alasdair MacIntyre charges that this fraud is built into the contemporary western political process:

> what I described earlier as the culture of bureaucratic individual-ism results in their characteristic overt political debates being between an individualism which makes its claims in terms of rights and forms of bureaucratic organization which make their claims in terms of utility. But if the concept of rights and that of utility are a matching pair of incommensurable fictions, it will be the case that the moral idiom employed can at best provide a semblance of rationality for the modern political process, but not its reality. The mock rationality of the debate conceals the arbitrariness of the will and power at work in its resolution.
>
> (1981: 68)

Many sociologists complain that scientists cultivate a similar myth of rationality. Scientists refuse to let their activities be analyzed as just another social practice. Instead, they present science as a qualitatively different institution privileged by its methodology.

Expressions of puzzlement also have rewards. G. E. Moore remi-nisced that he was impressed by the young Wittgenstein because he was the only student who looked puzzled during lectures. Bewilder-ment is a sign of comprehension. For the inquirer must have mas-tered the prerequisites for forming the frustrated expectation. So one ruse for getting others to overestimate your knowledge of x is to look puzzled about something that presupposes knowledge of *x*. For instance, students writing philosophy papers feign bafflement in the hope that the grader will infer that they have mastered background issues. The strategy has its risks. A pupil who is 'more clever than wise' may formulate his puzzlement so that it emerges as a merely stupid question. I recall a paper on the problem of other minds that contained much hand-wringing over 'How can I know I have a mind?'

Some students are taken in by their own role-playing. They spook themselves into thinking that they are really flummoxed. A portion of this self-deception may be an inevitable side effect of apprenticeship. The student strains to synchronize with the professionals. So like a fledgling songbird, he gives himself over to their patterns. The novice emulates the way teachers think to acquire their mental habits. This epistemic empathy heads into silly quizzicality when the model is misperceived. But on the whole, the ready resonations bring one into tune. Notice how cerebral tropism inverts the logical order of inquiry. Normally, puzzlement over p arises from the existence of background beliefs that implied $\sim p$. In the inversed case, one starts with puzzlement about p and then triangulates background beliefs that predict $\sim p$.

Some forms of insincerity can come to light without dissolution of the dispute. A worker who hopes to discredit his foreman, might back-talk about the way a job should be done. The aim of the fray is to show the foreman that the procedure is as the uppity subordinate contends. News that this is not the *motive* for the dispute fails to undermine the question of whether the foreman is competent. The worker can still decisively settle the issue in his favor. To think otherwise is to commit the intentional fallacy – inferring that a product is defective because it was made with a bad motive. This point can be applied to the attempt of some feminists to reject the abortion issue on the grounds that it is really motivated by a desire to control women by depriving them of their reproductive freedom. Even if anti-abortionists are as diabolical as alleged, their ethical and legal arguments could be as sound as a diving bell. Merely unmasking the ulterior motives of an adversary does not disarm him. James Boswell once asserted that the arguments of lawyers should be ignored because they are only propounded for pay. Samuel Johnson astutely disagreed: the cogency of an argument is not determined by the arguer's motives. Good arguments as well as bad can be bought in the marketplace of ideas.

Say what you mean and mean what you say! A man who habitually retracts statements acquires a reputation as a gabby fool. Thus a speaker who makes an irresponsible remark will be tempted to defend it against challenge as a matter of conversational honor – even if the challenge has justifiably shaken the speaker's confidence. So expect insincere disputes to rupture along the lines of loose talk: at bars, in political discussions, in emotional circumstances.

Speech act ambiguity causes insincere disputes because speakers often acquiesce to their challenger's mischaracterization of their utterance. This compliance may be conscious when the speaker is pugnacious or when he disdains a wimpy plea of being misunderstood. But acceptance of the distortion can also be unwitting. Habits of conversational cooperation make you go along with the speaker's interpretation of your speech act. (Fighting takes a lot of cooperation.) For example, a speaker who quotes the deflationary definition 'A language is a dialect with an army' is readily goaded into defending it as if were a serious assertion. The real function of epigrams ('Poetry is emotion recollected in tranquility', 'Rap is musical graffiti', 'An agnostic is a chicken atheist') is to direct attention to a few interesting features of the 'definiendum', not to assert literal generalizations. Anthony Flew claims that this misplaced literality underlies several metaphilosophical debates:

> people coin or seize on epigrammatic statements of what philosophy is; and proceed to rejoice or deplore that this is all that it comes to. This must always be mistaken: if only because 'philosophy' is one of those words (like 'poetry', 'nation', or 'genius') the whole meaning of which cannot be given in a definition. When Professor Ryle writes of philosophy as 'the detection of the sources in linguistic idiom of recurrent misconstructions and absurd theories' or Professor Price claims that 'all the great philosophical discoveries are discoveries of the obvious', they are to be taken as coining epigrams or slogans to draw attention to aspects of philosophical inquiry which had been neglected or overlooked.
>
> (1965: 223)

Ideological fanaticism may develop from this habit of defending slogans that were initially asserted for shock value or as entertainment or because of aesthetic merit.

MARKS OF INSINCERITY

An answer to 'What is an insincere debate?' need not imply an
answer to 'How can one know that a debate is insincere?' Nevertheless discussion of the nature and cause of insincere dispute puts us
on the lookout for signs of duplicity.

One sign is an irregular format. Frontrunners in elections avoid
debates. Why risk blowing the lead through a mistake? Why legitimate the opposition by sharing a forum with them? The only motive
to debate is to avoid the stigma of evasiveness. So most top dogs
agree to a small number of tightly controlled debates. For example,
in the 1990 New York election for governor, Mario Cuomo sheltered
his huge lead by insisting that the debate include a candidate from
a fringe party. He also scheduled the two debates to coincide with
two major sports events (the World Series and the New York Mara-
thon.) These are signs that Cuomo merely went through the motions
of debate. He really wasn't interested in persuading an already
secure electorate.

Historians ask 'How can we know where we are if we do not
know where we have been?' This suggests that knowledge of where
we are implies knowledge of how we got there. Although this
assumption rarely holds, deviant outcomes are *signs* of deviant origins. Hence, positions themselves can be signs of insincerity. Take
denials of the obvious. Some propositions are believed if understood. When $2 + 2 = 4$ is denied, we conclude that the speaker is
joking or misheard the statement or that he is being obstreperous.
This irresistibility has also been claimed on behalf of some contingent propositions. Rudolph Carnap's 'protocol statements' are
believed whenever understood. However, the notion has little application in debating contexts because Carnap confined protocol statements to records of one's own experiences such as 'Here now an
experience of red.'

Wittgenstein postulates a more substantive, social kind of agreement:

> Disputes do not break out (among mathematicians, say) over
> the question whether a rule has been obeyed or not. People don't
> come to blows over it, for example. That is part of the framework
> on which the working of our language is based (for example, in
> giving descriptions).
>
> 'So you are saying that human agreement decides what is true
> and what is false?' – It is what human beings *say* that is true and

false; and they agree in the *language* they use. That is not agreement in opinions but in form of life.

(1953: §240 and §241)

Agreement in form of life provides that backdrop for the paradigm-case argument. Ordinary language philosophers maintained that disagreement over paradigm cases was precluded by linguistic competence. Thus, Susan Stebbing (1937) took the solidity of a table to be incontestable because a table is a paradigm case of 'solid object'. Nor do they halt at the is/ought gap. Just watch how G. E. M. Anscombe chastises utilitarians who assert that punishing the innocent is just in emergency situations:

> if a procedure *is* one of judicially punishing a man for what he is clearly understood not to have done, there can be absolutely no argument about the description of this as unjust. No circumstances, and no expected consequences, which do *not* modify the description of the procedure as one of judicially punishing a man for what he is known not to have done can modify the description of it as unjust. Someone who attempted to dispute this would only be pretending not to know what 'unjust' means: for this is a paradigm case of injustice.

(1958: 16)

The flip side of this maneuver is to feign incomprehension of the opposition. Consider the questionable quizzicality of those who say they cannot understand how suicide could be in one's best interest. They query: how can you be better off dead if dead people do not exist?

Wittgenstein warned against the 'schoolboy pleasures' of pseudo-discoveries such as that space is curved or that real numbers fill the gaps between rational numbers. Aesthetic appreciation influences assent, so people sweet-talk themselves into positions that are merely beautiful. Or ugly – observe the horror show of Schopenhauerian metaphysics. Thus the artsier the position the more probable a posture.

We have no control over many of our beliefs. People cannot believe the people around them are mere automata or that the future will not resemble the past. Thus philosophical positions such as solipsism and skepticism about induction are dismissed as pseudotheses. Intellectuals can *say* that they believe these doctrines but their behavior gives them away. As Moore noted, the deniers of common sense are sometimes betrayed by their very act of expressing their position: 'We cannot know that other people exist', 'I do not believe that there are selves', 'Before demonstrating the nonexistence of time, I shall review past commentary on the issue.' As Cicero observed, a parallel point holds for irrepressible desires: 'Every noble man is led by glory and even the philosophers who write books despising glory place their names on the title page.'

Deconstructionists specialize in exposing this literary type of self-defeat. For example, Jacques Derrida finds it damning that Plato *writes* in support of the supremacy of dialogue and that opponents of metaphor make their case with metaphors. This preoccupation with how the medium contradicts the message makes deconstruction resemble dissolution. Both are negative, reactive, and parasitic. Nevertheless, deconstruction is a much narrower enterprise that only partially overlaps with dissolution. Moreover, deconstruction is a feeble form of refutation because charges of self-defeat can usually be tidied away by minor reformulations. The solipsist, for instance, can simply reword his arguments to avoid reference to others. At worst, the double-talker need only admit to being over-powered by misleading psychological mechanisms.

William James drew a distinction between live and dead issues. A live issue concerns a proposition that you might really come to believe. Dead issues, in contrast, are psychologically impossible. The contemporary western mind is closed to the possibility that brains are organic radiators. So if someone professes belief in a dead issue, we have an actuarial reason to doubt his sincerity.

Inordinate length is our final mark of insincerity. The purpose of deliberation is to reach a decision. So the failure to achieve this goal after being given ample opportunity is a sign that the process has fallen into the orbit of extraneous needs. Bureaucracies are notorious for commissioning studies as a pretext for delaying action. The dodge is also used by self-deceptive procrastinators and cowards. Their proper course of action is plain enough but they dawdle with 'doubts' and 'complications'. This gives Marcus Aurelius' admonition real purchase: 'Waste no more time arguing what a good man should be. Be one.'

Artificially long deliberations can also be induced by the refusal to think clearly. The indecisive hobble their own deliberations by shying away from elements of the problem. Hamlets are shaped by social forces. Onlookers take elaborate ponderings as a sign of virtues such as seriousness, sensitivity, and judiciousness. Florid introspection is also a significant economic sign. A person who thinks long and hard must have the time and money to indulge such a leisurely pursuit. ('We who have thought so much would not deign to act' (Villiers de l'Isle-Adam).) Cogitation can be a form of conspicuous consumption. Thus a praise-hungry thinker gets inadvertently shaped and shifted into mental and behavioral ruts. His wheels spin and spin but he stays put.

Since people monitor achievement as well as effort, they will withhold praise once it becomes apparent that the 'problem solver' is only busy in the way a gerbil on a running wheel is busy. So those who crave praise for their signs of activity are well advised to stick to problems in which resolution is hard to measure – or not even expected. Philosophical problems amply satisfy this desideratum.

10 Beyond our ken

> I suppose it may be of use to prevail with the busy mind of man
> to be more cautious in meddling with things exceeding its
> comprehension; to stop when it is at the utmost extent of its
> tether; and to sit down in quiet ignorance of those things which,
> upon examination, are found to be beyond the reach of our
> capacities.
>
> (John Locke)

What were Einstein's last words? Nobody will ever know because
his nurse did not understand German. The question lacks *knowable*
answers. Since 'knowable' means 'possible to know', inaccessibility
has to be relativized to different laws and initial conditions. So we
distinguish between the logically knowable, the physically knowable,
and so on.

kNOw limits

Bullish epistemologists, such as René Descartes, maintain that
knowledge knows no bounds: 'there can be nothing so remote that
we cannot reach it, nor so recondite that we cannot discover it'
(1967: 92). Descartes is up-front, can-do, forward-leaning. Yet
philosophers friendly to verificationist theories of meaning go
further; they make knowability a necessary condition for meaningfulness. They picture the universe as completely open to discovery.

The most dour epistemological pessimist is the universal skeptic.
However, most epistemological pessimists are moderates. They
think that some but not all propositions are knowable. Pessimists
are divided about where to draw the line between the knowable

and the unknowable. But they agree that recognition of such a boundary constitutes a form of maturity. Optimists regard such resignation as slothful defeatism. They relish stories in which proposed epistemic limits were smashed by triumphant discoveries. And indeed, the good news continues to roll in. Fifty years ago, physicists would have laughed at 'What was the universe like when it was one second old?' Now physicists know this early, surprisingly simple stage of the universe better than they know their contemporary universe.

But bad news also rolls in. Now we have fresh unknowables such as 'What goes on in a black hole?' In addition to revealing new ways to circumvent old limits, science discovers fresh obstacles (such as the speed of light). The appeal to future science is a double-edged sword. Science does not go down a fixed list of questions. New questions get added so ignorance isn't simply washed away by the rising tide of information. Even extreme epistemological optimists believe that some propositions are unknowable in the mild sense that there are obstacles to knowing them. If we regard these as the relevant limits, we gain a large area of consensus that can be cultivated with the concept of a *blindspot*.

COSMIC LUCK AND BLINDSPOTS

Why is a lost object always found in the last place you look? This question beckons for the notion of a blindspot – a consistent but inaccessible proposition (Sorensen 1988). My utterance of 'Here it is but I will continue to look for it over there' expresses the same proposition as my utterance of 'Here it is but Sorensen will continue to look for it over there' so it cannot be contradiction. The tension lies in the impossibility of me intending to do what I know I won't do, i.e. finding it there when it is here.

Inaccessibility is a matter of degree, varying with the strength of what stops you from reaching your destination. At the shallow end of this continuum is the ignorance enforced by brute contingencies. Many interesting animals went extinct shortly before zoology began. Had we evolved sooner, we would have had a better view of the moon because it used to be much closer to earth. Given the current distance, one cannot clearly see the moon's craters. The significance of this fact is evident from the impact of Galileo's telescope. Aristotelian astronomy drew a sharp distinction between terrestrial and celestial phenomena. Celestial objects were depicted as perfect with the earth at the center of the universe. Galileo's telescope revealed the moon's imperfections and its resemblance to terrestrial phenomena. When he turned his telescope to Jupiter, he discovered that Jupiter has its own moons. Their center of attraction was not earth. Had our moon or Jupiter been nearer (or our sight sharper), our ancestors would not have been misled into Aristotelian astronomy.

On the brighter side, there are 'gifts of nature'. These are helpful phenomena that invite insights into the nature of the universe. For instance, we have a simple solar system that facilitated the discovery of the law of gravitation. Most stars have twins that create complicated orbits for their planets. We only have the sun. This gives earth and its fellow planets simple elliptical orbits which helped Kepler to discover his first law. A second astronomical blessing is the existence of the earth's moon whose study serves as a stepping stone to the rest of the solar system and the universe. Physicists are also grateful for rare opportunities to test theories. The solar eclipse on 29 May 1919 provided Arthur Eddington with an ideal opportunity to test Einstein's General Theory of Relativity. He later remarked that if the problem 'had been put forward at some other period of history, it might have been necessary to wait some thousands of years for a total eclipse of the sun to happen on the lucky date'. Indeed, we should be grateful that there are any useful eclipses at all. Had the moon been a bit bigger or the sun a bit smaller, the moon would have blocked too much out. Happily, their relative sizes are just right for the study of the sun's corona.

At the microphysical level, we have the good fortune of hydrogen. Hydrogen is the simplest atom with a regular spectrum of light. The laws of the atom could be inferred rapidly from this simple case featuring one proton as the nucleus and a single electron in orbit about it. Had the simplest atom been oxygen (which has eight electrons and a complicated spectrum), quantum theory may have taken hundreds of years to develop.

Complexity is the inferential counterpart to intellectually unfortunate contingencies. Consider weather prediction which requires lots of data and lots of computing power. Great headway on the first problem was made with the development of aviation. High speed electronic computing provided a major advance on the second problem. By the 1960s, meteorologists were able to make reliable, short-term predictions. Hopes of extending the range of forecast beyond the one-week range were dashed in the 1980s by mathematical confirmation of the 'butterfly effect'. In the 1960s, Edward Lorenz had conjectured that minute errors of measurement could grow prodigiously over time so that long-term forecasts would be impossible. The flapping of a butterfly's wings in Tokyo could have profound effects on Parisian weather in a few weeks. Thus avalanching measurement errors impose a limited epistemic range. We can eventually learn the weather by waiting but there will always be unknowable weather on the horizon. So complexity alone is enough to establish a 'floating blindspot'.

The complexity problem draws us into deeper limits. For complexity is a limit only because laws of nature constrain the range of our perceptions, the length of time we may store them, and the depth and direction of our inferences. Perhaps these biological barriers will one day be explained in terms of physics. For example, super-computers are getting smaller because electricity cannot travel faster than the speed of light; it takes too long for information to flow from one side of a big computer to the other. Thus designers of artificial intelligence face a physical upper bound on computing power.

Physics has already accounted for limitations of the devices used to enhance our perceptual powers. Brownian motion imposes a limit on measurement accuracy. The motion was discovered by the Scottish naturalist Robert Brown when he looked through a microscope at pollen dust suspended in water. Individual dust particles continuously zigzag about, apparently at random. Einstein explained the motion of the particles as an effect of their collisions with invisible molecules. This implies that measurement devices will be disturbed by Brownian motion if they are made very small. Miniaturizing the needle of a galvanometer or thinning its suspending fiber could eventually prevent them from ever being at rest.

Sometimes blindspots are supported with the claim that a certain kind of metaphysical entity is a precondition for knowledge. Hence any theory that implies the nonexistence of these enabling entities condemns itself to unknowability. William Whewell, for instance, contended that evolutionary theory precludes knowledge of itself (1837: 626). Knowledge, said Whewell, only arises when we succeed in grasping essences. (Whence the importance of definitions which specify these essences.) Transmutation into new species is only possible if organisms lack fundamental, unalterable natures. So if evolutionary theory were true, no one could know it! In addition to epistemological critiques that base the unknowability on ontological requirements, there are some that base it on cosmology. For example, opponents of epiphenomenalism say that the causal impotence of the mind would prevent it from knowing anything because knowledge requires one mental event to cause another (as in inference).

The blindspots considered so far are at least open to contemplation. However, there may be propositions that are even closed to our imagination. J. B. S. Haldane suspected 'that the universe is not only queerer than we suppose, but queerer than we *can* suppose' (1927: 286). Evolutionary continuity provides one reason for agreeing. More developed animals can conceive of more possibilities than less developed animals. So we occupy one point on a continuing scale.

The preceding speculation makes the conceptual limit innate. Environmental limits are also possible. After all, conceptual development is stimulated and sustained by the contingent character of the external world. If the objects about us were highly unstable, we would not benefit from counting them. Thus concepts of arithmetic would never sprout. We owe our notion of matter to the concept of impenetrability. But we would never have the sensation of hardness if material things always retreated at the same velocity as our poking fingers.

Noam Chomsky (1975) has speculated that biological processes have made our cognitive capacities a mixed bag. Only certain kinds of problems had to be solved to survive. Therefore, there has been evolutionary pressure to form some cognitive capacities but no pressure to form others. This would explain our erratic scientific progress. Perhaps some issues are 'mysteries' for which we are just hopelessly ill designed.

Colin McGinn (1991) has gone beyond Chomsky's general claim and has argued that a specific philosophical issue, the mind–body problem, is due to a human deficiency of understanding. Extraterrestrial creatures may find the relationship between the mind and body as unproblematic as we find the relationship between objects and their shadows. McGinn marshals four pieces of evidence for his attribution of species-wide mental deficiency. Exhibit 1 is our inability to clearly express what puzzles us. Exhibit 2 is the universality of this puzzle amongst humans. They need little coaching to feel the difficulty. The third piece of evidence for our deficiency is the long history of failed attempts to solve the mind–body problem. Lastly, there is the apparent ease with which consciousness is manufactured by nature: it appears early in evolutionary history and across the animal kingdom. So there does not appear to be anything objectively difficult about the relationship between the mind and body.

McGinn further suggests that if the mind–body relationship puzzles us only because of a human conceptual deficiency, it is not really a problem. Genuine problems cannot be due to defects of particular species. The problem would be 'our fault', not an objective obstacle.

McGinn's idea can be generalized to defects within subpopulations. Some groups of people may have (perhaps ephemeral) cognitive disorders that create pseudo-anomalies. I once boggled at the Indian preoccupation with reincarnation. An Indian philosopher replied that when she came to America as a graduate student, she boggled at her professors' treatment of abortion as a *philosophical* issue. Just as an acorn is not an oak tree, a fetus is not a person. If that little reminder about the slippery-slope fallacy fails to dispel the puzzlement, well there is not much more to be said. True, one can invent fancier arguments but that is pandering to an intellectual weakness.

There is something appealing in the idea that there are objective problems on one side and on the other, difficulties that say more about us than the world. Consider the way David Hawkins criticizes the performance of motorists:

> It may sound odd to say it in this age of aeronautical and astronautical achievements, but the automobile has outstripped us in the intellectual, moral and aesthetic capacities we need for coping with it, and the result is chronic foolishness, bad taste and venality. It is essentially a 19th-century invention and represents a jump in vehicle speeds by only a factor of 10 or so over the speeds available before. A tenfold increase in speed, however, is a hundredfold increase in kinetic energy and peak forces. Our predominantly pre-Newtonian commonsense intuitions do not stand up against so great a change. Thus far we have done little to replace our primitive near-zero-velocity intuitions with properly Newtonian ones.
>
> (1969: 253)

Here, Hawkins is attributing a cognitive defect to human beings in general. However, he points the finger elsewhere when discussing the Park, Neutral, Drive, Low gear, Reverse automatic gearshift pattern common to the old Cadillac, Buick, Oldsmobile, and Pontiac. This pattern invites a dangerous confusion between L and R. Motorists approaching a steep hill would shift down too far causing accidents due to 'driver negligence'. But Hawkins insists that the real negligence was due to the engineers who designed the pattern.

Redesign to the current '**PRNDL**' pattern has ended this sort of accident.

The rule of diagnosis is to blame the most easily changed feature. That's why social activists protest the mild misdeeds of democratic governments rather than the barbarisms of intractable totalitarian regimes. We blame ourselves for our pre-Newtonian thinking because it is easier to change our thinking than the laws of physics. We blame the cars with the **PNDLR** gearshift pattern because it is easier to change the cars than the habits behind the mistake of shifting down too far. Thus our tendency to describe questions as pseudo-problems is influenced by our psychological theories (because that determines our opinion of human flexibility) and engineering (because that tells us how easily artifacts and surroundings are changed).

Indeed, any causal belief can make a contribution to our application of debunkers because it may activate the diagnostic rule. Perhaps some of the difference can be traced to the level of personality. Individuals who emphasize their own control and responsibility will tend to blame themselves rather than the questions they ask and so will have little use for the category of pseudo-problems. Externally oriented people who think they have little individual control, will trace their misfortunes to traps, temptations, and 'accidents waiting to happen'. They will make wide use of debunkers in order to redirect attention away from agents and towards our more easily reformed environment. Conceptual factors have a say in whether we 'blame the victim'. For theories of causation vary in how much of a role they assign agents and so influence whether the agent is the cause of trouble.

Relative blindspots

Two propositions that are not blindspots qualify as relative blindspots if they are co-possible but not co-knowable. Attention to relative blindspots corrects a misconception about confidentiality. We tend to think of secrecy as antithetical to knowledge. But what I refuse to divulge to others I have come to know myself. Total frankness would only increase knowledge in the short term. In the long term, people would clam up. People are discreet because they want to learn more, not because they enjoy withholding information. Social forces undermine the *co-knowability* of sensitive facts, hence people are forced to choose what will be known. Given this system of relative blindspots, one will have more *net* knowledge by exchanging rights of dissemination for knowledge of secrets.

Leo Szilard's analysis of Maxwell's demon suggests that relative blindspots are physically pandemic. The general idea is that since knowledge requires energy and energy is a limited resource, learning one fact will make other facts unlearnable. To see why this is so, visualize the universe in its final stage of heat death. You can't do it! To visualize is to imagine how it will look. But perception requires a contrast between things. When the universe reaches the stage of heat death, all the energy has run down to its lowest level. So everything is at a uniform temperature, everything is in a maximum state of disorder. At this moment, you are expediting this transition to ultimate entropy by reading this book. For your reading requires brain activity. This in turn requires energy to be released by biochemical reactions and this energy ultimately dribbles down to the level of heat. So the orderly organisms you ate to sustain your reading wind up disordered. Since information is just a measure of order, you can acquire information in one area only by destroying information elsewhere.

Information theorists like to say that we only manage to spread our ignorance around, that there is no net increase in our knowledge. This is overly gloomy. True, when you turn on a lamp to read, you lose the chance to learn about the positions and velocities of the particles in the light bulb and surrounding air. But that information is worthless. There is nothing wrong with sacrificing a mega-byte of useless information to get a bit of useful information.

GRAY MATTERS

Queen Victoria's son, Edward, was a philanderer. But he did have one principle: do not fornicate with a wife who has yet to produce a clear heir. This princely policy was a provision against unclear cases. In this section, we deal with unclear cases of a deeper sort, ones about which inquiry is fundamentally misconceived: indeterminacy.

To say that a term is vague is to say that it has borderline cases. Applying the term to one of its borderline cases gives rise to a statement that resists *all* possible inquiry. Thus everyone agrees that inquiry about the truth-value of a borderline statement is *pointless*. Since it is impossible to attempt what one knows to be impossible, no person can even be described as inquiring about a statement that he takes to be borderline. Of course, a teacher can ask 'Is a virus an organism?' as an intellectual exercise. This mock-inquiry prompts proto-biologists to think about the criteria for life just as a mock-trial leads proto-lawyers to think about the definition of 'assault', 'contract', and other key terms. However, those who believe the question is moot can only pretend to answer it. Thus there is a performative dimension to indeterminacy verdicts: to describe something as a borderline case is to renounce investigation. Thus judgments about what is and what is not a borderline case play an important role in intellectual resource allocation.

This dissolutional effect is equally potent for debates that turn on *commissive* borderline cases. The dominant conception of a borderline case is the shoulder-shrugging type in which one has no opinion. However, borderline cases are also pictured as points of linguistic *disagreement*. For example, about half of English speakers believe that handkerchiefs are clothing while the other half believe handkerchiefs are not clothing. But now suppose that two handkerchief debaters come to believe that handkerchiefs are borderline cases of 'clothing'. This would end the debate. Wide acceptance of the point would transform the commissive borderline case into an omissive borderline case because people cannot believe x is F while also believing that x is a borderline-F.

Consider the debate over 'When does a fetus first become a person?' If the answer set is formulated by the matrix 'A fetus becomes a person at the n-th week of pregnancy', it contains borderline statements. Under these conditions, the debate is defective because neither side can know that it is right. 'Person' is too vague to allow a knowable answer at this level of precision.

Derek Parfit has argued that vagueness also precludes answers to certain questions of personal identity. This is more controversial because most of us believe that there is always a yes or no answer to 'Am I about to die?' Parfit softens this belief with an analogy. Suppose a club is 'revived' after years of inactivity. Have the people reconvened the same club or have they merely started another (very similar) club? Unless the original club had rules specifying how it could be reconvened, there is no determinate answer to this question. 'Though there is no answer to our question, there may be nothing that we do not know' (Parfit 1984: 213). Likewise, there may be indeterminacy as to whether a person emerging from a teletransporter is the same person as the one who was 'sent'.

Historians of science also quit debates on grounds of vagueness. Thomas Kuhn (1977: 165–77) rhetorically asks when was the discovery of oxygen complete. If the criterion of discovery is the first collected sample of the gas, then the first person collecting atmospheric air would be the discoverer. If a pure sample is demanded, then the credit probably goes to Priestley in August 1774. But if we require recognition of what one has discovered, we also face vagaries as to how much one must know in order to constitute recognition. Priestley knew very little. Lavoisier gradually came to know much more about the gas between 1775 and 1777. Yet important errors about oxygen lingered on until the principle of acidity was abandoned in 1819 and caloric in the 1860s. Similar arbitrariness will be encountered in dating the discovery of X-rays, penicillin, and even the discovery of America. Arbitrariness should be expected because of the vagueness of 'know' in 'know for the first time'. Scientific knowledge requires both observational and conceptual elements that are normally supplied by many people.

Once the indeterminacy is recognized, debate on the original question ceases. This effect is especially welcomed by scientists attempting to defuse acrimonious priority disputes. However, the disputants may switch to the related topic of how the key term should be precisified. This transition from the context of discovery ('Is x an F?') to the context of invention ('Should x be stipulated to be F?') often goes unnoticed. Thus many of the techniques that are so handy in getting people to accept a convention can look like they are modes of *discovery*. For example, the construction of rules is greatly facilitated by extra concentration on goals. As John Wisdom notes, we are stymied by 'Is a flying boat a ship or an airplane?' when we consider it abstractly. But suppose we are trying to decide whether the captains of flying boats should have an airline pilot's license or a master mariner's certificate. The context brings the issue into focus. But not because the context leads us to *discover* the correct answer. For another context would lead us to the opposite answer. The context only helps by cuing us into certain goals and local conditions that make one answer the best *provisional* ruling for this type of case.

Divergent but stable goals can enable 'rival' precisifications to co-exist. The ordinary meaning of 'twilight' is the light from the sky between sunset and nighttime or between nighttime and sunrise. It has many standing precisifications because the distinction between twilight and nighttime can be tied to different purposes. For most of us, the key difference between twilight and nighttime is the need for artificial illumination. Thus civil 'twilight' ends when the center of the sun dips 6 degrees below the horizon because that's when outdoor activities need extra lighting. Sailors want to know when night begins because they want to know when the light will become too dim for their sextants. Thus nautical 'twilight' lasts until the sun's center is 12 degrees below the horizon. Astronomers, on the other hand, want to know when they can use their telescopes for the fainter stars. So astronomical 'twilight' requires an 18-degree dip.

The effectiveness of this appeal to vagueness is reflected by the degree to which it is overplayed. When Richard Truly headed NASA, he tried to quell the debate over how much emphasis should be placed on manned missions by portraying it as a quibble over borderline cases. Take the Venus mapping mission. Although no astronaut is inside the Magellan probe orbiting Venus, it is controlled by many people on earth. Is it a manned or unmanned mission? Truly asked this question rhetorically, as if it has no answer. But there is no genuine borderline case here. The project is clearly an unmanned mission; the ground control is a diplomatic red herring. Expect similar pseudo-dissolutions wherever there are stark either-or dilemmas that must be softened by administrators.

After the great religious turmoil of the sixteenth and seventeenth centuries, politics was redefined as a material affair rather than an application of spiritual principles. (Jennings 1985: 160). For social theorists had concluded that when human beings conceive of their rivalry in moral terms, they lose their capacity to compromise. This moral minimalism may be fueling current interest in indeterminacy. For once disputants view the matter as a borderline case, they avail themselves of less disruptive tools for conflict resolution. They negotiate rather than resort to the high-pressure tactics licensed by the judgment that a matter of principle is at stake.

THE ROOTS OF INACCESSIBILITY

Just as theoretical allegiances affect one's view of which questions have false presuppositions, theory also controls judgments of inaccessibility. A metaphysics of precision (determinism, mechanism, atomism) tends to make questions determinate while metaphysics of vagueness (gradualism, libertarianism, holism) tends to rule matters void for vagueness. For metaphysics breeds epistemology and epistemology breeds methodology.

However, first impressions are often reversed by the details. Which came first, the chicken or the egg? Evolutionary theory seems to dissolve this riddle. After all, 'chicken' is vague. The idea is that Charles Darwin demonstrated that the chicken was preceded by borderline chickens and so it is simply indeterminate as to where the pre-chickens end and the chickens begin.

However, this line of reasoning only dissolves 'Which bird was the first chicken?' (Surveillance must be extended to both problem *solvers* and *dissolvers* because both get sidetracked into servicing the wrong problem.) Rather than implying that the chicken-and-egg question lacks a definite answer, contemporary evolutionary theory favors the egg. Given Mendel's theory of inheritance, the transition to chickenhood can only take place between an egg-layer and its egg. For a particular organism cannot change its species membership during its lifetime. It is genetically fixed. However, evolutionary theory assures us that organisms can fail to breed true. So although it is indeterminate as to which particular egg was the first chicken egg, we can know that whichever egg that may be, it precedes the first chicken – whichever that may be. The egg's precedence is a biological rather than a logical necessity. Given Lamarck's theory of acquired traits, the chicken could have come first.

One might object that there can be no first F if the onset of F-ness is indeterminate. But consider a son who gradually grows bald in just the pattern that his father balded. The father became bald before the son even though there was no clear first stage of baldness. Here's a closer analogy. A sculptor who works on a marble block only during the mornings. There is no definite first day on which the block became a statue. However, we can say the block first became a statue during a morning. Indeterminate states can be determinately related. One of the virtues of the chicken-and-egg question is that it reminds us of this internal structure. The riddle also shows that there is hidden determinacy to complement the more common theme of hidden indeterminacy.

11 The edge of reason

> I can stand brute force but brute reason is quite unbearable. There
> is something unfair about its use. It is like hitting below the
> intellect.
>
> (Oscar Wilde)

Argument is a very general method of persuasion. Indeed, its scope
is so wide that many assume that any reasonable position can be
reached by rational discussion. Those who harp on the limits of
debate are suspected of being mystics or quitters or autocrats.

The existence of limits can be quickly proven from examples of
self-defeating reports. Behold the contradictoriness of 'The debate
established that no one has ever disputed anything.' Both parties
are committed to the belief in the possibility of debate, hence they
cannot *reach* this position through debate. Any thesis that conflicts
with a precondition of successful debate will smell of backfire: No
one ever makes a mistake, Everyone is omniscient, People can
never be reasoned into another belief. Hence, belief in fallibility,
partial ignorance, and corrigibility are indisputable. Like all persuasive media, disputation commits the participants to certain propositions. These commitments cannot be themselves established by the
medium in question. So there are definite boundaries to argument.
Like it or lump it.

The location of those boundaries is more contestable. Some of
the controversy derives from the skulduggery of the 'can' in 'can be
reached by rational discussion'. Can Sinead O'Connor dance the
can-can? She can can-can (in that she has the ability to learn the
dance) and she cannot (in that she lacks the opportunity). Like

'possible', 'can' must be relativized to background laws and initial conditions. Our freedom tends to shrink as more background information is added. Eventually we reach the determinist's position that identifies what we can do with what we actually do.

A speaker who wants to make our problems seem unsolvable will resort to the same contextual manipulation. People express impotent awe by formulating a question in impossible terms. I recall an exasperated university president who said that 'Anyone who thinks he has a solution does not comprehend the problem and anyone who comprehends the problem does not have a solution.' But having conveyed the magnitude of the challenge, he began to redescribe his troubles in can-do terms. After all, the practical person will only want to talk about problems that have some prospect of resolution. This pragmatic constraint ensures that our dominant use of 'can' will be far more discriminative than the determinist's.

In discussing what can be settled by discussion, we need to be mindful of the general difficulties posed by 'can'. Yet the focus has to be on limits that are peculiar to discussion. Thus I have raised the issue of cans chiefly to insure that it will be warily bracketed.

INCOMMUNICABLE EVIDENCE

The feel of a morning stretch must be experienced from the inside to be known. Sense modalities may also shape the kinematics of belief change. In his 'Letter on the Blind', Denis Diderot argued that sight reinforces concrete thinking and blindness enhances abstract thinking:

> the famous argument from design and wonder of nature has little force to the blind. The ease with which we seem to create new objects by a looking-glass is infinitely more mysterious to them than the stars which they are destined never to see. The bright sun moving from the east to the west causes them less astonishment than the small fire which they can augment or diminish as they please. And since they habitually think of matter more abstractly than we do, they have less difficulty in believing it to be sentient.
>
> (1977: 38)

Diderot goes on to meditate on the imprudence of reporting your visual perceptions in the country of the blind. Claims of sight would be met with justified skepticism. Better to remain silent than be dismissed as a madman.

Self-professed psychics also face the problem of private evidence. But at least the psychics and Diderot's man in the land of the blind can disseminate evidence that they do have special perceptual abilities. The matter becomes desperate when you cannot provide public predictions or perform amazing feats with your special mode of perception. Such is the case with introspection. Recall George Berkeley's criticism of John Locke's conceptualism. Locke proposed that general concepts such as that of triangularity and cathood arise from a process of elimination. Starting with a particular idea of a triangle, one deletes those features not held in common with other triangles. The result is the abstract idea of a three-sided figure that 'must be neither oblique nor rectangle, neither equilateral, equicrural, nor scalenon, but all and none of these at once' (Locke 1690: IV.vii.9). Berkeley doubted the feasibility of the procedure and challenged his reader to visualize such a triangle. Admittedly, if someone reported a success, there would be no disputing the matter. Since introspection provides access to only one mind, the British Empiricists had to grant the possibility of different results. When two introspectors report different results, they can ask each other to check for misdescriptions, but they cannot go beyond this. Since the possibility of misdescription or insincerity is never wholly eliminable, introspectors can reach an impasse if their results differ dramatically. For the introspector must ask himself which is more likely: a genuine radical divergence of our inner lives or some unreliable reporting. The more dramatic the divergence the less credible each other's testimony becomes. Hence Hume had to resign himself to an uneasy stand-off in his investigation of the reality of the self. Hume's introspective search for his self was fruitless; he could only find a stream of particular perceptions of heat, light, etc. But if someone else reported perception of something simple and continued, a self, then Hume had to 'confess I can reason no longer with him. All I can allow him is that he may be in the right as well as I, and that we are essentially different in this particular' (1777: I.4.6. 252). Later thinkers were less sensitive to the limits of introspection. Early psychologists were frequently drawn into irresolvable disputes about the qualities of conscious states: 'there is always to be remembered that famous session of the Society of Experimental Psychologists in which Titchener, after a hot debate with Holt, exclaimed: "You can see that green is neither yellowish nor bluish!" and Holt replied: "On the contrary, it is obvious that a green is yellow-blue which is exactly as blue as it is yellow" ' (Boring 1946). Frustrated psychologists eventually repudiated introspection because of its penchant for starting dead-end disputes. Behaviorism promised to keep issues resolvable by restricting debate to publicly observable features of organisms.

Religionists seeking to resolve the faith/reason dilemma have assimilated mystical experiences to introspected ones. Indeed, whole life-styles are matched with sensory modes. Only *experience* of the religious life can show the truth of, say, Christianity. This puts momentum behind St Augustine's claim that certain religious propositions must be believed before they can be understood.

UNSHAREABLE INFERENCES

People often have difficulty stating their reasoning. Education remedies much of this inexpressiveness but there is inarticulate residue. Physicists who know how to skateboard cannot describe how they manage the feat. So it may be that there is little to be said on some issues. You may know that p and be entirely unable to persuade me even though we agree on all the data.

Usually, we can unroll enough reasoning to satisfy ourselves that the opposition should be won over. But in some cases, we realize that the expressible portion of the issue leaves the matter unsettled; only the inexpressible nuances settle the question. So frank recognition of the indecisive nature of the *public* aspect of the issue may lead us declare it a matter of 'judgment'. This appeal to dumb intuition presupposes that there really is a fact of the matter and that people might have knowledge. So it is not a counsel of subjectivism, relativism, or noncognitivism.

There might not even be any reasoning behind the judgment. A person leaving his home for a vacation checks it over before leaving. Just how much review is appropriate? The difference between reasonable checkers and ones who are too superficial or too anxious is not a difference in *reasoning*. Eventually, the reasoning of all three characters fades away and they just act. After all, if there were a reason behind each bit of reasoning, an infinite regress of reasons would follow. What really separates the reasonable checker from the irrational worrier and the reckless Roger is that the moderate man has been built and conditioned to go just far enough. There's calibration behind the cogitation!

Perhaps this is what Pierre Duhem had in mind when he appeals to the physicist's 'good sense'. Duhem pointed out that theories only imply predictions when supplemented with background assumptions (such as the belief that the laboratory equipment is functioning and that the constants have been accurately measured). So if the prediction is mistaken, the scientist could finger these assumptions rather than the theory itself. Of course, it is irrational to dogmatically cling to your pet theory by tearing up ancillary beliefs and tacking on amendments. Duhem's point is that this irrationality is not purely a matter of logic. We have 'reasons which reason does not know'. Good physicists have a rough but reliable sense of when loyalty to inarticulate sources shades off into dogmatism. But since this is a vague matter, Duhem thinks they should allow each other discretion and await future developments.

Wisdom about the limits of debate is frequently abused. Consider the dispute between nineteenth-century physicists and geologists over the age of the earth. Following Darwin, the geologists accepted an indefinitely long time scale. (T. H. Huxley thought the age of the earth was beyond human imagination and so not amenable to scientific investigation.) Biologists always felt free to help themselves to as much time as they pleased when proposing evolutionary explanations. Thus Darwin conjectured that 300 million years had elapsed since the beginning of the Tertiary. Lord Kelvin thought this vague awe toward time was scandalous. He declared that the solar system had a definite beginning and is undergoing chemical developments at measurable rates. In particular, Kelvin calculated that a molten globe that cooled by convection from outside inward could only acquire a solid crust between 20 and 400 million years ago. Within this range, 100 million years was the most probable. Geologists were shocked by Kelvin's short time span but could not puncture his arguments. Many defended their continued incredulity by provincializing inference. For instance, Andrew Ramsay told Kelvin that 'I am as incapable of estimating and understanding the reasons which you physicists have for limiting geological time as you are incapable of understanding the geological reasons for our unlimited estimates.' But Kelvin felt quite up to geological argumentation and expressed parallel confidence in Ramsay: 'You can understand physicists' reasoning perfectly if you give your mind to it.'

CIRCULARITY AND BEDROCK ASSUMPTIONS

Some propositions are too fundamental to figure as *conclusions*: the universe has existed for many years, it is possible to know some things by memory; some propositions are more likely than others. Each of these propositions is associated with a philosophical controversy. Those who believe that these propositions are indeed fundamental will view disputes about them as defective. The point is that although the propositions are knowable, they cannot be known by means of good arguments. They can only be known in the way that axioms are known. Thus dissolutionists dismiss challenges to ground these beliefs. For instance, Richard Price declined to support his contention that the understanding has original and self-evident ideas. He maintained that if a man denies the existence of these ideas, then 'he is not further to be argued with, for the subject will not admit of argument, there being nothing clearer than the point itself disputed to be brought to confirm it' (1758: I, 2).

Similar scorn greets the invitation to justify inference rules. For instance, David Lewis declines to debate with 'relevance logicians' about whether the law of contradiction holds. Lewis asserts that he knows this principle *a priori* and with certainty, yet nevertheless concedes that 'it is indefensible against their challenge. They have called so much into question that I have no foothold on undisputed ground. So much the worse for the demand that philosophers always must be ready to defend their theses under rules of debate' (1982: 434–5).

This passive resistance has been practiced in nondeductive realms. According to Max Born, science has codified inductive inference into a set of rules that has been instrumental to the success of physics, chemistry, and so on. He describes members of anti-vaccination societies and believers in astrology as methodological dissidents who simply fail to accept the rules of science. Born again:

It is useless to argue with them; I cannot compel them to accept the same criteria of valid induction in which I believe: the code of scientific rules. For there is no logical argument for doing so; it is a question of faith. In this sense I am willing to call induction a metaphysical principle, namely something beyond physics.

(1949: 7)

Thomas Kuhn (1970: 94) has applied the idea to an explanatory entity that is a hybrid between a belief and a rule of inference, the paradigm. This is a loose form of guidance that often takes the form of a model achievement. These conquests acquire status as emulatable works largely in the subjective way that forms of political authority become entrenched. Since these exemplars constitute the standard by which scientific work is to be appraised, debate about paradigm choice is circular. Since scientists nonetheless switch sides, Kuhn's philosophy of science assigns an important role to non-rational factors.

One might try to make a virtue out of necessity by taking pride in one's nonrational factors. James Rachels, for instance, concludes his discussion of the ethical egoist's challenge to ordinary morality with a pair of pugnaciously circular explanations. The reason you ought to perform actions that will help people is because those actions help people. The reason you ought not to perform actions that hurt people is that those actions hurt people. Rachels goes on to acknowledge that the egoist will balk.

> He will protest that *we* may accept this as a reason, but *he* does not. And here the argument stops: There are limits to what can be accomplished by argument, and if the egoist really doesn't care about other people – if he honestly doesn't care whether they are helped or hurt by his actions – then we have reached those limits. If we want to persuade him to act decently toward his fellow humans, we will have to make our appeal to such other attitudes as he does possess, by threats, bribes, or other cajolery. That is all that we can do.
>
> (1986: 393)

An epistemology that attributes rich connections between all of our beliefs will portray most circularity as avoidable – especially if those beliefs are widely shared and stable. For then there are apt to be plenty of exploitable connections between your conclusion and your audience's beliefs. But circularity will be hard to avoid if our beliefs are loose and separate or if they are only connected in patches or if they are readily revised. For then one is apt to be marooned on isolated convictions or only able to argue within one's immediate neighborhood; one is then powerless to move the audience's beliefs in the direction of *your* conclusion (because they are free to revise in other directions). So whereas foundationalism and global holism dissolve few problems on grounds of inevitable circularity, intuitionism and relativism view reason as impotent over a wide range of issues.

Local holisms will also make the related point that beliefs have overwhelming inertia. For if a conviction is richly integrated within a body of other beliefs which are themselves isolated from other clusters, then a single belief will be like the tip of an iceberg. Thus a debater may be unable to budge an anti-abortionist because the conviction is part of a massive world view (Luker 1984: 159, 191).

COMPULSIVE BELIEF

We cannot help but believe that the future will resemble the past. We cannot abjure the belief that we act freely. Since an unchangeable belief cannot be changed by dispute, dispute over compulsive beliefs is futile. For example, when Hume reached the question of whether bodies existed independent of our perceptions, he stated that debate about the matter was futile. We are built to believe that external things exist:

> Nature has not left this to [the skeptic's] choice, and has doubtless esteemed it an affair of too great importance to be trusted to our uncertain reasonings and speculations. We may well ask, *What causes induce us to believe in the existence of body?*, but it is in vain to ask *whether there be a body or not*. That is a point which we must take for granted in all our reasonings.
>
> (Hume 1739: I.iv.2.187)

Wittgenstein took a similar stand on the question of other minds. We might be able to entertain the possibility of other people being mindless automata, but it is difficult to sustain the supposition:

> Just try to keep hold of this idea in the midst of your ordinary intercourse with others, in the street, say! Say to yourself, for example: 'The children over there are mere automata; all their liveliness is mere automatism.' And you will either find these words becoming quite meaningless; or you will produce in yourself some kind of uncanny feeling, or something of the sort.
>
> (Wittgenstein 1953: §420)

There is probably a biological basis for this incapacity (Levin 1984b). Early primates who readily attributed beliefs and desires to others would outperform solipsistic rivals. For belief–desire explanations make other people more predictable and so are avenues to social success. Thus human beings should be strongly predisposed to attribute mentality. Skepticism about other minds just cannot take root in the human mind-set. Such an asocial hypothesis can be entertained but not believed.

There may also be a biological grounding to the issues that arise for people at different stages of life. Curiosity amongst all animals is highest in youth. This stage of life is greatly prolonged in human beings and contributes to the wide intellectual interests of young people. Indeed, the general youth-likeness of human beings, neoteny, may be a precondition for all intellectual endeavor. Konrad

Lorenz (1973: 224–48) maintains that the rebelliousness of adolescents fosters independence. Cultural and biological outbreeding is facilitated by their curiosity about foreign customs and the ease and enthusiasm with which they assimilate to another social group. So perhaps some of the contentiousness of adolescents is inevitable. Since many men never seem to fully outgrow adolescence, the counter-suggestibility of some intellectuals may be equally ineradicable. The boyishness of a Richard Feynman or a Bertrand Russell may have driven their intellectual projects.

Desires can be as compulsive as beliefs. Emotivists argue that since morality involves our deepest, most robust desires, we are unlikely to be reasoned into or out of morality. Furthermore, a desire might be compulsive for one subpopulation but not another. Sociobiologists analyze the 'war between the sexes' in this fashion. Evolutionary pressures select men who maximize sexual intercourse because this increases their chance of passing on their genes. Women can only pass on their genes by the costly process of bearing and raising a child. Hence, a woman will be pickier than her mates, favoring men who will help her raise offspring. Thus men and women are forced to work out an uneasy compromise: she acts in a way that assures him of paternity in exchange for his help in raising their children.

Biologically enforced disagreement may also arise at the intrapersonal level. Lorenz (1973: 238–9) suggests that mood swings bestow the benefit of cognitive diversification. When on a downswing, we are better at detecting problems. When on an upswing, we are better at detecting opportunities. Lorenz thinks that swings in public opinion may also have this scanning function.

KEEP OFF THE PREMISES! IRRATIONALITY AND ARATIONALITY

Jonathan Swift glumly averred 'It is useless for us to attempt to reason a man out of a thing he has never been reasoned into.' This is *too* Swift. People are argued out of many unreflective prejudices and inconsistencies. However, Swift's pessimism is plausibly weakened to the thesis that *some* beliefs are so strongly warped by irrational forces that they cannot be rationally straightened out. Arguing over these Swiftian beliefs is like trying to recover control of a plane caught in a hopeless spin.

Intellectuals have suggested that a number of issues are caught in this storm of irrationality. Witness Sigmund Freud's sulky skepticism about attempts to support psychoanalysis with statistical arguments. After raising technical objections, Freud unburdens his main reservation:

> The strongest reason against it, however, lay in the recognition of the fact that in matters of therapy humanity is in the highest degree irrational, so that there is no prospect of influencing it by reasonable arguments . . . Against prejudice one can do nothing as you can now see once more in the prejudices that each group of the nations at war has developed against each other. The most sensible thing to do is to wait and allow them to wear off with the passage of time. A day comes when the same people regard the same things in quite a different light from what they did before; why they thought differently before remains a dark secret.
>
> (1949: 386–7)

Philosophers sometimes express frustration with their colleagues' ability to escape refutation by rejecting premises. Indeed, some philosophers have claimed that this freedom to endlessly question premises is unique to philosophy. However, anarchical questioning can always be found in border clashes between scientists and pseudo-scientists.

The ideology of science claims that its results are publicly demonstrable. Hence, many scientists feel obliged to take on all comers. However, those who actually try to fulfill this obligation frequently conclude that they have overestimated human rationality. According to Martin Gardner, the best advice on dealing with cranks was given by H. L. Mencken: one horse-laugh is worth ten thousand syllogisms.

> In discussing extremes of unorthodoxy in science I consider it a waste of time to give rational arguments. Those who are in agreement do not need to be educated about such trivial matters and trying to enlighten those who disagree is like trying to write on water. People are not persuaded by arguments to give up childish beliefs; either they never give them up or they outgrow them. If a Protestant fundamentalist is convinced that the earth was created six thousand years ago and that all fossils are records of life that flourished until Noah's Flood, nothing you can say will have the slightest effect on his or her ignorant mind-set.
>
> (Gardner 1981: xv)

Notice that fruitful generalizations about reasoning are highly dependent on psychological premises about human beings. Martians might be more (or less) open to argument. This might make Martians better (or worse!) philosophers than us.

The factors influencing a belief are sometimes neither rational nor irrational. Often these belief-makers herd us into consensus. For instance, communities rally in the face of disasters (Dynes and Quarantelli 1971). Residents adopt a present orientation that de-emphasizes concerns about the past and future. They become egalitarian, so status-driven conflicts dissipate. Debate is further curtailed by the appearance of obvious, urgent, concrete remedies. This threefold reorientation (presentism, egalitarianism, practicalism) is *collectively* rational in the sense that the psychological transformation of community members bestows a large *group* benefit. However, each *individual's* conversion is neither rational nor irrational. The consensus inspired by earthquakes and floods has little to do with the argument or rational calculation of self-interest or moral reasoning. But why stop here? Wittgenstein's later writings suggest that the bulk of normal human consensus simply arises from sharing forms of life. Philosophy becomes a series of footnotes to anthropology. Whoa!

Scientific consensus can also blossom from arational sources. One of Max Planck's most important contributions to physics at the turn of the century concerned the study of heat. At the time, it received little attention. But then the spotlight of scientific attention moved to the controversy between atomists, led by Ludwig Boltzmann, and advocates of a purely phenomenological theory of heat (Wilhelm Ostwald, Georg Helm, and Ernst Mach). The atomists needed to counter the phenomenological theory and so recruited Planck's theory. Thus Planck concluded that his idea was finally accepted because of its association with a quasi-ideological commitment rather than because of its specific merits as an explanation of heat. Atomism proved much more popular amongst young physicists, so it eventually prevailed by attrition: 'This experience gave me an opportunity to learn a remarkable fact: a new scientific truth does not triumph by convincing its opponents and making them see the light, but rather because its opponents eventually die' (1949: 33–4). Other scientific turns are the epiphenomena of social trends or simply matters of fashion.

Arational factors also lead to disagreement. Philosophers such as F. C. S. Schiller (1934: 10–12), William James, and Peter Strawson (1985: viii) maintain that many philosophical disputes are not rationally resolvable because they rest on personality differences. (Think of Leibniz's optimism and Schopenhauer's pessimism.) James contends that

> The history of philosophy is to a great extent that of a certain clash of human temperaments. Undignified as such a treatment may seem to some of my colleagues, I shall have to take account of this clash and explain a good many of the divergences of philosophers by it. Of whatever temperament a professional philosopher is, he tries, when philosophizing, to sink the fact of his temperament. Temperament is no conventionally recognized reason, so he urges impersonal reasons only for his conclusions. Yet his temperament really gives him a stronger bias than any of his more strictly objective premises. It loads the evidence for him one way or the other.
>
> (1977: 363)

Temperament may also be relevant at a meta-level. The founder of analytic philosophy, G. E. Moore, had a distinctive presence. (The historic role of his character is fleshed out in the first chapter of Warnock 1969.) Moore was attentive but calm, wide-eyed but common sensical, concrete yet careful. This unblinking, child-like simplicity starkly contrasted with the convoluted escapism of British Idealism. Moore lacked the motives of a metaphysician. He was at home with the ordinary world. His interest in philosophy was stimulated by the amazing assertions of philosophers, not spontaneous, personal puzzlement about time, morality, or science. Moore constantly pressed for explanations of why ordinary features of the world were thought to be problematic. He was bewildered by challenges to trivial truths such as 'Some things change.' In short, Moore had the *personality* of a de-problematizer.

Although temperament surely has a significant role in the history of philosophy, James should not portray the philosopher's reluctance to admit the role of temperament *in one's own* thinking as an arbitrary, rationalistic prejudice. The refusal is essential to sincere dispute. If I think that my belief is due to mere temperament, I cannot regard the belief as well grounded. So the discovery that temperamental differences are the ineliminable cause of our divergence ends the debate.

The same applies to a semantic counterpart of James' thesis; W. B. Gallie's notion of 'essentially contested concepts'. These are 'concepts the proper use of which inevitably involves endless disputes about their proper uses on the part of their users' (1955–6: 172). 'Religion', 'culture', 'artwork', and 'democracy' head Gallie's list of examples. If rival definers of 'democracy' really believed that it was an essentially contested concept, they would have a compelling reason to abort their debate as futile.

AUTHORITATIVE IMPOTENCE

After Hitler's suicide, German resistance had been annihilated. However, Grand Admiral Dönitz attempted to continue the government. New officials were appointed, meetings were convened, fancy cars ferried dignitaries to and fro. Albert Speer recalls:

> We composed memoranda in a vacuum, trying to offset our unimportance by sham activity. Every morning at ten a cabinet meeting took place in the so-called Cabinet Room, a former schoolroom . . . A hot debate arose over the question of adding a Minister of Churches to the cabinet. A well-known theologian was proposed for the post, while others regarded Pastor Niemöller as the best candidate. After all, the cabinet ought to be made 'socially acceptable.' My tart suggestion that a few leading Social Democrats and liberals be brought forth to take over our functions went unnoticed. The Food Minister's stocks helped to liven the mood of the meeting. We were, I thought, well on the way to making ourselves ridiculous; or rather, we already were ridiculous.
>
> (1970: 498–9)

Speer goes on to chronicle how the Allies nonchalantly picked up members of the government for questioning and how low-level British and American officers turned up at the schoolhouse to rummage about in the 'seat of government': 'Our government was not only impotent; the victors did not deign to notice it' (1970: 498).

The efforts of the Dönitz government were farcical because they lacked the *authority* to settle anything. In practical reasoning, the conclusion is an imperative rather than a declarative. No special standing is needed to describe facts but special standing is often needed for the performance of prescriptive speech acts such as commanding, marrying, and christening.

The problem here is institutional, not cognitive. The participants of a simulated trial may have the same information and inferential prowess as participants of the genuine trial. Yet the mock-jury has no power to render a verdict. Of course, pretend verdicts and simulated decisions are often capable of bestowing other benefits.

These pragmatic observations extract a grain of truth from Sartre's austere assertion that no one can solve another individual's moral problem. Practical moral problems have conclusions that are resolutions, acts of forgiveness, apologies, admissions of guilt, and so on. Only the agent himself is in a position to make those commitments. The conclusions cannot be made by proxy.

THE ILLUSION OF PHILOSOPHICAL STAGNATION

When we conjoin the foregoing themes about the limits of arguments with philosophy's reputation for endless debate, we naturally wonder whether philosophical problems are simply intractable. Happily, there is reason to re-think the reputation of philosophy as a static field.

General nature of the clinician's illusion

There is a puzzling divergence of opinion between those who treat disorders and those who analyze them in abstract statistical terms: clinicians are more pessimistic than epidemiologists about problems such as schizophrenia, alcoholism, and obesity. Patricia Cohen and Jacob Cohen (1984) have given an intriguing diagnosis of the disagreement that attributes an illusion to the clinicians. The illusion has four causes. First, people with bad cases of the disease are more apt to seek treatment. Second, they are each more likely to patronize several clinicians – a practice that courts double-counting. Third, the worst cases are the most memorable ones. Fourth, bad cases require longer periods of treatment and so have a higher probability of appearing in a sample of the disease. These four factors collude to bias the clinician's sample in favor of the more severe cases and so entice him into the conclusion that the disease in question is worse than it really is for the general population.

The clinician's illusion can be generalized beyond the medical domain. For parallel factors are at work in appraisal of other conditions. Especially bad criminals are more likely to wind up in prison, have longer and more frequent terms, and are more memorable because of the severity of their crimes. This should lead prison staffs to overestimate the severity of criminality just as clinicians overestimate the severity of diseases.

The clinician's illusion does not always generate overly *pessimistic* conclusions. We tend to be overly optimistic about the average level of talent of past people. For we tend to judge their talent by the artifacts that have been preserved over a long period. So our sample is biased in favor of artifacts that have passed the test of time. Most things must be of above average quality to pass this test. Mediocre writing and art will not be passed from generation to generation. Nor will inefficient techniques merit transmission. And ill-constructed artifacts are not worth repairing and so disintegrate. Hence, we overestimate our forefather's ingenuity, practicality, and tastes. Happily, our virtues are also destined to be overestimated by posterity.

The application to research problems

The clinician's illusion also infects the theoretical realm. When researchers estimate the difficulty of problems in their field, they form their opinions on the basis of a sample biased in favor of severe problems. The easier the problem, the less likely it will enter the research literature. Harder problems will be published and will enter more publications more frequently and will be under discussion for longer periods. And the harder problems will be the more memorable ones. In most fields, however, the pessimism bred by the clinician's illusion will be diluted by the presence of successes. In addition to the initial publicity of a victory, the solved problem will continue to receive exposure by its status as a paradigm of good research. And great successes, like catastrophic failures, are memorable. Furthermore, success breeds success along with selection biases that magnify the appearance of success. Thomas Kuhn summarizes the mechanism:

> the development of a mature scientific specialty is normally determined largely by the closely integrated body of concepts, laws, theories, and professional education. That time-tested fabric of belief and expectation tells him what the world is like and simultaneously defines the problems which still demand professional attention. Those problems are the ones which, when solved, will extend the precision and scope of the fit between existing belief, on the one hand, and observation of nature on the other. When problems are selected in this way, past success ordinarily ensures future success as well. One reason why scientific research seems to advance steadily from solved problem to solved problem is that professionals restrict their attention to problems defined by the conceptual and instrumental techniques already at hand.
>
> (1977: 261–2)

It is as if scientists approach nature with a questionnaire while others use unstructured interviews. This pickiness about what counts as a good question increases the ratio of answered to unanswered questions. But since answerability itself is used to determine what counts as a good question, some scientific progress is an artifact of what scientists choose to be graded upon.

History does not put much of a brake on this circular measurement. For scientists ignore past failure. When scientists pursue unprofitable lines of research, their fruitless efforts are forgotten. Only efforts that are perceived as successful merit dissemination. If a fruitless pattern of inquiry continues to be pursued by die-hards (mesmerism, phrenology, parapsychology) the area will be labeled pseudo-science. Thus, the ratio of success to failure in science is boosted by the vigorous use of this waste-basket category. Fields outside science, must take the bad with the good. (Little is dismissed as pseudo-ethics and pseudo-history.) So in science much of the failure can be discounted by book-keeping devices while other types of failure are overlooked because of the bias against reporting failure caused by scientific ahistoricism. Of course, much of our amazement at the success of the natural sciences is fitting. Stealth bombers are not kept aloft by positive thinking. My point is only that a surprisingly large portion of scientific progress is illusory.

Interestingly, the factors counteracting the influence of the clinician's illusion in science are muted in philosophy. Since philosophy is taken to be a speculative enterprise, there is a tendency to count a problem as unphilosophical once a solution wins agreement. For an answered question becomes part of the background against which we speculate rather than an object of speculation. The same tendency can be discerned with terms such as 'experimental therapy' and 'news'. Once a therapy is established as safe and effective, it no longer counts as experimental therapy. And once a report becomes widely known, it is no longer news.

The tendency of solved philosophical problems to become non-philosophical has been used to explain the apparent lack of progress in philosophy. For example, Bertrand Russell maintained that the apparent scarcity of solved philosophical problems

> is partly accounted for by the fact that, as soon as definite knowledge concerning any subject becomes possible, this subject ceases to be called philosophy, and becomes a separate science. The whole study of the heavens, which now belongs to astronomy, was once included in philosophy; Newton's great work was called

'the mathematical principles of natural philosophy.' Similarly, the study of the human mind, which was a part of philosophy, has now been separated from philosophy and has become the science of psychology. Thus, to a great extent, the uncertainty of philosophy is more apparent than real: Those questions which are already capable of definite answers are placed in the sciences, while those only to which, at present, no definite answer can be given, remain to form the residue which is called philosophy.

(1912: 155)

Philosophers will have difficulty providing examples of solved philosophical problems because of the verbal illusion created by 'philosophy'. This illusion will give free reign to the clinician's illusion in philosophy. Hence, it should be expected that philosophers will systematically underestimate the prospects of fruitful philosophical controversy.

How philosophy makes progress

Those who persist in philosophy tend to justify participation in philosophical disputes in eccentric ways. Some deny that the participants really aim at knowledge of the answer to the disputed question. Romantic defeatists affirm the aim but revel in its quixotic nature. Others externally justify the dispute in terms of its good consequences (intellectual training, therapy, etc). Still others stand pat on the intrinsic value of contemplating the Eternal Questions.

None of these answers differentiates philosophical investigation from pseudo-scientific diversions. The correct justification of philosophy is the same as for all fields; it produces knowledge by resolving problems and exposes ignorance by revealing new problems.

Most thinkers grant that philosophy unearths new problems. Historians credit David Hume with the discovery of the problem of induction and the is/ought gap, John Stuart Mill was the first to appreciate the problem of other minds, and we can thank Nelson Goodman for the grue-bleen paradox. The reason why we feel enlightened by these puzzles is that they liberate us from error. It is bad knowing that you do not know but worse to not know and think you know. As Russell noted, there is value to uncertainty as well as to knowledge. The value of uncertainty is not peculiar to philosophy. People, ranging from intelligence analysts to farmers, pay informants and experts to expose what they mistakenly believe they know.

The second half of the thesis, that philosophy is also justified by its production of knowledge, is a controversial claim. Some of the resistance to this thesis may have been eroded by the appeal to the clinician's illusion. But most readers nevertheless yearn for some solved philosophical problems.

There are plenty of questions that were asked by past philosophers which now have settled answers. For instance, the ancient Greeks wondered 'Which organ is the source of intelligence?' Plato favored the brain, Aristotle the heart. Philosophers also debated whether the earth moved and the permissibility of slavery. The trouble with these examples is that they tend to be rejected as nonphilosophical by the book-keeping trick exposed by Russell.

The only cases that will look completely convincing are freshly solved philosophical problems – ones that have yet to cross over into another field. For example, the existence of infinite numbers and classes is now well established even though they still resonate with philosophy. Several of Zeno's paradoxes now have textbook solutions which are being absorbed into the mathematical curriculum.

Twentieth-century research in philosophical logic has also been fruitful. In recent history, Saul Kripke provided the semantics for modal logic and established the necessity of identity. The semantics for sentence and predicate logic were established by philosophers early in this century. Russell's theory of descriptions earned the title of 'paradigm of philosophy' because it is a masterfully executed, correct analysis. The fact that it continues to be challenged does not show that it is not *the* solution. Solutions to scientific problems rarely win total and immediate assent. Some of the dissent comes from incompetents and crackpots. But there is also brilliant, well-informed resistance (such as Lord Kelvin's rejection of evolutionary theory and standard geology). Defenders of Russell's theory of descriptions rightly regard the challenges of Peter Strawson (1950) and Keith Donnellan (1966) as valuable and insightful. As in challenges to scientific truths, their objections have stimulated refinements and further discoveries, most notably, H. P. Grice's theory of conversational implicature.

Consensus is only a rough measure of truth. There has been philosophical consensus on falsehoods and overwhelming opposition to truths. Consensus only works under the delicate conditions that sustain the appeal to authority. The authority must be an expert in the given field, he must be impartial, sincere, and attentive to the issue at hand. Consensus is an indicator of truth just to the extent that these conditions are satisfied by the research community as an epistemic collective.

Occasionally, philosophical truths are immediately recognized. The solution to Ross' paradox is a capital instance. Suppose Alf ought to mail a letter. If 'ought' is closed under implication, then Alf ought to either mail the letter or burn it. But it is absurd to say that Alf satisfies this latter obligation by burning the letter. After Grice's theory of conversational implicature became widely disseminated, philosophers agreed with the solution given by D. Follesdal and R. Hilpinen (1971). They note that although it is *misleading* to make a weaker claim when in a position to make the stronger, the infelicitous claim is not thereby false. Since the speaker knows that Alf has an obligation to mail the letter, he should not say that Alf fulfills his obligation by burning the letter because it suggests that the disjunctive duty is the strongest that the speaker knows of. Nevertheless, the misleading statement is still true.

When outsiders look at a field's problems, they tend to see only the big ones or gestalts of small problems that look like a single big one. But most of a field's problems are shrimps. The researcher's vocabulary, like the carpenter's, teems with words for classifying this multitude of minor problems: glitch, hitch, snag, snafu, . . .

Many small solutions are little known because the problems only arise within philosophical specialties. Alvin Plantinga (1974: 23–6) won no fame for solving Quine's mathematical cyclist. This puzzle only circulated amongst modal metaphysicians. Likewise, Paul Benacerraf's (1970) solution of Thompson's lamp paradox only made him a *local* hero.

Most small problems arise as satellites of other problems. One standard mini-problem is the task of exposing a spurious solution. For example, truth-gappers suggest that the liar paradox springing from 'This statement is false' can be solved by denying that it has a truth-value. Many dissatisfied philosophers thought that this 'solution' exploited a dispensable feature of the paradox. So the problem was reformulated as 'This statement is not true.' Another illustration is a response to Gilbert Ryle's 'solution' to the liar. Ryle maintained that 'This statement is false' is meaningless because it is impossible to completely specify what the demonstrative 'this statement' refers to. Substituting the sentence itself just produces another ungrounded demonstrative: 'This statement is false' is false. Quine steps in with quick fix:

The problem is to devise a sentence that says of itself that it is false without venturing outside the timeless domain of pure grammar and logic. Here is a solution:

(3) 'Does not yield a truth when appended to its own quotation' does not yield a truth when appended to its own quotation.

(1987: 148)

That does the trick. Since the eleven-word quotation is a noun rather than a demonstrative, the reformulated liar is put out of reach of Ryle's objection.

Here is a correlativity argument for solvability. The dialectic of objection, reply, and rejoinder, generates indefinitely longer links between philosophical problems. Witness the problem of defining knowledge. Before 1963, there was a consensus that the problem was solved by 'JTB' analysis: knowledge is justified true belief. Edmund Gettier counterexampled the definition to the satisfaction of nearly all epistemologists. But there were a few replies, then rejoinders to those replies, and so on. Once the dependence of some problems on others is noted, we acquire decisive reason to reject 'No philosophical problem is solvable.' Some philosophical problems concern the rebuttal of proposed solutions to other problems. A rebuttal problem is unsolvable only if the original problem is solvable. So it is impossible for both to be unsolvable. Since there are rebuttal problems in philosophy, it follows that some philosophical problems are solvable.

Full-blown pessimism about philosophical problems requires them to be co-unsolvable. Since rebuttal problems show otherwise, a pessimist must retreat to a more cautious position. A natural alternative is to defend the thesis that no *major* philosophical problem is solvable. But this smacks of arbitrary extremism. For the flip side of grave pessimism about major problems is chirpy optimism about minor problems.

We should also be mindful of the contribution a field makes to other fields. Philosophy makes external contributions by eliminating some alternatives and adding others. Empiricists contributed to the discussion of action at a distance by releasing physicists from the presupposition that all causation is ultimately mechanical. Hume argued that interaction by impact is no more causally necessary than other types of interaction. The important factor is the sequence of observable motions, not the inner nature of the causes. This opened the path to alternatives such as field theories.

Of course, there is no need to oversell philosophy as the *sole* liberator. William Clifford's interest in non-Euclidean geometries was stimulated by evolutionary theory. In particular, Clifford was impressed by the idea that if our spatial intuitions are merely a product of natural selection, they may be useful oversimplifications. The help has also flowed in the opposite direction. John von Neumann's mathematical model of self-reproducing machines enabled biologists to reconcile mechanism and reproduction. Having conceded this reciprocity, I still venture to say that philosophy's preoccupation with conceptual knots makes it an *especially* altruistic discipline.

The organization of knowledge

The coupling of Russell's historical insight with the clinician's illusion also suggests lessons about the way research is channeled. As Russell asserts, solved problems tend to be re-classified as non-philosophical. But the re-classification is prompted by even weaker stimuli. For problems are counted as unphilosophical upon learning of methods that *could* solve it. Actual knowledge of the solution is not needed. Knowledge is organized like a system of files devoted to problem solving. Almost all of the files contain problems that resemble each other. A key point of resemblance will be the pragmatic one, the method of solution. But we will also have a miscellaneous file for those problems that can't be paired with a method. This file contains questions that are unanswered in a stronger sense than 'Is there an odd perfect number?' and 'Does the sun have a distant twin star?' The twin-star question lacks an answer but is approachable by standard astronomical techniques. These procedures are such that if anything would deliver the answer, they would. (Unanswerable questions can still be paired to approaches by virtue of their resemblance to questions that are successfully answered by the approach.)

The problems in the miscellaneous file do not have any *actual* problem solving unity. They have some *potential* problem solving unity. One can group problems together by virtue of the fact that a solution to one would solve the rest. So the unity is conferred by problem solving conditionals, not actual solutions. Philosophical problems are always solved by refiling. Sometimes a new file is created by philosophers. This is the sort of solution emphasized by Russell. Much like any file system, our knowledge began from one big miscellaneous file – all inquiry was philosophy. Although the early files were the work of philosophers, new files are increasingly the product of old files. Biology and chemistry are the parents of biochemistry; philosophy is only the grandfather. Lastly, the refiling may feature a pre-existing file.

Once a file, always a file? No. Some approaches are subtly defective. These pseudo-answering files are the pseudo-sciences. Pseudo-sciences as well as sciences separate from philosophy. Astrology and alchemy are just as much a part of the history of philosophy as astronomy and chemistry. Sometimes the separation of a pseudo-science is due to an overestimation of its promise. But on other occasions, the pseudo-science is expelled from philosophy as a cognitive pariah. Mesmerists and phrenologists, for instance, were actively persecuted by mainstream philosophers.

More commonly, philosophers merely shun perceived cranks. This refutes the conception of philosophy as an arena of intellectual anarchy in which one is expected to consider every position, no matter how far out or crazy. An illusion of pan-tolerance is fostered by the philosopher's preoccupation with extreme positions such as solipsism and moral nihilism. One infers that if the philosopher is willing to take these extreme positions seriously, then there is no limit to their open-mindedness. But as statisticians stress, the *range* is a poor measure of central tendency. Just as the grades on a test can be homogeneous even though there is a great distance between the highest and lowest score, opinions can be in rough agreement when there is a great distance between the few extremists. We also need to be alert to the entertainment value of extreme opinions. Radical and rare views tend to be more interesting than moderate or common ones (rather like zoo animals). This makes extremists more salient. So just as television news comes to exaggerate controversy, so too do the commentators on philosophy. We must also bear in mind that the interest in the weird positions is part of methodological strategy. Builders of a bridge assess it by loading it with huge deadweights. But this does not mean that the bridge is designed to bear any kind of traffic. Likewise, the philosopher is often interested in extreme opinions only in the way economists are intrigued by pure command economies and pure free-market economies. The philosopher's closed-mindedness manifests itself along most of the intermediate part of the continuum. The creation scientist will get as hostile a hearing in a philosophy department as in a biology department.

I have argued that the appearance of stagnation within philosophy is the product of interlocking illusions. When we correct for these errors, philosophy looks more like other disciplines. So to a large extent, my account supports metaphilosophical gradualism, the view that philosophy differs from science in degree rather than kind. My only disagreement with gradualism is that I deny that philosophy has a unified subject matter. Following (or perhaps amplifying) Russell, I maintain that it is essentially a miscellany. But happily, a progressive one!

12 Undermining the undeserving

Is your cucumber bitter? Throw it away. Are there briars in your path? Turn aside. That is enough. Do not go on to say, 'Why were things of this sort ever brought into the world?'

(Marcus Aurelius)

So far, I've focused on the *tractability* of problems. A negative answer to '*Can* the aim of the dispute be achieved?' doubles as a negative answer to '*Should* the disputants try to achieve the aim?' However, the normative question can also be addressed with an appeal to values rather than facts.

ABSENCE OF BENEFIT

Since the aim of a dispute is to change your adversary's mind, indifference to his beliefs prevents you from undertaking this aim. Witness Mach's insouciance:

I have read somewhere that I am leading a 'bitter struggle' against the concept of cause. Not so, for I am no founder of religions. For my own needs and goals I have replaced this concept by that of function. If somebody does not find this more precise, liberated and enlightened, he can simply retain the old concepts. I neither can, nor wish to, convert everybody to my views. On learning that somebody had been indicted for not believing in the resurrection, Frederick II is said to have decreed: 'If on Judgment day he does not want to rise with the rest, let him stay put for all I care'. This mixture of humor and tolerance is on the whole to be recommended. Our successors will one day be amazed at the things we quarrel about and even more at how excited we grew in doing so.

(1976: 210 fn)

Detachment is more fragile than Mach intimates. Our social nature ensures that interest in each other's beliefs and desires grows with contact. Coordination becomes more important, hence there is a longing for predictability and pressure for agreement. Since any discussion triggers our socializing instincts, the very act of debate heightens concern about your adversary's beliefs and thereby kindles a desire to win the debate. This emotional engagement explains why we are more apt to lose our tempers with those who have a hidden divergence in beliefs or inferential patterns. Prior to debate, we tolerate alien outlooks with anthropological equanimity. But if we overestimate our prospect for conversion, we will invest in a series of mis-targeted arguments. The absence of return on our persuasive efforts builds frustration that is apt to fracture our decorum.

There are familiar forces that offset the drive for attitudinal homogeneity. We back off when there are signs that the debate is generating more heat than light (though sunk costs fallacies prolong the friction). After all, if the goal of debate is to increase agreement, then the process backfires when it causes social rifts. So debaters break off discussion when signs of divisiveness surface. Instead of sacrificing the good in the pursuit of the perfect, we resign ourselves to our differences.

The decision to agree to disagree can also be triggered by events that affect our scale of appraisal. Many quarrels shrink into insignificance when a major disaster grabs our attention. In 1889, Germany and the United States were enmeshed in a long dispute over Samoan independence. Then a hurricane hit the island sinking each side's warships and killing 100 seamen. This tragedy cooled tempers and led to the formation of a tripartite protectorate over the Samoan Islands (with Great Britain making up the third leg). Conflict managers realize that debates take place in an emotional climate and so try to indirectly control the debate by manipulating the atmosphere. 'Irrelevancies' such as emotional displays, theatrical posturing, and publicity stunts can be understood as elements of a campaign for a favorable context of resolution. Shocking behavior can also jolt one's adversary into a adopting a different standard. For example, acts of self-destruction may be attempted in the hope of gestalt switching enemies into helpers.

To be worthy, is to have *net* worth. Recall the joke about the two chemists at work on a universal solvent. A skeptic asks 'When you fellows get that stuff that will dissolve everything in the world, just what are you going to keep it in?' The point of the skeptic's challenge is that the problem can only be solved by creating another problem that cannot be solved. Nor can one get ahead by continually swapping one problem for equally severe problems. Consider ecologists who warn against the introduction of exotic species as 'pest control'. They tell comic horror stories of how one species was introduced to control a pest only to become a pest itself – thereby necessitating another round of inconclusive pest control.

INTRINSICALLY BAD DISPUTES

A few philosophers (Friedrich Nietzsche, John Stuart Mill, John Dewey) view disputation as natural, life-affirming, even inevitable. They may concede the need to control and formalize conflict but they view it as basically healthy. For them, the mystery may be the extent of human agreement. However, most philosophers (Descartes, Leibniz, Spinoza) regard disagreements as abnormal, as deviations from the proper course of harmony, coordination, unity. Thus disagreement becomes an embarrassment to reason – a disorder calling for explanation and remedy.

Belief in the intrinsic evil of dispute is compatible with disputation. Descartes viewed dispute as a regrettable but necessary means to end dispute. Interestingly, the philosopher who most influenced Wittgenstein, Arthur Schopenhauer, viewed dispute as bad *and* inevitable. Wittgenstein finessed this deep pessimism by conditionalizing it: *if* one persists in philosophy, *then* one faces interminable disagreement and fruitless research.

Dispute is rarely charged with being an *overwhelming* intrinsic evil. One explanation is the transparent hypocrisy of arguing that all argument is absolutely wrong. However, self-refutation can be skirted by classifying disputation as immoral for groups that do not include oneself. Disputation (especially public disputation) used to be considered unladylike just as boxing continues to be considered unladylike. Since men are not obliged to be ladylike, men could consistently, though implausibly, argue that women should not argue.

Another avenue to consistent prohibition lies in inter-group restrictions. Hierarchical institutions have norms against debate between superiors and subordinates but they tolerate argument between equals. Thus the acceptance of cross-rank debate (as in business–labor negotiations) erodes social-status differences. (For an application to the 1960s civil rights movement, see Himes 1966.) Your adversary is not a supplicant or advisee. For the time being at least, he is a rough equal. Thus egalitarian reformers rightly view half of their battle as simply securing official 'dialogue' with the elite group.

A consistent but weaker prohibition of debate can be formulated in terms of a quota. For instance, contentiousness can be defined as the vice of being too prone to argue. So an argument against argument could be consistent if the prohibition were only against exceeding a certain limit of argument. Weakening the prohibition to an overridable presumption opens further options. For one can consistently argue that disputation has some presumption against it – but a presumption that is sometimes overridden. One could regard disputation as a *prima facie* wrong. For example, one might claim that disputation is as bad as, say, gossip. Robert Nozick, for instance, criticizes philosophers for an overemphasis on argumentation (1981: 4–5). Philosophical training molds arguers. Yet, argument is coercive. You force your opponent into changing beliefs by marshaling overwhelming arguments that have punch. The martial metaphors are foreshadowed by etymology. 'Debate' used to mean 'fight' or 'strife'. In Isaiah 58:4, 'ye fast for strife and debate' means that you fast in order to squabble and fight'. And 'this debate that bleedeth at our doors' in *King Henry IV*, Part II (IV.iv.2) refers to an insurrection. Nevertheless, Nozick can consistently object to argument by treating the infringement on autonomy as only presumptively wrong.

Most critics of disputation only condemn subclasses of disputes. Stephen Clark, for instance, objects to disputes over what is morally obvious. While admitting the value of an open mind, he insists that

> it is difficult to escape the suspicion of treason to other and perhaps higher values if one pretends to debate with proper detachment questions which hardly seem open to debate. It may seem merely foolish to engage in philosophical, and insincere, discussion, say, of solipsism or of the existence of the material world. Not because these are empty questions, but because those who actually experience their full challenge, for whom they are living options, are unlikely to be assisted by the rhetoric of disputing philosophers. It seems more than foolish, rather it seems disgusting, to pretend to disinterest in certain moral affairs.

We are committed to decency in argument, but there are other decencies than those of logic.

(1977: 1)

Other inquiries are impertinent. For example, Benjamin Franklin's research into lightning exemplifies the hubris of science. To many eighteenth-century figures, Franklin's investigations had a distinctly Faustian character: he was trying to steal God's thunder and even to evade divine retribution by installing lightning rods.

Many people feel that there are areas better left unexplored. Thus the criticism of nosy reporters who snake into the private lives of celebrities. Medical procedures were resisted when they involved probes of 'private parts'. Nietzsche assures us that 'Science offends the modesty of all real women. It makes them feel as if one wanted to peep under their skin – yet worse, under their dress and finery' (1886: §127)

The complaint in yet other cases is about *who* is conducting the debate. People need *standing* to enter a debate. Those without a stake in the situation are perceived as intrusive, as busybodies who butt into other people's problems. In addition to wanting their problems solved, people generally want them solved in a certain way. So outside help can cause resentment by violating metalevel preferences about self-reliance and autonomy. The 1960s civil-rights movement irritated white southerners partly because northerners were perceived as paternalistic meddlers, 'self-appointed spokesmen' horning in on local matters.

DIAGNOSTICALLY BAD DISPUTES

Some disputes are taken as signs of a flaw. Consider feminist appraisals of the medieval controversy over whether women had souls. The intellectual underpinnings of the dispute can be traced to the view that women were imperfect men or at least their marked inferiors – a view fueled by biblical talk of man being made in God's image and pressure to economize on one's postulation of forms. It was obvious to the medievals that men had souls, but women? Hmmm. Feminists maintain that this selective curiosity is a symptom of an ethical blindspot. They say the question could only be asked by a sexist. Likewise, Elizabeth Anscombe takes the willingness to argue certain ethical points to be a sign of depravity:

But if someone really thinks, *in advance*, that it is open to question whether such an action as procuring the judicial execution of the innocent should be quite excluded from consideration – I do not want to argue with him; he shows a corrupt mind.

(1958: 17)

Anscombe does not specify why she does not wish to contend with the corrupt. There could be several legitimate reasons. Maybe the corrupt resist correction by argument. Maybe it is immoral to associate with the immoral. But it is also possible that Anscombe is confusing signs of badness with the badness itself.

EXTRINSICALLY BAD DISPUTES

Most critics concentrate on the instrumental value of the issue rather than its inherent moral defects. For this form of appraisal sidesteps fractious ethical premises and even may admit of empirical testing.

Sometimes we approve of the effects of a false belief and so are reluctant to correct it. An atheist may think that belief in God helps some people cope. So he criticizes a fellow atheist's refutation of a troubled theist on the external grounds that the loss of faith might ruin a life. Ignorance has its charms. The North Pole has a mystique that the South Pole lacks because of the on-going controversy about whether Robert E. Perry's 1909 expedition really reached the North Pole. Chroniclers of the debate conclude that the debate's irresolvability is a blessing because it stimulates new generations of explorers.

Issues are more commonly criticized for leading to bad consequences rather than for depriving us of benefits. For instance, critics of the nature/nurture controversy over intelligence try to impale debaters on a dilemma. If the dispute is resolved in favor of nature, the value of the result will be swamped by the ensuing social strife. If the dispute is resolved in favor of nurture, our egalitarian social assumptions are vindicated but it makes no practical difference. So a victory would be either pernicious or redundant. If neither side wins, the dispute is a waste of time. Hence, conclude the critics, the issue is best left undebated. Similar dilemmas have been constructed against research into extra-terrestrial communication, aging, and gender determination of human offspring.

Another common moral criticism of disputes claims a need for a united front against a shared opponent. Vegetarian reviewers of Tom Regan's *The Case for Animal Rights* decried his tenacious and protracted attack on the utilitarian case for humane treatment

(Sumner 1986: 429). Why pick on someone on your own side? Condemnation is also triggered by the fear that debate about a questionable practice will arouse interest and thereby its frequency. Some sociologists, for instance, propose limits on public discussion of suicide on the strength of statistics suggesting that it causes suicide.

Addressing an issue tends to 'dignify it'. For example, some pro-abortionists lament their brethren's tendency to describe abortion as morally problematic. Barbara Ehrenreich complains that anti-abortionists have 'succeeded in getting even pro-choice people to think of abortion as a "moral dilemma", and "agonizing decision" and related code phrases for something murky and compromising, like the traffic in infant formula mix' (1984). Those who get involved in an issue tend to fall under the sway of conventions encouraging conflict resolution. So businessmen duck dialogue with representatives of incipient unions because norms of cooperation suck them into concessions. Henry Kissinger defended the elaborate pre-negotiation negotiations on the structure of the Paris Peace Talks on the grounds that the formalities of who is represented, the agenda, and so forth greatly influence the feasibility and outcome of an agreement. Structure fixes content. Is talk cheap? Measure it by what people will exchange in order to get addressed.

Disputation involves target selection. The debater is expected to pick issues and sub-issues that offer the best expected yield. Thus appraisal illusions divert us into 'nonissues'. For example, an evolutionist who debates with a creationist may be tempted to point out that Archbishop Ussher's calculation of the date of creation is off by 46 years even given his Biblical premises. But this could sidetrack the debate into calculative trivia and so is better left unbroached. The evolutionist has bigger fish to fry.

Appeal can also be made to goals that are more lucrative than the resolution of the issue at hand. Hence, normative criticisms of disputes often amount to the claim that the value of resolving the dispute has been overestimated. The value of a dispute's resolution is proportional to the difference between the alternatives. So disputes between very similar alternatives are described as petty, piddling, or picayune. The complaint is not that the questions are answerless or that they are too easy to answer. Consider the question of whether you cool your coffee faster by immediately adding the cream or by waiting until just before you drink it. The correct but nonobvious answer is to wait. Newton's law of cooling says that the rate of cooling is proportional to the difference in temperature between the substance and its surroundings. Pouring the cream into the coffee immediately will therefore slow the rate of cooling.

Trivial disputes are literary favorites. Swift's *Gulliver's Travels* chronicles a war over whether a hard-boiled egg should be cracked open at the small end or the large end. Although charges of triviality are amusing, they are apt to rest on a failure to properly relativize 'trivial'. The value of a problem may lie in the *process* of solution rather than the *product*. For example, the question about cooling coffee might have merit as a physics exercise. Our result-oriented thinking makes us undervalue questions in which the answering rather than the answer is key.

One must also relativize 'trivial' to varying interests. What makes a small difference to you may make a large difference to me. I recall a Marxist scholar being amused at the interest American students showed in the 1977 presidential debates between Jimmy Carter and Gerald Ford. She thought the question of who would make the better president was trivial because the two candidates were practically identical. From her vantage point at the far left of the political spectrum, there was indeed little difference. But from the vantage point of centrist students, the distance between Carter and Ford was significant.

The charge of triviality is not always defeated by relativizing. Criminologists who scoff at the debate over capital punishment will admit that the issue seems momentous to the public. Their complaint is that the public is under-informed. The significance of the death penalty shrinks against the grand panorama of the underworld. Many other criminological questions have higher priority. If we are to relativize 'important', we should relativize to these well-informed perspectives.

THE PRACTICAL MAN'S PUZZLING INTEREST IN SOCIAL ISSUES

Ironically, most people who pride themselves on their practicality have an enduring interest in issues over which they have virtually no control. Politics, social trends, and disasters are news because millions of individually powerless people are curious. In addition to spending the time and money necessary to acquire information about events outside their sphere of influence, ordinary people spend further time and patience hotly debating their significance.

Some people regard such discussion as fulfillment of their duty to be an informed citizen. But purely moral explanations of social behavior are rarely acceptable because morality is only a weak force; prudence is the strong force. (Notice how civil-war historians scout for ways to replace moral explanations with economics.) That's what makes interest in current affairs puzzling: lack of a self-interested reason to debate issues beyond one's control. It might be suggested that there is prudential value in keeping abreast of uncontrollable events because they make good topics of conversation. It pays for me to be interested because others are interested. But why are the others interested? Maybe the answer is that news of big events is like money: no one directly values money but everyone indirectly values money because they know others indirectly value it.

In any case, we still need to explain what makes the discussions rewarding. Perhaps people debate social issues because it gives them the illusion of control. Control illusions are most noticeable in gambling situations (Langer 1982). Dice players throw dice softly to get low numbers and hard to get high ones. They believe that their performance will be better with concentration and effort. Lottery participants carefully select their number. This makes people feel in control because it assimilates the selection task to skill situations. Control is a valuable psychological commodity because it figures in the 'equation' Problem severity = Distress × Uncontrollability × Frequency. Habits that increase my estimate of my control will be reinforced by their appearance of decreasing the problem's severity. Perhaps people talk about big issues because such discussions resemble planning. By treating the issue as one over which I can make a difference, I gain a sense of control and thereby hush anxieties about large scale social events.

Although the attribution of illusions dispels some of our puzzlement about why ordinary people take an interest in uncontrollable social issues, it cannot account for enough of it. Perhaps the residue can be explained as a relic of the days when social groups were smaller. For 99 per cent of human history, we lived in small hunter-gatherer bands. A chap who paid attention to his little society's problems could predict and influence collective behavior. Given that this social tendency is heritable, it will prevail over the psychology of apathy and so pass down to the citizens of giant nations.

AN EXPECTED-UTILITY ANALYSIS OF DISPUTES

Our choices are not always choices between good and bad alternatives. Often, we have the pleasure of choosing between two good alternatives – and too often the pain of choosing between two bad options. In these pure cases, we aim for the greater good or the lesser evil. Sometimes life is more complicated. We confront alternatives offering uncertain mixtures of goods and evils. These decision problems are most simply analyzed in terms of their expected value.

The expected value of an option is obtained by multiplying the option's pay-offs with its probabilities. Criticisms of decisions can be organized around the above model of decision making. Thus complaints about the decision to debate can be cast as an accusation of deviation from the behavior of an ideal chooser.

The epistemic entrepreneur's miscalculations

In the case of a formal error, you are aware of the relevant probabilities and values but you misfigure the result. Some people who are told that they have less than a probability of 1/1,000,000 for winning the single million-dollar prize of a lottery will nevertheless pay a dollar for a ticket *as an investment*. Their failure to correctly multiply the probability of the gain by its value leads them to pay a dollar for something worth far less than a dollar. Instead of calculating expected value by multiplying, they use rules of thumb. They acknowledge that the probability is small but appeal to the compensating effect of the large potential gain.

Misderived probabilities

The category of probability fallacies is lush. Some of the fallacies have earned their own labels: gamblers' fallacy, regression fallacy, and biased sampling are staples of statistics courses. Experimental psychologists have documented our tendency to overestimate conjunctions and underestimate disjunctions, to ignore base rates, under-revise prior probabilities, and a tendency (even on the part of trained statisticians) to slip into primitive representativeness thinking. Although all of these fallacies create pseudo-problems, I shall concentrate on three especially fertile sources of error.

One symptom of miscalculation is the hypnotic draw of big questions. Queries into the meaning of life and the perfect form of government captivate people because of their enormous potential payoff. But there are rational grounds for interest in big questions. After people become curious about a large, unwieldy set of questions, they naturally seek a way of reducing this large set of problems to a smaller, more manageable set. So they try to formulate central, fundamental questions.

Answers to these big questions lead to answers to the original, smaller questions. Isaac Newton made a revolutionary advance in physics by grouping together mysteries about the movements of planets, rocks, and tides. In 1869, Dmitri Mendeleyev gave chemists a synoptic vision of their subject matter by constructing the periodic table. Charles Darwin did the same for biology by providing a theory that unified questions about fossils, the age of the earth, species differentiation, and animal breeding.

Advantages accrue from broadening an issue. First, unification often reveals a new pattern in much the way aerial photographs reveal the path of a lava flow, suburban sprawl, or patterns of traffic congestion. Second, generalizing helps us extend an old pattern to new cases (as when germanium was predicted by interpolating between known elements). Broadening the issue may reveal new cases that are easier to handle and which can serve as stepping stones to more difficult ones. Finally, generalizing tends to produce the conceptual virtue of internal coherence, that is, the components of the theory have rich inferential connections. For instance, Ptolemaic astronomy was a piecemeal approach to determining the positions of the planets; each planet was calculated independent of the rest. Copernicus' heliocentric theory dealt with the planets simultaneously. Although the observational data available at the time did not favor either theory, Ptolemaic astronomy could only produce a big picture as a three-dimensional montage of little pictures. To obtain a Ptolemaic 'system', one would have to take the calculating charts for each of the planets, superimpose and center them through the earthpoint, and use a special technique to scale the orbits to avoid collisions. By placing the sun at the center, Copernicus transcended this jumble.

The successes of the top-to-bottom strategy are impressive. But we must also remember its failures such as the nineteenth-century attempt to unite biology and electricity. A number of fallacies feed our fascination with grand visions. Just as lottery participants downplay their small probability of winning by dwelling on the size of the grand prize, bold thinkers downplay the small probability of resolving a big question by emphasizing the intellectual payoff of an answer to the big question. Obsession with grandiose issues runs through much of the history of philosophy. The philosophers most preoccupied with the big question strategy are by no means ignorant of its long history of disasters. Descartes, Kant, Hegel, Husserl, and Wittgenstein all express disgust at endless wrangling. But rather than taking millennia of failure as providing overwhelming inductive evidence against a future success, they emphasize the benefits that accrue from big answers. They then propose their own secrets of success, usually a master method intended to finally put philosophy on the right track. Descartes advocated the method of doubt, restricting the conscientious philosopher to 'clear and distinct ideas'. Leibniz had a lifelong fascination with the 'alphabet of thought', a universal algebra by which all knowledge could some day be derived. Once issues were translated into this ideal symbolism, disagreements would be ground out by mechanical calculations. After Leibniz, there appears Kant's transcendental method, Husserl's bracketing, and the logical positivist's verification criterion of meaning.

One need not endorse grandiose designs to be a proponent of thinking big. Even picky analytic philosophers frequently complain that a problem has been formulated in an overly narrow fashion. They say that the 'problem' is just a special instance of a more general problem. Indeed a whole subset of problems may have this character. Philosophers frequently dismiss topics such as sexual ethics on the ground that they do not raise *special* problems – sexual ethics is just ethics applied to sex and so no more a genuine topic than culinary ethics.

Analytics dodge the problems posed by borderline cases by broadening the question. For instance, 'What is a disease?' is hampered by cases that are borderline between 'disease' and 'injury'. The indeterminacy is finessed by broadening the problem to 'What is a pathological condition?' The original point of asking whether a condition is a disease was to decide whether it should be corrected or its treatment reimbursed. This practical issue is settled just as well by the more general question.

Our preoccupation with big issues may be rooted in a 'counter-bias' that offsets our tendency to ignore low-probability events (Goldman 1986: 342–3). An organism that paid attention to marginal possibilities would be overwhelmed by details. This clutter can be eliminated by restricting attention to likely events. But now the creature is blind to possibilities that have a low probability but high value (or disvalue). So Mother Nature strikes a compromise by introducing an attentional bias in favor of possibilities with extreme values. Now we will shy away from risks and gravitate toward speculative opportunities. Unfortunately, we will also tend to overreact and to be constitutionally vulnerable to fearful and wishful thinking.

Opponents of philosophy in the grand style warn that we should be more attentive to the odds. Instead of pursuing a few large questions, caution counsels attention to a large number of smaller ones. The per capita payoff is much lower but the probability of some success is much higher. J. L. Austin advocates the study of excuses over a direct attack on the problem of free will, the nature of reality, or the difference between good and evil:

> Here at last we should be able to unfreeze, to loosen up and get going on agreeing about discoveries, however small, and on agreeing about how to reach agreement. How much it is to be wished that similar field work will soon be undertaken in, say, aesthetics; if only we could forget for a while about the beautiful and get down instead to the dainty and the dumpy.
>
> (1961: 131)

The piecemeal approach was also promoted by formal analytic philosophers. Bertrand Russell (1957) pined for the benefits of successive error recognition and correction associated with science.

Wise researchers monitor their issue for signs of degeneration. Many issues sour because of a failure to revise probabilities in light of new information. Consider criticism of the unification problem in physics. Newton's unification of celestial and terrestrial movements in terms of gravity and James Clerk Maxwell's unification of electricity and magnetism in terms of electromagnetism led many physicists to wonder whether gravity and electromagnetism could themselves be unified. These unified field theories presented the two forces as aspects of a single force. This initially promising problem occupied Albert Einstein and Werner Heisenberg even after most of the physics community concluded that it was no longer promising. One reason for the revised estimate was that their many years of failure boded badly for future effort. The other was the discovery of a strong force and a weak force (radically different from each other). These new wrinkles revealed that the problem was even more difficult than initially supposed. Persistence in light of such bad news made the unified field theorist look like Captain Ahab doggedly pursuing Moby Dick.

Of course, new evidence can have the opposite effect by increasing the probability of resolution. In 1967, Steven Weinberg and Abdus Salam revived the grand unification problem by showing how the electromagnetic and weak forces could be viewed as aspects of a single 'electroweak' force. Einstein may have the last laugh! However, a successful reduction would not show that his tenacity was rational. Rational researchers choose their problems in accordance with their *expected* value, not their actual value.

The fact that certain ideals become outdated is a sign that they are closer to being empirically based strategies rather than *a priori* values. For instance, our forefathers took understandable pride in self-sufficiency. A settler should be able to make and repair essential artifacts, to live off the land, to protect his own property. Lingering loyalty to the frontier ideal leads to criticism of contemporary Americans for their dependence on others. However, this complaint is merely quaint. The virtue of self-sufficiency is no longer important in our highly specialized society. Similarly, the intellectual ideal of the 'Renaissance man' who has broad knowledge of all fields is just out of date.

Overestimates of the expected return on a problem often turn on its relevance to another problem. A task that is a necessary condition for another task must be completed in order to accomplish the more ultimate end. When the derivative task is only an illusory necessary condition, then an alternate route will let us *abandon* the original problem. This can happen in two ways. The mild way occurs when solution to a subproblem is part of a *sufficient* condition for solving the original problem. Discovery of another sufficient condition that is easier to satisfy will mean we can skip the difficult subproblem. Engineers praise this maneuver as 'lateral thinking': instead of digging the hole deeper, you relocate to a new excavation site.

The severe way of abandoning a problem occurs when the perceived 'subproblem' is totally irrelevant. Debaters get sidetracked into this kind of useless subdebate by red herrings passing as useful lemmas. Consider the controversy over whether formal student evaluations of teachers leads to lowering of academic standards. This has spawned a subdebate over whether teachers can improve their evaluations by lowering standards (by either giving higher grades for the same work or the same grade for less work). After noting how hard it is to empirically resolve this sub-issue, Kenton Machina (1987) goes on to criticize the debate on grounds of irrelevance. If faculty *think* that lowering standards will produce higher ratings, then the belief alone will produce damaging consequences. For faculty will then fall into two dispirited groups; those who cravenly lower standards and those who hold the line – and a grudge. So the question of whether teachers can improve ratings by lowering standards is a pseudo-problem – there was a false need for its solution. The subjective heart of the problem was overlooked.

And mind the *direction* of the relevance. The parties to the euthanasia debate have long agreed that the killing/letting die distinction is crucial. They reason that *passive* euthanasia would be permissible if the distinction is sound. However, Holly Smith Goldman (1980) has pointed out that the killing/letting die distinction only concerns evils; letting a bad event occur is better than actively promoting that event. Letting a good event occur is not better than actively promoting it! Since 'euthanasia' means a *beneficent* death, the moral relevance of the killing/letting die distinction would *favor* active euthanasia if it had any bearing at all.

Our gratitude for the news that a problem is a red herring swells with our estimate of how difficult that problem is. So this type of dissolution is especially prized in philosophy. Judith Jarvis Thomson (1971) earned fame for her daring argument that abortion is permissible even under the assumption that the fetus is a person. Participants in the controversy had long agreed that the issue turned on the status of the fetus. Thomson's challenge offered a way of sidestepping this metaphysical problem.

Clever conflict managers *make* divisive issues bypassable. In *The Sand Pebbles*, a dispute breaks out when a hostess in a Chinese bordello (just prior to the communist revolution) refuses an offer from an American sailor. The hostess denies that she is a prostitute. The pugnacious sailor insists that any woman working in the bordello is a prostitute and so is obliged to accept a fair offer. At this point, the house pimp intervenes by making the price $200 on the grounds that the hostess is a virgin. Since the sailor can only afford the customary $10 fee, he is forced to drop the issue.

Proposals to ban words often amount to the claim that certain problems can be bypassed. Some epistemologists, for instance, say that 'know' should be dropped because everything we want to do with the concept can be done with its better understood components 'belief', 'justification', and 'truth'. Proposals to add words can also be motivated by diplomacy. Movie producers had frequent disputes with censors over whether a movie should be rated R (under 17 only admitted with parental permission) or X (no one under 18 admitted). The X rating was chiefly assigned to sexually explicit films. This meant that many artistic films got lumped in with pornographic movies. Furthermore, most theaters refuse to show X movies and most newspapers refuse to carry advertisements for X movies. So there were lots of battles to get artistic but sexually explicit films rated R rather than X. Censors did not want to make quality judgments of films and so resisted. The solution was to invent a new category 'NC–17' (no one under 17 admitted) to cover the troublesome intermediate case.

Like other extrinsically unworthy problems, bypassable problems are *relational* pseudo-problems. Their failure to be relevant to one problem is compatible with their relevance to another problem. Thus it is a mistake to assume that defectiveness of a pseudo-problem is always an *intrinsic* feature.

Misderived values

The next arena for miscalculation is the value judgment. The value of a solution is the sum of its intrinsic value as an act and the value of its consequences.

Classical conditioning explains some of the pleasures of dispute. People who excel at an activity find it followed by rewards and so come to enjoy it for its own sake. There may also be evolutionary mechanisms that lend luster to debate. Fights, chases, and courtship rituals test prospective mates. Lovers' quarrels may also serve this function. That is, the process of sexual selection may have favored those who took pleasure in verbal tussles and pursuits. For these arguers would be able to test the wit and character of potential partners and to pass the tests of others in the mate market. Zest for argument, like a taste for combat, could also be enforced by the social power conferred by persuasiveness.

Just as there are moral intuitions about the inherent disvalue of debate, there are moral intuitions about its inherent value. Many people who agree that a guilty verdict is inevitable will nevertheless insist that the defendant 'get his day in court'. They view the adversarial process as a requirement of procedural justice. Similar deontological intuitions undergird the ritual debate of committee members 'deliberating' over the inevitable. This performative dimension of the joint speech act of debate is apt to be neglected by those enamored by the expected-utility model.

Parallel points can be made on behalf of all acts associated with issues. For instance, people love to gripe. What would people talk about if they had no problems? By complaining about their shared woes, they gain at least the pretext for social communion and often genuine solidarity. A witty critic makes unity through adversity positively enjoyable by stylishly fingering absurdities. Grousing and commiseration can also be edifying. For in addition to presenting new facts and connections, the negative thinker articulates vague discomforts into specific objections. Thus the process of complaining spirals into a constructive diagnosis of what ails us.

Given a broadly evolutionary outlook, one should expect to find hidden functions to our constitutional negativism. This expectation is reinforced by developmental psychology. After the middle of the child's second year, toddlers become concerned about flaws. The child will bring a broken doll to his mother and say 'Fix' or 'Yucky' (Kagan 1984: 125). This betokens a grasp of standards – an appreciation of how things should be.

We should be reluctant to view our preoccupation with defects as merely useless *whining*. This optimism about our pessimism is partly vindicated by the prevalence of protest among those who have difficulty solving their problems any other way, namely, children, the elderly, and the incapacitated. Consciousness itself is oriented toward trouble-shooting. When things are running normally, affairs are handled most efficiently by automatic processes. Consciousness is only called for when habit and routine de-rail (Bach 1984). Therefore, thinking beings are always on the lookout for trouble. We fasten onto what is wrong and take what is right for granted.

Disputes acquire extrinsic value from the wide range of beneficial consequences. The disputants get to blow off steam and publicize their beliefs and desires. In addition to their nonintellectual benefits, there are many that are internal to the pursuit of knowledge. Often, a solution to a curio is also an answer to a wide range of important questions. For example, in 1872 Leland Stanford, ex-governor of California, bet Frederick MacCrellish $25,000 that a running horse sometimes has all four legs off the ground. He hired one of the state's top photographers, Eadweard Muybridge, to settle the wager. Muybridge produced shadowy images that were enough to prove that the horse was not always in contact with the earth. But this only whetted Muybridge's appetite for a distinct representation of the galloping horse. Stanford was also intrigued and so commissioned Muybridge to continue research into speed photography. By 1879, he had photographs that revealed the exact orientation of the horse's legs. Since these postures conflicted with theories of animal locomotion and artist's representations, Muybridge's photographs revolutionized these fields. Further research led to the construction of the 'zoopraxiscope'. This projection lantern contained a sequence of photographs printed on a glass wheel. When spun past a shutter, the illuminated wheel produced an image on a screen that seemed to move. Thus it was one of the forerunners of the contemporary motion picture. So although the initial question about the horse's legs was a piffle, answering it led to an enrichment of billions of lives.

A controversy can be useful even if it goes unresolved. Paul Feyerabend's (1965) defense of the principle of theory proliferation contains many appeals to the advantages of the dispute process. Rival theorists expose each other's hidden assumptions and expand our range of options. Moreover, debate entertains and encourages the virtue of intellectual individualism.

One important source of value error is a static conception of problemhood. Just as a changing probability can make a problem worth pursuing, a changing desire can make or unmake an issue. When the Nazis were bombing England at night, the British yearned for radar accurate enough to shoot down the hidden bombers. This generated intense research into microwave radar at the Massachusetts Institute of Technology. But after a few months, the bombing stopped, interest waned, and research slacked off. This episode illustrates the mercurial nature of problems and thus, of pseudo-problems.

Since desires change through the stages of life, some problems wax and wane with the rhythms of childhood, youth, adulthood, and old age. These 'outgrown' problems often look like they are solved by ineffable insights. The same illusion holds for life-styles. For example, Leo Tolstoy intimates that the meaning of life emerges when one adopts the simple ways of the peasant. Tolstoy was not able to articulate this meaning and so presented it as a sort of mystical folk wisdom. But actually, the problems are just sweated out of laborers. Farm-life smothers the desires that launch esoteric problems. Strenuous, outdoor work in the fields builds a hearty appetite, a tired body, and preoccupation with practical tasks. So curiosity about abstruse matters is supplanted by concrete desires.

What happens accidentally can also be orchestrated. Instead of just hoping you acquire more easily satisfied desires, you can actively reform your wants. This was the Stoic's secret of happiness. The fool tries to solve his problems by changing the world. The wise man dissolves his problem by changing his desires to fit the world. Buddha occupies the logical limit: his metaphysical reservations lead him to advocate the annihilation of *all* desire.

The Stoic strategy is often discernible in one form of optimism. The active, positive thinker operates on the assumption that an optimistic outlook will bring the world around to his wishes. The passive positive thinker tries to make himself believe that the world is already the way it should be: 'What is, is good.' This is incredible enough to create a market for metaphysical crutches such as Pangloss' belief that this is the best of all possible worlds.

Bad inputs

When Saddam Hussein invaded Kuwait on 2 August 1990, westerners debated whether he was rational. One side emphasized his ruthlessness, his megalomania, his insularity. The other side agreed that Saddam was extraordinarily cruel and audacious, but countered that his reasoning from his (albeit repugnant) premises was logical. This debate illustrates the looseness of 'rational', not a factual disagreement. Economists and political analysts tend to interpret 'rational' in a purely structural way. For them, rationality is merely a function that yields beliefs and desires (and in the case of practical rationality, decisions) on the basis of other beliefs and desires – any beliefs and desires. So if a man wants to collect as many bottle caps as possible and if he uses his beliefs to efficiently procure bottle caps, then he is as rational as Socrates. It is merely closed-minded to ridicule his passion for bottle caps. A desire is a desire. Period.

The same nonjudgmental attitude has been directed toward the agent's basic probability assignments. Subjectivists say that basic probability judgments only record one's degree of confidence in the proposition. They do not correspond to any external facts. So subjectivists maintain that only your derived probabilities can be irrational. So no matter how eccentric your initial judgment is, you count as rational just as long as you revise them in accordance with the probability calculus. Often we are reassured that any initial 'craziness' in the probability judgments evaporates as new evidence comes in: two people with radically different initial opinions will converge as they rationally process more information.

Most thinkers condemn this narrow conception of rationality as evasive. They agree that there are lots of problems with evaluating ends and at picking prior probabilities. But they nevertheless insist that these are problems to be solved; they are not superstitious pseudo-problems that deserve to be lambasted as symptoms of intolerance. So according to this broad conception of rationality, one can be irrational even if one is a perfect calculator. For one may have assigned a false probability or a false value. Garbage in, garbage out!

Consider a pig-headed man whose basic probabilities are all 1s and 0s. He can easily follow the probability calculus because it simply tells him to never change his mind. But this does not vindicate dogmatism! Or consider Duhem's fanatic who always revises background beliefs to save his pet theory. The zealot's consistency does not immunize him from irrationality.

An inclination to condemn prior probabilities is also stimulated by the delusive origins of those probabilities. The paranoid man is regarded as irrational even though he is credited with being more consistent than the average person. The fears of the insane are dismissed because they are so out of touch with reality, not because they don't fit the probability calculus.

Genuine problems only issue from nondefective desires. Sufferers of Lesch-Nyhan Syndrome have an overwhelming desire to mutilate themselves. Paternalistic intervention frustrates this desire without making genuine trouble for the diseased individual.

A desire needn't be insane to be discounted as a false value. A sudden yen for moldy worms isn't taken seriously. Drunks become pugnacious or overly affectionate. We say it's the liquor talking. We also discount the dispositions that give rise to false values. People become grumpy when their blood-sugar level drops. When this is recognized as the source of the complaints, we don't fend them off, we feed them. Existentialists are sometimes dismissed in the same spirit. After hearing them fuss and fret and flutter about their 'thrownness', contingency, and sundry abstracta . . . well, you just want to say 'Cheer up!'

Since there is variation in standards for what counts as a correct desire, there is great potential for verbal dispute over what is a pseudo-problem. Catholics think that there is no genuine match-making problem for homosexuals. Pacifists think that the technological problems posed by the Strategic Defense Initiative are bogus. People who are absolutely opposed to suicide do not think that the Hemlock Society solves a problem by disseminating copies of *Final Exit* (a manual on how to painlessly and reliably kill yourself). As foreshadowed in the discussion of false desire, 'pseudo-problem' will be applied to questions emanating from desires that have aberrant origins or objects.

Disapproval is compatible with the ranking of lesser evils. Morality has a system of fall-back positions so that unprevented evil can be moderated. Hence the existence of 'contrary to duty imperatives' such as 'If you burglarize a home, then at least leave sentimental items.' The burglars' question 'How should we divide the loot?' seems like a pseudo-problem because it only arises among those who misbehave. But since there is still scope for moral instruction, there are answers to questions about contrary to duty requirements. Morality never quits. Of course, there is the (misguided) worry that giving advice on how to do something immoral is tantamount to condoning the immorality. Thus safe-sex programs are resisted even by those who prefer that abominations be conducted hygienically rather than infectiously.

Lack of good inputs

'Your problem is that you have no problems.' So said the hero of *10* to the hedonistic adulteress he finally bedded. His point is that her untroubled conscience was a sign that she lacked the standards that worry us into genuinely good lives.

Of course, the adulteress had lower-level problems of eating, health-care, transportation, etc. The lamentable fact was that these more basic desires were overgrown. Her superficiality was caused by omission; no higher values checked her lower values. For all her beauty, the adulteress' life was grotesquely misshapen.

10 provides a riposte to an initially compelling kind of solution to social problems. De-criminalizers maintain that certain behaviors, especially victimless crimes such as prostitution and recreational drug use, are only problems as long as we feel them to be such. Why not simply alter our desires? Thus our persistence in prosecuting these behaviors is portrayed as a sort of mulishness. However, problems can persist even without any actual desires to sustain them.

THE DEONTOLOGY OF DEBATE

I am a chicken utilitarian; I think utilitarianism is the least worst theory but I'm unnerved by its conflict with common sense. This state of half-belief is behind my side-glancing, expected-utility analysis of unworthy disputes. Even deontologists will see some value in this exposition because they acknowledge the relevance of consequences. They just insist that other factors are also relevant and hence would urge me to round out my ambivalence by fully reviewing the anomalies of the expected-utility model. Fair enough.

Folks care about the *variance* of that utility. More specifically, most people are 'risk-averse'. They prefer a 9/10 chance of getting $1000 over a 9/100 chance of getting $10,000 even though the expected dollar return is the same. Defenders of the expected-utility model reply that this is not a genuine counterexample to the principle that rational people maximize expected utility. For the law of diminishing marginal utility states that each new dollar is worth a bit less. (A dollar is worth more to a poor man than a rich man.) Opponents of the model then concede the relevance of the diminishing marginal utility but insist that it is not enough to explain all risk aversion.

Regardless of how the issue of variance gets resolved, we can appreciate how it makes situations problematic in a way that does not *obviously* turn on probabilities and values. Consider the opposition encountered by *radical* proposals. Risk-averse people would rather stick with a known amount of evil than fool with a remedy that might make things much better and might make them much worse. The legalization of recreational drugs is a good example. People complain that they do not know what the heck will happen. Legalizers respond by lowering the variance. They emphasize continuity with the past: opium, cocaine, marijuana, and other drugs were legal until the turn of the century. Legalizers go on to preen the analogy with the American prohibition of alcoholic beverages in the 1920s. Promoters of new products also rely on this strategy of finding hidden precedents. The perfume industry has been keenly interested in the biochemist's deepening understanding of sex attractants. Worry about the manipulative potential of this research is soothed with appeals to the history of perfumes. Musk, civet, and castoreum are natural attractants that have been extracted from animals for thousands of years.

The objection from variance alleges that the expected-utility model of issues is too *narrow*, that it made some worthy issues look unworthy. Now we address an objection running in the opposite direction.

The self-aware neurotic realizes that no one is hiding under the bed but feels compelled to look. After he gets in bed, his curiosity once again becomes unbearable, so he takes a second look. The neurotic realizes that these inquiries are worthless. He has not miscalculated the expected return on the effort. It's just that he can't translate his beliefs and desires into action (or in this case, inaction). Even sensible people can be stressed into this empty checking behavior. For instance, the nervous traveler keeps checking for his ticket while driving to the airport (Stocker 1987). So the expected-utility model seems incomplete. It cannot articulate the unworthiness of these problems in terms of miscalculations or bad values. Consequently, it overestimates our *control* over problem selection.

There are rational ways of coping with irrationalities (Elster 1979). Thus one may wittingly address a pseudo-problem because that is the best of one's practical alternatives. A neurotic intent on getting a good night's sleep might indulge his obsessive curiosity about how many tiles make up the ceiling. It is irrational to root out every little irrationality.

The expected-utility model is also analytically harsh. For it seems to imply that any problem that is resolvable by analysis is *ipso facto* a pseudo-problem. Anyone who abides by the probability calculus assigns each tautology a probability of 1 and each contradiction a probability of 0. Hence he is logically omniscient. That means that any problem that turns on a hidden inconsistency is a pseudo-problem. However, this would mean that half of logic and mathematics is bogus.

Anyone who abides by the probability calculus will never find old evidence informative. Hence, any problem that can be resolved by reminding you of a fact is *ipso facto* an unworthy problem. However, appeals to precedent are all instances of analogical reasoning between past disputes and a present one.

Philanthropists are frequently criticized for neglecting more pressing charities. If they donate to animal protection, they are told to switch to aiding the local poor. If they donate to the local poor, they are informed that the ill are in more desperate need. And if they donate to the sick, they are introduced to the greater reduction of misery offered by global famine relief. These critics are dismissed as fanatics. However, the expected-utility model legitimates their extremism. There are opportunity costs to working on a problem, hence the existence of highly lucrative options ensures that most of our ordinary problem solving is inefficient.

Satisficers offer a moderate alternative to optimizing. Michael Slote (1989) says that an option need only be good enough. Thus a project that promises a fair return might be rationally undertaken even though one is aware of more lucrative projects. One crosses the threshold into pseudo-problemhood only when the expected value of the project falls below quota.

A defender of the expected-utility model will portray satisficing principles as mere rules of thumb. The problem solver needs to simplify his selection task and so will adopt heuristics that stop his research as soon as he finds an alternative that meets his quota. The expected-utility model also allows us to introduce psychological constraints. Most human beings undertake projects because they have been touched by the problem. For example, the basketball star Magic Johnson became an AIDS activist after contracting AIDS himself. Only a minority of people adopt causes by sheer logic. We are biologically directed to concern with self, kin, and friends. So the value revealed by abstract reasoning tends to be overwhelmed by the influence exerted by vivid, concrete, present, familiar needs. Thus a utilitarian will dismiss alternatives such as heroic famine relief as psychologically unrealistic.

Of course, the debate continues. Why can't the utilitarian approach fanaticism in easy stages? (Perhaps a holiday to a famine zone will stir the needed sympathy.) My purpose is not to contribute to this debate. I merely wish to draw attention to the way that this meta-issue of dispute worthiness comes to be subsumed under the issue of moral fanaticism. Ethics as well as science has a say in the nature of dissolution.

13 Enlightened tasks

I believe that I am not overstating the truth when I say that half the time occupied by clerks and draftsmen in engineers' and surveyors' offices . . . is work entailed upon them by the present farrago of weights and measures.

(Lord Kelvin)

I was introduced to the game of Twenty Questions by an excellent player. He was so reliable an interrogator that I suspected he was planting the answer in me or that I was giving away unconscious clues. But the artful questioner was merely adept at dividing his search space; twenty pair-wise divisions excludes falsehoods at a geometric rate. This systematic progression is far more efficient than the amateur's wandering inquiry.

An efficient question can be lodged within an inefficient strategy. Indeed, the wastefulness of the whole could be solely due to how the questions are organized. Inefficiency only makes a question a pseudo-problem when there is waste in how that particular problem is being handled. Since 'efficient' is relative to one's goals and constraints, pseudo-dissolutions can arise from deviations from these ground rules.

An unworthy problem should be abandoned. An inefficient one should be modified. The most moderate reform is to apply a different method, say, a switch from field studies to laboratory work. Somewhat more severe is the idea that the problem is missituated. Here one urges that the problem be rescheduled or that it be moved to another forum, say, off the street corner and into a conference room. The charge of misdelegation is similar in spirit. But instead of changing the time or place at which you address the problem, you change the personnel working on the problem. A tad sharper is the complaint that the issue is cumbersomely packaged – that there is an easier, equivalent formulation. The most severe efficiency critique demands a change in the content of the question. We now take up these five efficiency criticisms in order of increasing severity.

NEW APPROACH

Persuasion by argument is intellectually taxing and socially hazardous. (That explains why debate tends to take place in controlled settings such as classrooms and conference rooms.) So this slow, exacting process should only be used as a last resort – only when the point cannot be made by observation, testimony, or some other easy method of demonstration.

Historians of science find it telling that the sides chosen on the issue of continental drift correlate well with the terrain in which the geoscientist was trained. Had the disputing scientists concentrated on disseminating observational evidence, they would have reached an earlier consensus. What one thinks can be influenced by how one thinks. Anthony Flew traces the disagreement between E. Titchener and J. B. Watson over the existence of mental imagery to the fact that Titchener was one of those people who had vivid mental imagery and Watson one of those who had little or no image life (1956: 392). Each overgeneralized from his own case. Perhaps other disagreements within psychology reflect 'the uneven distribution of raw facts, with psychologists diverging on the sources of phenomena to which they are exposed – animal versus human, abnormal versus normal, laboratory versus natural, behavioral versus introspective, developmental versus differential, and so forth' (Simonton 1988: 20).

Mis-tooling can be caused by a mischaracterization of the issue. For example, different conceptions of background facts make a factual disagreement look like a conceptual one. J. L. Austin gives the example of the dispute over whether ghosts are illusions or hallucinations. One party assumes that ghost-seers are taken in by reflections, shadows, and tricky lighting. The other assumes that ghosts are conjured up by a disordered nervous system. Since the parties think they agree on the facts, they vainly attempt to resolve their difference by definitions of 'illusion' and 'hallucination'.

PREMATURE ISSUES

It is smart policy to resolve the routine factual aspects of an issue before delving into the more contentious conceptual and normative features. Thus investigators like to 'let the dust settle' before offering serious opinions. When the problem lacks subquestions that can be solved by standard techniques, we are apt to forge ahead wildly with 'shots in the dark'. This often results in a comical series of failures like those enshrined in the history of flying machines.

Since we have many issues and the order in which those issues are pursued affects their resolution, we often have preferences among agendas. An agenda is a queue of issues. An item can work its way to the head of our agenda by virtue of its urgency or priority. Another issue might be placed last because it can only be achieved after all of the preceding issues are settled. A third issue might rise to the top of the agenda because it is easy to resolve and so will set a precedent of cooperation. There are many orderings: temporal, pedagogical, informational, etc. Since the kind of order is usually left tacit, equivocation is frequent. For example, Socrates slides from the semantic priority of 'What is the definition of F ?' over 'Is x to be classified as F ?' to its epistemological priority and so concludes that definitions must precede classifications. Thus in Plato's dialogues Socrates constantly turns the discussion back to questions such as 'What is virtue?', 'What is knowledge?', 'What is justice?' Just as the *Republic* lays down a blueprint for a controlled society, the earlier dialogues prepare a program for all research.

Central planners are embarrassed by the prevalence of unintended solutions. The invention of the locomotive unexpectedly solved social problems such as inbreeding and famine. The Victorian fear of waking up in a coffin is now groundless because current embalming techniques kill anyone who is misdiagnosed as dead. Sometimes these bonuses are foreseeable, making direct approaches to the problem needless. Why pay for what will soon be gained for free?

The appeal to prematurity is frequently an evasive stall. So the dissolver runs the danger of being called out at the metalevel. In the 1980s Canada and the United States quarreled over acid rain. The Canadians maintained that American smokestack industries were obviously sterilizing their lakes. The Reagan administration replied that more research was needed. Thus the US refusal to debate the issue prompted a meta-debate on how much research is appropriate.

Higher-order disputes can be just as acrimonious as lower-level ones. The anthropologists Donald Johanson and Richard Leakey had cordial disagreements until they divided over a methodological matter (Johanson and Shreeve 1989). Johanson proposed that *Australopithecus afarensis* was the ancestor of all later hominids and so required a redrawing of the human family tree. Leakey believed that the so-called species mistakenly yoked two separate species under a common title. However, the real trouble erupted when Leakey refused to debate the issue on the grounds that more fossil evidence was needed. Johanson thought this a dishonest dodge and so kept prodding Leakey to debate. Leakey felt badgered and insulted. The result was mutual annoyance and a broken friendship.

In the case of negotiation, prematurity tends to be mixed with insincerity. Typically, the parties agree to address procedural matters before substantive ones but then make the procedural points proxies for the substantive issues. For instance, at the outset of the 1991 Middle East peace negotiations in Madrid, there was fierce debate over the site of future meetings. The Israelis wanted the Palestinians to meet in Israel because that would nudge them towards recognition of the Israel state. Neither side wanted to admit violating the agreed protocol, so the site debate had to be conducted with surrogate rationales.

Issues can also be broached too late. Sometimes this defect is preempted by the criticism of false presupposition. Those who 'close the barn door after the horse has already run away' are simply operating on a false assumption. But in other cases, the trouble is the extra burden of handling an overly ripe problem. These overdue but still tractable problems bring out a curious asymmetry between later and early charges. When I complain that the problem is premature, blame is centered on the problem. But when I complain that the problem is tardy, blame focuses on dawdling agents. In short, premature questions are pseudo-problems but tardy questions are genuine problems. The asymmetry even applies to the self-same question – one that begins premature but then becomes late. The question of how one's crop should be harvested is premature in the winter (before one has decided what to grow) and tardy in the fall (as it begins to pass its peak). This asymmetry in pseudo-problem-hood between premature and tardy questions is grounded in the pragmatic conventions behind the deployment of debunkers. Late treatment makes problems more severe and so they are helpfully labeled as problems to underscore their urgency. Premature treatment attaches to problems that need no treatment now (and may need no attention at all) and so are only misleadingly described as problems. This also explains why preventable problems (such as running out of fuel) and near-misses of nonproblems (such as injuries due to freak accidents) are nevertheless genuine problems. As much has to be done about a stupid problem as a problem that does not arise from hang-ups or quirks or plain bad luck.

RE-DELEGATION

Stagnation is often blamed on bad personnel. Richard Feynman thought this explained the lack of progress on the quantum theory of gravity:

> There is a great deal of 'activity in the field' these days, but this 'activity' is mainly in showing that the previous 'activity' of somebody else resulted in an error or in nothing useful or in something promising. It is like a lot of worms trying to get out of a bottle by crawling all over each other. It is not that the subject is hard; it is that the good men are occupied elsewhere.
>
> (1988: 91–2)

Other inquiries are conducted by *irrelevant* disputants rather than underqualified ones. This is frequently just a species of a fallacious appeal to authority. But sometimes one confronts a hard case that can't be settled with casual clear thinking (Laudan 1977: 19). The fact that the moon seems larger near the horizon has been passed around from astronomy to optics to psychology. Crystal growth sits uneasily between chemistry, biology, and geology. This uncertainty complicates the assessment of theories that are responsible for solving problems. It also leads to misbalanced research. For when a field falls between two specialties, it will be overresearched when both fields claim the borderline territory. The intermediate field will be neglected when each specialist views it as the domain of the other. For example, the history of hydraulics falls between the cracks of the history of science and the history of engineering.

It is natural to think that question delegation is determined by the nature of the field and so the problem reduces to that of defining that nature. And indeed, many definitions of fields are offered with question delegation in mind. From about 1950–75, most ethicists defined their field as the study of moral language. They denied the following questions were in their domain: 'Is abortion ever permissible?', 'Is euthanasia murder?', 'What sort of life should I lead?' For these are not questions about moral discourse. The answers to these questions would be *in* moral language, not *about* moral language. The ethicists affirmed that the following questions were in their domain: does 'ought' imply 'can'? Do moral statements have truth-values?,' Is 'pacifism' contradictory? For these are second-order questions; comments on the features of moral discourse.

However, definitions of fields are hard to come by. Even when people agree on the definition, it is often too vague to settle the matter. Consider the question of whether fallacies should be studied by logicians or psychologists. People who agree that logic is the study of argument and psychology is the study of mind will still be puzzled because fallacies are bad arguments that look like good ones. Should we give precedence to the argumentative aspect or to the aspect of illusion?

Some thinkers break the deadlock by appealing to the pragmatic criterion: a question belongs to the field that has the best chance of resolving it. This criterion makes the recalcitrance of a problem a powerful reason for delegating it to another field. For example, many philosophers advocate re-delegating the study of fallacies from logic to psychology by emphasizing that logicians have studied fallacies for thousands of years with meager success. Successful resolution of the problem thus tends to reassign the problem – as emphasized in Bertrand Russell's metaphilosophy.

To the victor goes the spoils. However, it must be a fair competition. A problem does not change fields when the success of one field is due to favoritism or to suppression, neglect, or external contingency. The progress must be explained as a positive effect of more effective methods. Thus an *F*-ologist who solves a problem does not automatically make that problem belong to field *F*. It was the astronomer Christopher Wren who invented transfusion in 1659, as well as the intravenous injection of drugs. Nevertheless, these results belong to medicine, not astronomy. To go completely by an *extensional* pragmatic criterion would run against the insight that outsiders are frequently able to solve key problems because they import expertise needed solve a key subproblem or they simply lack the distractions of insiders.

Similarity plays a strong role: questions that resemble questions that clearly belong to field *F* belong to field *F*. 'Do all human beings have a common female ancestor?' is a biological question even though biologists have no hope of answering it. Resemblance often overwhelms the pragmatic criterion. For example, 'Is an Aquarius cat more docile than a Leo cat?' is an astrological question even though *astronomy* decisively answers: no, the stars are totally irrelevant to personality. Origin also plays a role in question delegation. Philosophy retains many questions by inertia. Of course, if a problem's history were decisive for field membership, there would be no re-delegation.

We care about problem delegation because we want to solve problems. But we also care about the delegation when appraising problem solvents (that is thinkers, instruments, and theories). A solvent earns demerits when it fails to solve the problems it was intended to solve. So one way to excuse a solvent is to show that the unsolved problem is not its responsibility. For example, defenders of physics say that it can hardly be faulted for not solving the political problem of how to control dangerous technology. Of course, problem appraisal is a comparative affair. If a competitor can solve a problem that it was not intended to solve, it gets extra credit and so its rivals suffer a *de facto* loss of relative merit. Since our allegiance is won by the most effective solvent, any solution by one alters the criteria for all. Conversely, a problem that resists all solvents leaves none of them worse off.

Notice that the strategy of re-delegation has an intrapersonal counterpart. Our problem solving strengths vary during the course of a day – and the course of life. Temporal delegation is also used to quarantine problems that trigger compulsive overattention. For instance, a workaholic learns to 'leave his problems at the office' when he realizes that his business affairs are invading his personal life. This internal division of labor also consolidates tasks. An individual can work more effectively by temporarily becoming a specialist on one kind of problem. Hence, the wise home-owner spends one hour on bills, another on lawn care, etc.

REPACKAGING

Logically equivalent questions are not equally easy to answer. Merely changing one's point of reference can make the problem easier to solve. What is the probability of getting at least one head on three tosses of a fair coin? Statistics instructors advise their students to reframe the question as 'What is 1 minus the probability of getting no heads?' The probability of getting no heads is easy to calculate since it is only a single point in the sample space; 0.5^3. Since the no-heads event is the complement of the at-least-one event, $1 - 0.5^3$ equals the probability of getting at least one head. Behold the power of negative thinking! Formulation effects extend to mindless machines. Programmers are taught to minimize processing time by re-writing computer programs. Computational speed also varies with hardware, hence technological advances can make questions obsolete.

Repackaging a problem sometimes reveals that it is identical to a previously solved problem. This is maximal frugality. The mathematician's fondness for this maneuver is epitomized by Raymond Smullyan's (1978: 190) test for whether you are a mathematician or a physicist. Suppose you are in a cabin containing an unlighted stove, a box of matches, a working faucet, and an empty pot. How would you get a pot of hot water? Both mathematician and physicist answer 'I would fill the pot with water from the faucet, light the stove with matches, and place the pot on the stove.' The following question separates them: suppose that everything is the same as the first problem except that the pot is already filled with cold water. The physicist says that he would light the stove and put the pot of cold water on it. The mathematician says he would pour out the water, reducing the case to the preceding problem which has already been solved.

Repackaging can even have a point if the reduction is another unsolved problem. Reducing two mysteries to one prevents us from overcounting our troubles and enriches our adequacy conditions for a solution – a solution to one problem must be a solution to both.

Notational advances ease the burden of calculation and mental book-keeping. According to Papyrus records, Egyptian arithmeticians had a long struggle with 'What number added to one fifth of itself equals 21?' The enigma was eventually conquered in 1600 BC more or less through trial and error. Nowadays, a beginning algebra student can answer it quickly by formulating the question as an equation: $x + x/5 = 21$, therefore, $x = 17.5$. The problem was formidable for ancient Egyptians because they lacked efficient notation, i.e. digits for numbers and the variable x for the unknown value. Although one can solve the problem with ordinary words for the numbers and operations, the process is slow and cumbersome. Mental drudgery breeds fatigue, fatigue breeds error, error hampers progress.

Consider the difficulty of multiplication with alphanumeric expressions such as Roman numerals. Even modest multiplication problems in this system require lots of tabulation. Multiplying large numbers requires extraordinary patience and care. Historians of astronomy conjecture that difficulties in calculating large products produced a systematic bias against conceiving of the heavenly bodies as lying enormous distances from the earth. Such a bias affected questions such as 'Does the earth orbit the sun?' Aristotle correctly deduced that the orbit would produce the parallax phenomenon in which the 'fixed stars' would appear to move from the perspective of the moving earth. Since no parallax was observed, the theory that the earth orbited the sun was rejected. However, the parallax would not be readily observable if the stars were at mind-boggling distances from us. Thus a prejudice against large numbers led astronomers away from the truth.

Division was also difficult and contributed to philosophical problems. Consider Zeno's problem of Achilles and the tortoise. Since Achilles runs ten times faster, the tortoise is given a 100 yard head start. Given that the tortoise runs 1 yard per minute, how long before Achilles overtakes the tortoise? Zeno's paradoxical answer was 'Never.' His reasoning began with the observation that by the time Achilles made the first 100 yards, the tortoise will have traveled 10 more yards. When Achilles covers these 10 yards, the tortoise has moved another 1 yard. And once that yard was made up, the tortoise still has a lead of 1/10 yard. Thus the tortoise will always be ahead even though his lead constantly diminishes. But since Achilles will obviously reach the tortoise, alert students calculate that the tortoise only gets 11 and 1/9 yards before Achilles comes abreast. Students see this quickly but the Greeks missed it because they could not do sums on paper and had to rely on an abacus for long division. The Greeks knew that adding ever larger amounts to a quantity made it grow larger at a faster rate. This invited the belief that adding ever smaller amounts increased the quantity indefinitely at a slower and slower rate. Their notation for the distance covered by the tortoise before Achilles came abreast does not correct this impression: $X + I + I/M + 1/C + 1/X + \ldots$ However, Hindu-Arabic notation draws attention to a 'barrier': $10 + 1 + 0.1 + 0.01 + 0.001 + \ldots$ or $11.111 \ldots$ Adding extra 1s at progressively lower place-holders will never raise the number to 11.2. Thus the notation exposes the possibility of adding ever decreasing amounts without exceeding a given threshold. This in turn invites the idea of the convergence of an infinite series to a limiting value. Thus the notation solves a philosophical problem and points us toward important mathematical concepts.

QUESTION REVISION

Exchanging one question for a synonymous (but easier) question is a tame reformulation. The bolder replacement proceeds without any claim to strict synonymy. In place of the original question, we address one that is free of some of the original's shortcomings. The importance of content changes is reflected in the ubiquity of retorts such as 'Don't ask where we can dump garbage; ask how can we prevent its production.' Interestingly, a riposte like 'The question is not *whether* Los Angeles will have a major earthquake, but *when*' tweaks our presuppositional timidity rather than our temerity. It exhorts us to presuppose more, not less. The example also sheds light on ostentatious question begging. The proponent of naturalized epistemology often responds to radical skeptical challenges by flamboyantly deploying premises from science. He is aware that the skeptic will refuse to allow these premises, so he is not aiming at the usual style of persuasion. The naturalized epistemologist is instead evincing his methodological position that science provides a perfectly reasonable point of departure – that it is not in need of any philosophical support. The attempt to shore up science is characterized as intellectually gratuitous, as akin to the fussy double-checking of a neurotic.

In addition to these timidity criticisms, there are ones independent of presupposition. These recommend overlooked alternatives and invite attitudinal changes. Consider Jeremy Bentham's comment on debates over the ethical treatment of animals: 'The question is not, Can they *reason*? nor Can they *talk*? but Can they *suffer*?' (1789: 411n).

After rejecting an attempt to dissolve the problem of induction by an appeal to the paradigm-case argument, Urmson concludes that the failed attempt compels

> us to reformulate the traditional problems in a healthier way. This is no matter of pedantry; in philosophy the correct formulation of problems is half the battle. To move from the question 'Are any inductive arguments valid?' to the question 'What good reasons can be given for rating arguments of a certain type higher than arguments of another type?' is to make a real advance, before any answer is found. Above all, we get away from bogus doubt into methodical philosophical research. Above all, these arguments compel us to take seriously the need for careful analysis of the nature of the inductive, ethical, and other types of argument that we actually use.
>
> (1974: 83)

How much can a question's content change before it constitutes a complete change of topic? Since this requires a judgment of the resemblance between the new and the old question, there will be a borderline area where it is unclear as to whether we have altered the original debate or just abandoned it for another. But there are clear cases. We are addressing the same issue if we switch from 'Are bachelors happier than spinsters?' to 'Are unmarried men happier than unmarried women?' We are not addressing the same issue if the switch is from 'Was Babe Ruth a better baseball player than Hank Aaron?' to 'Is Alaska as cold as Siberia?' We can't allow radical differences. But Charles Stevenson wisely warns against tight requirements:

> we must not expect the substituted question to be strictly 'identical' with the original one. The original question may embody hypostatization, anthropomorphism, vagueness, and all the other ills to which our ordinary discourse is subject. If our substituted question is to be clearer, it must remove these ills. The questions will be identical only in the sense that a child is identical with the man he later becomes. Hence we must not demand that the substitution strike us, on immediate introspection, as making no change in meaning.
>
> (1963: 10–11)

A dispute can survive small changes to its content. Of course, precise specification of the threshold at which content changes constitute a change to a different dispute is impossible. But nothing crucial turns on the question of whether the dispute is described as having merely evolved or is described as having been supplanted by a similar but distinct dispute.

Nevertheless, we must be vigilant against pseudo-resolutions that turn on a logical sleight of hand. Larry Laudan accuses C. S. Peirce of this kind of illegimate topic change. Peirce defended an affirmative answer to 'Is all science self-corrective?' by arguing that the methods of science are self-corrective. They are like the method of long division. At each step, we multiply the divisor by the assumed quotient and check whether it matches the dividend. If not, we change the assumption, and check again. In the case of science, the methods are deduction, induction, and abduction. So if Peirce can show that these three methods are self-correcting, he will have proved his thesis. But his discussion becomes confined to the matter of proving that induction is self-corrective. The issue becomes further narrowed by his distinction between crude, qualitative, and quantitative induction. For Peirce's attention becomes monopolized by this last kind of argument, in which the distribution of properties in a larger population is inferred from the properties of a sample population. The self-correction thesis becomes centered around this subcase of a subcase. In other words, the issue has changed from 'Is all of science self-corrective?' to 'Is quantitative induction self-corrective?' And that's changing the topic.

FROM TALK ABOUT THINGS TO TALK ABOUT TALK

Content changes are sometimes recommended as a matter of policy. Instrumentalists advise us to routinely ask whether a theory is useful rather than whether it is true. Indeed, revolutionary changes in a field often amount to the widespread adoption of policies of erotetic metamorphosis. For example, philosophy took a mentalistic turn when disputes about F-ness were transformed into disputes about our ideas of F. The mood turned grammatical in the twentieth century. The key policy change was semantic ascent: philosophical disputes should be changed from disputes about things to disputes about talk of those things. It is common for the linguistic philosopher to broach a discussion of F by switching the topic to 'F'. Instead of analyzing the universal Truth, they focus on the abstract noun 'true'. For statements about universals have clearer, linguistic counterparts. The foremost exponent of semantic ascent is W. V. Quine. He points out that the method is in principle universal but only outperforms alternatives when the subject matter is more controversial than the words used to describe it. This tends to be the case when the subject matter is abstract and unfamiliar, so philosophy profits from it most.

Although semantic ascent requires a shift in the dispute's content, it is not intended as a complete topic change. However, it does strike many laymen and professional philosophers as illicit subject switching. They protest that the linguistic counterparts of the original philosophical questions are largely irrelevant to the originals. Since they take the originals to be the only ones that are philosophically pertinent, critics of linguistic philosophy allege that semantic ascent is an irresponsible junket into the domain of the linguist. The popularity of linguistic philosophy is bemoaned as an abdication of philosophy. Linguistic philosophers defend semantic ascent against the charge of irrelevance in various ways. The boldest is to claim that philosophical questions are essentially linguistic and that the original questions are just garbled versions of linguistic ones.

The thesis that *all* philosophical problems are linguistic is false.

Defenders keep the thesis alive by either monkeying around with 'philosophical problem' or by distending the extension of 'linguistic' so that nearly any nonempirical question counts as linguistic. If we stick to plain English, we find many philosophical problems that turn on our desires. Consider the perennial issue of death. If we were not mortified, we would not find mortality philosophically interesting. Fear of death is adaptive in obvious ways. But death is not universally catastrophic. The aphid is an edifying exception (Owen 1980: 102–4). Most aphids reproduce sexually in autumn but by parthenogenesis in the spring and summer. Since the females are producing daughters identical to themselves and the geometrical birth rate produces tons of offspring, individuals matter little to the perpetuation of the gene type. From the biological point of view, sister aphids are one organism. The death of particular individuals is of no more significance than a tree's loss of some leaves to caterpillars. This explains why aphids have such poorly developed anti-predator strategies. Death of the individual doesn't matter. If human beings reproduced like aphids, fear of death would not be so deeply ingrained. Although there would be many thinkers, few would find death an engrossing topic.

FURTHER TECHNIQUES

Most analytic philosophers employ a variety of methods for dispute modification. Disinterpretation resembles semantic ascent but is restricted to logic and mathematics. The method was motivated by the danger of mistaking deductions based on unobtrusive outside knowledge for deductions based on a designated set of axioms. For example, geometers frequently erred by relying to heavily on diagrams. Instead of reasoning about any triangle, they would slip into reasoning about the isosceles triangle that had been picked to represent 'any triangle'. To guard against polluted proofs, the disinterpreter pretends to understand only the logical vocabulary and not the descriptive terms of the axiom system.

There are also 'divide and conquer' techniques. Lawyers separate conjunctive questions into their conjuncts, calling each an issue. Linguistic philosophers are also fond of breaking down questions into subquestions. The quickest way of verifying this tendency is to read the introduction of anthologies devoted to special issues. The editor will almost always review how the authors of the various articles have disassembled the vague and familiar issue into precise and novel ones.

Sometimes the method of question division yields a collection of subquestions that have *more* content than the original question. This is the case when the method is used to cope with underspecific questions. People have a strong tendency to think concretely. So rather than sticking to an abstract question, they will use a mental counterpart that fills in the missing details (Johnson-Laird 1983: 237–9). When people happen to use the same supplement, there is the danger of 'convergence' to a pseudo-consensus. When the supplements diverge, we get an effect quite similar to an ambiguous dispute. For the parties will argue as if addressing distinct questions. A pollster who asked 'How long should a rapist spend in prison?' is apt to get a wide range of answers because people have different mental pictures of the rape. Since the mental models vary in how severe a crime they depict, the wide range of answers fails to demonstrate any substantial disagreement.

Theorists must also be wary of the superficial disagreements spawned by underspecific questions. Consider the feasibility of measuring well-being. James Griffin (1986: 93–5) maintains that different theorists read different content into the question. Some visualize the attempted comparison intrapersonally while others read it as between people. They also assume different kinds of scales. The least demanding scale is just any assignment of numbers to things. Others assume an ordinal scale, still others an interval scale. Lastly, some theorists read the question as a practical one ('Can we measure well-being as easily as we measure room temperature?') while others assume the question is purely theoretical ('Can well-being be measured *in principle*?'). So given the tendency of people to color in the blanks, the underspecific question should be replaced by a set of specific subquestions.

Other disputes are resolved by issue linkage. For example, one tactic of negotiators is to draw all the issues into a single-package proposal. The hope is that the advantages of the whole will overwhelm reservations about the parts. That's why legislation designed to stiffen immigration requirements is usually balanced with an amnesty provision for established illegal immigrants.

Linguistic obscurities can be remediable and irremediable. Even when remediable, it may not be worth remedying our ignorance. This inclines many to conventionalize the debate, switching from the descriptive question 'Is x an F?' to the normative question 'Should we begin to talk in a way that would count x as F?' 'Pseudo-problem', like most words, is vague. And we now encounter the borderline area where it becomes impossible to tell whether the problem's defect is substantial enough to merit the term. Since it would be an error to push our inquiry further, it is fitting that we stop here.

14 Depth

Science has grown almost more by what it has learned to ignore than by what it has had to take into account.

(Ernst Mach)

The previous chapters have addressed 'What is a dissolution?' This final chapter will address the evaluative issue of what makes a *good* dissolution.

Actually, the question of appraisal is partly answered by the discussion of the purpose of dissolution: a good dissolution is one that rationally undermines the point of pursuing the issue. However, this functional reading of 'good dissolution' does not completely explain why we value certain dissolutions. For a pacifist can know that the function of chemical weapons is to poison the enemy without thereby approving of good chemical weapons. So what do we *fundamentally* want from a dissolution?

Perhaps we want a variety things. However, I shall concentrate on the most central and powerfully motivating prize: depth. The way to understand deep dissolution is to start from the simpler case of deep solution. To speak of deep solutions is to invite the question 'What makes a problem deep?' 'Problem' here should be read in the sense of a *question*, not a defect. When we ascribe deep problems to an automobile or a home or a relationship, we are not committing ourselves to the existence of correspondingly deep questions. Notice the ambiguity in 'There are deep problems in sociology.' Conversely, deep questions can exist without any deep things – indeed no object is deep in the same sense that questions are deep.

The interesting thing about deep questions is that all fields have them and all researchers within these fields agree that their deep problems are among the most important. Why all this trans-disciplinary agreement and high regard? One dismissive answer is that 'deep problem' is merely an expression of approbation. However, I shall argue that it has a surprisingly large degree of descriptive content and that it explains research patterns. Thus the expression 'deep problem' goes well beyond cerebral cheerleading.

THE VERTICAL MEANING OF DEPTH

A deep problem is a revealing but qualitatively difficult question. This definition will only be acceptable once we fill in the meaning of the key terms.

A *qualitatively* difficult problem is a hard problem that satisfies two conditions. First, the difficulty must be one that can only be surmounted by *ingenuity*. This rules out questions that are answered by physical exertion and tests of character. For instance, 'What is the source of the Nile?' was a hard geographical question for nineteenth-century Europeans. For the Nile was a long river that ran through uncharted African wilderness. John Speke and Richard Burton only managed to discover the source, Lake Victoria, by overcoming grueling hardships. Nevertheless, the problem fails to be deep because there was no need for intellectual innovation.

The ingenuity requirement also excludes problems that yield to mechanical solutions. C. S. Peirce eked out a living by doing immense astronomical calculations for navigational almanacs. But none of these titanic efforts numbers among the deep problems addressed by Peirce. Problems that yield to 'brute force' methods fail to be qualitatively difficult because there is no originality. Of course, the presence of routine does not *disqualify* a problem from being qualitatively difficult. Johannes Kepler's 'war on Mars' had lots of mind-numbing mental drudgery. The point is that there must be some other intellectual obstacle that confers depth on 'How does Mars move?' (in Kepler's case, the need to discover the law that all planets move in ellipses that have the sun at one focus).

Second, a qualitatively difficult problem must be *inherently* difficult. Thus hitches and glitches cannot make a problem qualitatively difficult even though they make it harder. Charles Babbage's attempt to build an 'analytical engine' was dogged by a myriad of financial and technical difficulties – none of which deepened the problem one whit. The requirement of inherent difficulty also quarantines bad breaks. For instance, Plato never bothered to take fifteen minutes off and write down the order in which he wrote his dialogues. This omission has led centuries of scholars into elaborately reasoned but inconclusive chronologies. This historical problem fails to be deep because it is rooted in a misfortune. Lastly, the requirement of inherent difficulty excludes troubles that arise from mental abnormalities.

The requirement of difficulty does not conflict with the well-known fact that children ask deep questions. For the challenge is in the answering, not the asking. No special insight is needed to be puzzled by why the sky is blue (only answered in the 1860s by Lord Rayleigh) or why people age (still unknown). We are inclined to give credit to some askers of deep questions because their question presupposes special knowledge or skill. Since askability is relative to a body of knowledge, we can see how insights formed in response to a deep problem can open new and deeper questions.

To say that a problem is revealing is to say that its resolution has high merit as a hypothesis. This intellectual value can be understood in terms of standard explanatory virtues: universality, completeness, fruitfulness, testability, simplicity. Consider Newton's hypothetical question 'What would happen if an object were lobbed higher and higher without limit?' Newton answered that it would eventually fall (unless some other body acted upon it). Thus gravity has no limit. This in turn suggests that objects which are at great distances from earth are nevertheless attracted to it. Since this exercise can be performed from any other body, the attraction must be mutual. Thus Newton's question put him on the path to recognizing the universality of gravitation; that every body is attracted to every other body.

Reserve 'revealing problem' for problems that have revealing *resolutions*. (A resolution of a problem is either a solution or a dissolution.) But notice that a problem can have other revealing aspects. For instance, critics of the Carter administration found it telling that the President was working on scheduling problems for the White House tennis court. The problem revealed that he was too busy with minutiae. Here the *resolution* isn't the telling part; what's revealing is the *delegation* of the problem.

THE NEED TO WED REVELATION AND QUALITATIVE DIFFICULTY

A qualitatively difficult problem need not be deep. The Sphinx asked Oedipus which creature walks on four legs in the morning, two legs in the afternoon, and three legs in the evening. This riddle stumped a sequence of highly motivated questionees because it has a double track of metaphor and a self-referential twist. So when Oedipus cracked the allegorical code by answering 'Man', he had surmounted qualitative difficulties. Nevertheless, the riddle of the Sphinx fails to be deep because its solution has no broader implications.

Researchers relegate many problems to the status of 'curios'. Although these enigmas can only be resolved with considerable ingenuity, they fail to be deep because they 'go nowhere'. For instance, mathematicians suspect that 'Is there an odd perfect number?' is unrevealingly stiff. The question is perfectly clear once one understands that a perfect number is defined as an integer that equals the sum of its divisors. Thus even the ancient Greeks knew there are *even* perfect numbers: $6 = 3 \times 2 \times 1 = 3+2+1$. Nevertheless, the search for an odd perfect number has yet to be completed or to be called off on grounds of nonexistence.

Similarly, a revealing problem fails to be deep if it is easy. The negative answer to 'Does ice sink in liquid water?' makes water a chemically interesting substance. But since the answer is obvious to anyone who lives in a freezing climate, it fails to be a deep question. The possibility of revealing but easy problems is exploited in most attacks on deep problems. For thinkers use accessible questions as steps down to deeper questions.

A student fresh from philosophy class might take issue with my claim that all deep problems are qualitatively difficult. For philosophy lectures are populated with questions that have obvious answers. Consider Chuang Tzu's 'Am I a man who dreamed he was a butterfly or a butterfly dreaming he is a man?' The answer is easy: Chuang Tzu is a man who dreamed he was a butterfly. However, the appearance of ease is due to the professor's penchant for posing epistemological questions as requests for proof or as queries about facts. Instead of asking 'How do you know that other human beings have minds?', the philosopher asks 'Do other people have minds?' We know that other human beings have minds; the mystery is in *how* we know it. Likewise, skeptical questions such as 'Will the future resemble the past?' and 'Did the universe double in size last night?' are only deep when read indirectly, as requests for justification. So when measuring the depth of a question, be mindful of which question is really being asked.

The identity of a question is often obscured by our use of unstated qualifications. Many geometrical problems, for instance, are tacitly restricted to the use of a straight edge and compass. Ancient mathematicians realized that the problem of doubling the volume of a cube could be easily solved if one is free to deploy other proof techniques. However, their research tradition restricted them to the means endorsed by Euclid. Now recall the problem about dating Plato's dialogues. Although this problem is not deep, a closely related one is deep: 'Given only the evidence offered by the dialogues themselves, determine the order in which they were written.' Notice how easily Plato scholars could lapse into a verbal dispute as to whether the chronology of the dialogues constitutes a deep problem.

The meaning of an interrogative often varies from context to context. Note how 'Who am I?' expresses a shallow question when the range of alternatives is composed of names but expresses a deep question when the alternatives are roles in life. Such ambiguities are exploited in pseudo-resolutions. The sophist first surreptitiously reinterprets the interrogative so that it expresses a shallow question. He then answers this mimic and takes credit for resolving the 'deep question'. For example, clever ethicists argue that 'Why should I be moral?' amounts to the tautologous 'Why should I do what I should do?' They obtain this trivializing interpretation by relativizing 'should' to *moral* requirements. But this triviality is itself reason to prefer other groundings such as to the standards of rationality or prudence. We should prefer interpretations that increase the depth of the question. Thus the concept of a deep problem figures into an important principle of disambiguation.

THE HOLISTIC ASPECT OF DEPTH

Even when the meaning of a question is unambiguously fixed, we must attend to other relativities. One such dependence springs from the fact that a proposition is only revealing when conjoined with ancillary assumptions. Physicists can infer nothing of interest from the bare principle that energy is conserved. The illusion that they can is created by the retiring nature of background beliefs. What we presuppose becomes invisible. So all the illumination seems to shine from the proposition in the foreground. Thus what strikes us as a deep question is influenced by the order in which propositions happen to be learned. The early components of the solution get far less credit than the final one that brings about the breakthrough. Currently, 'Do neutrinos have appreciable mass?' is pivotal to the great cosmological question of whether the universe will expand forever or eventually collapse in on itself. But now suppose that the neutrino question had been answered earlier in the history of physics. Then another question would have developed as the one crucial to the fate of the universe.

The relativity of revelation is made manifest by switching between belief systems. *The Name of the Rose* anticlimaxes by finally specifying the question that threatens to divide Christendom: 'Did Jesus own the clothes he wore?' The 'vexed' question initially strikes the reader as a ridiculous piffle. How could anyone think this makes a difference to anything? And indeed, the question is a piffle relative to contemporary belief systems. But as Umberto Eco draws you deeper into medieval creeds, the reader begins to appreciate how the poverty of Christ would be a deep question if the asker's background beliefs were correct. For given the conviction that Jesus is God incarnate and his acts are signs of his beliefs, then 'Did Jesus own the clothes he wore?' becomes the crucial test of whether the Vatican's treasures are legitimate.

This dependence on background assumptions does not mean that background agreement is always necessary for agreement on the depth of the problem. The cultures of India and Europe sharply differ but they nevertheless agree on the depth of 'Is the ordinary world illusory?' Atheists and theists agree that 'Why is there so much evil?' is a deep question. The atheist's background leads him to trace its depth to its implication that God does not exist. The theist's background leads him to explain the depth in terms of implications about the *nature* of God and man.

Although disparate belief systems sometimes converge on the same depth judgments, we should brace for diverging verdicts. Too often, we make ancient thinkers appear foolish (and occasionally too prescient) by reading in a contemporary context. We must also bear in mind that subjective depth does not imply objective depth. When one enters into the mind-set of a Zionist, one readily appreciates how 'What is a Jew?' can *seem* like a deep question. But this kind of conditional depth (depth given certain assumptions) only translates into real depth if those assumptions are indeed true. After all, any question is revealing relative to *some* background assumptions.

HIDDEN DEPTHS AND MUDDIED WATERS

The most charming questions are those that *look* straightforward. 'Why is the sky dark at night?' appears quickly settled by 'Because the sun goes down'. But as Wilhelm Olber noted in 1823, there are other light sources in the night sky. Indeed, there is a shining star anywhere you point. So why isn't the earth as bright as the surface of a sun? One reply is that the more distant stars are too far away to make a difference. However, this fading is exactly compensated by the greater number of stars at greater distances. (At distance r, light decreases at a rate of $1/r^2$ but the number of stars increases as a factor of r^2.) Another pseudo-solution is that the starlight is blocked by a cosmic cloud. The trouble with this is that blocked starlight would be absorbed by the cloud until it too began to radiate like a star. Olber's question is not as easy as it looks! Long dialectical sequences also lie coiled within pseudo-trivial queries such as 'Why are there two sexes?'

We tend to assume that deep questions must be intended as such. However, many profound questions arose as purely practical matters. 'What is the most efficient heat engine?' was first broached by the cost-conscious operators of mines and factories. Sadi Carnot's answer required seminal insights into the foundations of thermodynamics. Sometimes science is the shadow cast by technology.

Questions can be deep even when intended as silly. In Lewis Carroll's *Through the Looking-Glass* Alice's adventures take place in the nonsense world behind the looking glass. Before stepping through the mirror she asks her kitten 'How would you like to live in Looking-glass House, Kitty? I wonder if they'd give you milk in there? Perhaps Looking-glass milk isn't good to drink . . .'. In the *Ambidextrous Universe*, Martin Gardner remarks that the question is deeper than Carroll assumed. Milk contains asymmetric carbon compounds such as fat and lactose. It is doubtful that a mammal could digest the reversed molecules because its digestive chemistry is oriented in the opposite direction.

The Lewis Carroll example is a colorful counterweight to the intuition that the depth of a problem must be *felt*. Depth cannot be a qualitative psychological state that is recognized by introspection. For depth depends on an array of objective factors: the nonexistence of a trivializing alternative, the correctness of one's presuppositions, the solution's long-term impact on the field. Nor is exaltation sufficient for depth. Nitrous oxide and Wagnerian opera inspire feelings of profundity more reliably than contact with deep problems. This is painfully evident to teachers. Perhaps our tendency to project inner psychological states on to external objects is responsible for talk of deep music, landscapes, people. The projection may also be on to psychological states. Thoughts, in the sense of propositions, can be deep but not as mere brain events. Once creativity is de-psychologized, we can continue to insist that deep problems demand novel solutions.

Many problem solving techniques look mechanical when viewed from afar. For example, those unfamiliar with the subtleties of experimentation view the laboratory as a sort of fancy kitchen. Just as cooks follow recipes, experimentalists follow the instructions dictated by theorists. However, those on the inside of the practice realize that there is room for ingenuity. Experimentalists are heavily constrained by the need to screen off interfering variables and to make the intended effect as noticeable as possible. Thus the fact that 'Can magnetism produce electricity?' was settled by Michael Faraday's *experiment* is compatible with the question being deep. For Faraday's experiment required ingenious stage-setting and the affirmative answer unified two puzzling phenomena.

Other problems acquire a reputation for shallowness by their associations with a failed research program. 'How can lead be transmuted into gold?' lay at the core of alchemy and so shared its ignominy. Chemists contended that the question falsely presupposed the possibility of transmutation. Thus it was relegated to the status of an unilluminating misconception. But in 1919 Ernest Rutherford reinstated the question by demonstrating that its presupposition was true after all and that transmutation implies much about the innards of atoms.

Just as deep problems manage to look shallow by displaying marks of mechanism and triviality, shallow problems manage to look deep by bearing marks of ingenuity and theoretical merit. (They also pass by displaying pseudo-marks of depth such as inspiring fine feelings – thus the admixture of rhetoric in research.) 'What is the sound of one hand clapping?' resembles esoteric questions because the audience is at a loss as to how to proceed. But you're stymied only as long as you fail to challenge the presupposition that one-handed clapping is possible. So the Zen *koan* only has phony depth.

'No pain, no gain!' is an apt slogan for deep problems. But people tend to fallaciously infer 'If pain, then gain.' That is, they use the sheer difficulty of a question as a depth indicator. This explains the success of those 'who muddy the waters to make them look deeper'. Epictetus devised the proper antidote for this kind of mental masochism two thousand years ago: 'When a man is proud because he can understand and explain the writings of Chrysippus, say to yourself, if Chrysippus had not written obscurely, this man would have had nothing to be proud of.'

It is tempting to say that one can only know that a question is deep once it has been resolved. 'The Owl of Minerva only flies at dusk.' For we might find that our inability to resolve the issue was due to bad luck or a lack of creativity. This line of reasoning is too optimistic in one respect, too pessimistic in another. The bad news is suggested by the deflationary effect of hindsight. The existence of an ingenious and revealing solution does not guarantee that the problem was deep. For we may discover that the ingenuity was superfluous; that there was an easy way of solving the problem. It is also possible that the easy solution will remain forever unknown.

The good news is that sometimes the flight path of the Owl is irrelevant. For we sometimes know that *any* resolution would be revealing: Are there other forms of intelligent life in the universe? Is space Euclidean? Is there life after death? These switch-hitters contrast with questions that are only revealing in one direction: is cold fusion feasible? Did Troy really exist? Was Abraham Lincoln afflicted with Marfan syndrome? On the surface, switch-hitters look like counterexamples to holism. However, these unconditionally interesting questions are only 'sure-things' relative to a system of background beliefs. Consider 'Are we reincarnated?' Nearly all Indian philosophies assign reincarnation a central role in their ethics and metaphysics. Hence, a proof of reincarnation would be a powerful vindication and a refutation would be a foundational crisis. However, a negative answer to 'Are we reincarnated?' would make little impact on western philosophies because they regard reincarnation as a farfetched possibility. Only a positive answer would be revealing to westerners.

The uni-directionality of most deep questions explains how a question can be regarded as deep at one stage of history and not at another. 'Were the continents once united?' had long been asked by geographers who were impressed by the congruence between the Atlantic coastlines of South America and Africa. Alfred Wegener earned a major hearing for the issue in 1926 when top geologists convened in New York to debate his theory. But his adversaries assembled counter-evidence that led to a consensus against the possibility of continental drift. By 1935, the answer to 'Were the continents once united?' appeared to be an unsurprising 'No'. So the question was dismissed as undeep. But by 1970, new evidence had accumulated which established that the answer was an amazing 'Yes!' So now the question is (correctly) regarded as having been deep all along.

IDEAL HUMAN BEINGS

For *whom* is a deep problem difficult and revealing? Let's try the obvious answer: *normal* human beings. This reference frame readily explains why idiosyncratic perceptual and mental shortcomings only make problems irrelevantly hard. It also explains how a universally difficult problem could fail to be deep. For it is possible that everyone slip below the human norm. Lead pollution might inflict universal brain damage without deepening any of humanity's questions.

The relativization to normal human beings fares less well with species-wide cognitive defects that concerned us in the chapter on inaccessibility. For instance, people have inordinate difficulty understanding spinning objects and are slow to grasp the concept of a valid argument. Yet it would be absurd to conclude that these human weaknesses suffice to make spin and validity deep problems.

We cannot relativize 'qualitatively difficult' and 'revealing' to an *ideal* thinker for fear of losing our grip on the concept. If 'ideal' excludes all intellectual shortcomings, then the thinker would have no pockets of ignorance. But since an omniscient being has no difficulty with any problem, there would be no deep problems! Clearly, we need to strike a balance between mental defectives and know-it-alls. And it must be a *stable* balance – one that will keep us from toppling down a slippery slope toward omniscience.

The same balancing problem confronts definers of 'health' (Reznek 1987). They don't want any inability to count as a disease. The inability to fly is compatible with human health even though flightlessness is a disease of pigeons. Yet definers of 'health' can't say all *normal* human beings are healthy because there are species-wide diseases (such as dental caries and minor lung irritation). The solution is to *mildly* idealize in *two* directions. First, imagine a human being who has the benefit of minor design corrections. That gets rid of the appendix, the intersection between food and wind pipes, and other biological fumbles. Second, place these tuned-up human beings in a hospitable environment, one without 'unfair' hazards such as pollution and unwholesome food. But remember that fairness is a double-edged sword: any unfair advantages must also be subtracted from their environment. For example, some meteorologists conjecture that we have been the beneficiaries of unusually good weather during the past few centuries. If so, we'll be obliged to situate our hypothetical humans in a climate more in line with the historic norm. Thus the idealized environment is no utopia. Indeed, it could be worse for your health than the actual environment. With all this said, define 'disease' as a condition that plunges performance below the baseline set by our hypothetical population of human beings.

Now make the same sort of adjustments for human cognition. This eliminates universal mental quirks and bypasses the intellectual bad breaks imposed by our environment. But fairness also demands that we filter out our good luck. In particular, we need to exclude chapter 10's 'gifts of nature' that soften hard problems. Since ideal thinkers lack these bonuses, they will have a harder time with astronomy and physics. Since *their* level of difficulty sets the baseline for 'qualitatively difficult', some deep problems could be downright simple for us.

The above analysis predicts the conditions under which we become unsure as to whether a problem (or pseudo-problem) is deep. The first class of cases turns on unclarity as to which flaws get idealized away. Our idealized humans are immune to superficial logical gaffs such as the gambler's fallacy and are vulnerable to well-rooted ones such as those dealing with infinite quantities. But many other fallacies are difficult to assess. Early ophthamologists were puzzled by how we manage to see objects right side up when they appear upside down on the retina. George Berkeley eventually dissolved the problem by denying any need to re-invert the retina's image. We only appear to need re-inversion as long as we picture ourselves as peering at the world from within our skulls through our own eyeballs. Since we model phenomena on what's familiar, and nothing is more familiar to us than human beings, it is no wonder that we have an anthropocentric bias that makes us suscep- tible to this homuncular fallacy. But why do we have such a high degree of susceptibility? If the strength of the fallacy is due to a quirk of human nature, then Berkeley's dissolution only overcomes an obstacle that fails to be qualitatively difficult. But Berkeley's dissolution is as deep as Australia if the fallacy is an inevitable structural weakness of our hard-pressed cognitive architecture.

We should also experience difficulty gauging depth when there is a string of lucky and unlucky reversals behind a problem. For instance, the meaning of Egyptian hieroglyphics was made a mystery by decaying mastery of the language. This bad luck was followed by the good fortune of unearthing the Rosetta stone. So was the problem of translating Egyptian hieroglyphics a deep problem? Our ambivalence is caused by the rival ways of resolving the issue of luck. Nearly all discoveries involve serendipity, so there is often a jumble of perspectives that make the depth measurement dauntingly arbitrary.

We also flounder when philosophical considerations lead us to dilate the meaning of key terms used in the analysis of 'deep problem'. This can be illustrated by asking whether a computer can answer a deep question. An immediate negative answer is tempting because computers are machines, thus their solutions are inevitably mechanical. However, computers have supplied crucial assistance in the solution of deep problems. The best known example is the Appel-Haken-Koch proof of the Four-color Theorem. Part of the proof relied on an IBM 370–160A to determine the reducibility of certain configurations that were too long to be checked by people. One can imagine the computer's share of an important proof becoming so large that it becomes the sole author. Would the computer proof automatically show that the problem wasn't deep? Science-fiction writers convincingly depict computers as engaged with deep problems. In *2001*, HAL grapples with a wide variety of questions such as the meaning of the black monolith and of his own existence. Computerphiles supplement these cases with the thesis that human beings are also machines. True, our intelligence rests on a carbon-based natural design rather than silicon-based engineering. But so what?

One reaction to this challenge is the dry-ice vision of hard determinism. Given the mechanistic view of minds, it seems that all appearance of depth is illusory. Feisty metaphysicians jerk free of this bleak outlook by embracing a libertarian vision of the mind. They say innovation requires an irreducible free will that computers lack. However, metaphysical free will is an irreparably vague notion. If it is precisified to mean randomness, then it is of no help because a problem is not made deep by the fact that it can only be solved by luck. If free will boils down to self-causation, then it is just an incoherent wheeze of defiance.

The best remedy for this grim dilemma is to allow that there can be mechanism behind ingenuity. 'Mechanical' can be pried apart from 'mechanism' by distinguishing between different degrees of causal complexity. The idea that our mental lives are machine-like is disheartening when we follow our natural inclination to picture the underlying processes as simple and uninteresting. But mechanism is more hospitable to the concepts of creativity when we conceive the system in all its engaging intricacy. The general point of calling a process 'mechanical' is to ward off the attribution of high complexity; we are encouraged to instead think that there is an elementary trick that is responsible for the apparently complex behavior. For example, one can dampen admiration for a home heating system by explaining how the appearance of paternal vigilance is the effect of the thermostat's simple, negative-feedback loop. Description of our immune system's sophisticated response to invading viruses does not have the same debunking effect.

HOW 'DEEP PROBLEM' HELPS TO EXPLAIN RESEARCH PATTERNS

We have already noted that the notion of a deep problem guides our interpretation of questions by privileging deeper readings. It also plays an important role in *appraising* solvents. This in turn provides insight into the researcher's choice of topics.

Researchers pick questions that have some promise of being revealing. That's obvious. But why would they also be drawn to qualitatively difficult questions? Why not stick with the easy but revealing problems? The answer lies partly in a filtering effect; the easy but revealing problems receive early resolutions. So all but the early birds are left with the residue of hard problems. Even so, there is some positive attraction to qualitatively difficult problems. The allure is partly a matter of the pure joy of tackling tough problems; many thinkers are mental mountain climbers. But there is also an institutional function. The ambitious researcher has an appetite for qualitative difficulty because it provides an opportunity to display problem solving prowess. Since resources go to those with a reputation for talent, there is professional reward in solving a tough problem. The problem need not be revealing to serve this purpose of one-up-manship. For instance, in the sixteenth century, Niccolo Tartaglia ('the Stammerer') gained fame by discovering a solution to cubic equations. The discovery had little theoretical significance but it showed that a European could solve a problem that had proven too tough for the revered ancient Greeks. Although qualitative difficulty is sometimes enough to confer prestige, the self-promoter is well advised to combine difficulty with revelation because revelation increases the dissemination of the feat and satisfies conservatives who think rewards should be confined to those who *actually* get results (rather than those who merely demonstrate their ability to get results). Thus ambitious researchers go gunning for deep problems.

We can also understand why researchers get credit for *raising* deep questions. The ability to ask a novel deep question betokens much of the talent that goes into answering it. But in addition to being diagnostic of intellectual ability, new deep questions *create* new opportunities for advances in knowledge.

The concept of a deep problem also explains research behavior by enabling us to distinguish between tolerable anomalies and worrisome ones. An anomaly for a theory is an apparent counterexample to it. For example, Newtonian physicists had no explanation of the fact that all the planets orbit the sun in the same direction. This surprising uniformity was especially vexatious because a rival theory, Cartesian physics, neatly explained the uniformity of orbital direction as the effect of a grand vortex centered about the sun. So one mark of a worrisome anomaly is its selectivity. When a question goes unanswered by your theory but is answered by the competition, your theory loses face. For allegiance to a theory is earned by its *comparative* problem solving power.

This analysis of 'deep problem' lets us further detail the difference between worrisome anomalies and tolerable ones. For it predicts that even selective anomalies will be tolerable when they are shallow problems – ones that are not both qualitatively difficult and revealing. These offer the competition little opportunity to disgrace you. The worrisome anomalies are deep problems. For example, Darwin fretted about Lord Kelvin's objection that no known physical process could enable the sun to remain hot for the time needed for evolution. He also worried about Fleeming Jenkin's objection that favorable traits would be diluted into insignificance. For neither of these were objections to Darwin's rival (divine design biology) and neither could be resolved without an impressive display of problem solving power. In contrast, Darwin brushed aside the equally unsolved problems of man's 'missing link' and reconciling biology with Christianity. Of course, not any deep objection attracts interest. For there must be the perception that the problem is resolvable. Thus Darwin had little interest in specifying how the original life forms arose because he thought this deep problem was beyond our ken.

Happily, matters are not as desperate as Darwin thought. Progress in biochemistry has revived interest in spontaneous generation. This revival illustrates a general pattern. Questions once dismissed as hopelessly difficult become feasible in light of surprising advances. Of course, new knowledge and skills also cause the reverse. Lesson: scientists discover obstacles as well as enablers. Thus deep problems are interrelated in positive *and* negative ways.

These connections form the basis for three predictions. First, current depth perceptions will strongly influence the course of future research. This research will in turn yield insights that will revive questions that we now discard – and will retire some that are now actively pursued. Finally, the holistic nature of depth confers a large degree of uncertainty in predictions about which questions will be perceived as deep. Hence, reflection on the nature of deep questions reinforces pessimism about our ability to predict the course of future research.

Happily, such reflections also bring out the affinity between problems and pseudo-problems. By and large, I have adhered to the stark contrast between solution and dissolution. The solver *accepts* the problem, works within the questioner's framework, and produces an answer that vindicates seed curiosity. The dissolver *rejects* the problem, repudiates the questioner's set-up, and undermines the motivation for the inquiry.

Despite these profound differences, there are illuminating similarities. Both solutions and dissolutions rely on ancillary assumptions that tend to be concealed by figure/ground illusions. The bias this creates for insight models of solution are even stronger for dissolution. For the negative character of dissolution fortifies one's incuriosity about its infrastructure. We are like the witnesses of a demolition who only show for the most spectacular stage of what is actually a program of reverse architecture.

Both solvers and dissolvers make (sometimes fallacious) inferences from (sometimes false or implausible) assumptions. Thus they are challengeable in the way that arguments are. 'Solution' and 'dissolution' have parallel ambiguities and indeterminacies. Each can be ingenious, ingenuous, or injudicious.

Even their differences can be harmonized by recognition of their division of labor. An efficient problem solver must also be an efficient problem dissolver. For as a creature of limited resources, he can only cut to the heart of the matter by clearing away debris and dispelling distractions. The problem solver's toolbox needs a brush along with the chisel.

Bibliography

Amis, K. (1960) *New Maps of Hell*, New York: Harcourt, Brace and World.

Andreski, S. (1972) *Social Science as Sorcery*, London: Ebenezer Baylis and Son.

Angene, L. E. (1978) 'False judgment in the *Theaetetus*', *Philosophical Studies* 33, 4: 351–65.

Anscombe, G. E. M. (1958) 'Modern moral philosophy', *Philosophy* 33, 124: 1–19.

Aqvist, L. (1975) *A New Approach to the Logical Theory of Interrogatives*, Rubingen: G. Narr.

Austin, J. L. (1961) *Philosophical Papers*, ed. J. O. Urmson and G. J. Warnock, Oxford: Oxford University Press, 44–84.

—— (1962) *Sense and Sensibilia*, Oxford: Clarendon Press.

Ayer, A. J. (1936) *Language, Truth, and Logic*, New York: Dover.

—— (1986) 'Philosophy and the meaning of life', in E. D. Klemke, A. D. Kline, and R. Hollinger (eds), *Philosophy: The Basic Issues*, 2nd edn, New York: St. Martin's, 359–64.

Bach, K. (1984) 'Default reasoning', *Pacific Philosophical Quarterly* 65, 1: 37–58.

Barker, S. (1974) 'Is there a problem of induction?', in R. Swinburne (ed.), *The Justification of Induction*, Oxford: Oxford University Press, 57–61.

Barnes, J. and Robinson, R. (1972) 'Untruisms', *Metaphilosophy* 3, 3: 189–97.

Belnap, N. and Steel, T. (1976) *The Logic of Questions and Answers*, New Haven Conn.: Yale University Press.

Benacerraf, P. (1970) 'Task, super-tasks, and the modern Eleatics', in Wesley C. Salmon (ed.) *Zeno's Paradoxes*, New York: Bobbs-Merril, 103–29.

Benjamin, M. (1990) *Splitting the Difference*, Lawrence, Kansas: University of Kansas Press.

Bentham, J. (1789) *Introduction to the Principles of Morals and Legislation*, Oxford: Basil Blackwell, 1960.

Berkeley, G. (1710) *A Treatise Concerning The Principles of Human Knowledge*, La Salle, Illinois: Open Court, 1986.

—— (1930) *Philosophical Commentaries, generally called the Commonplace Book*, ed. A. A. Luce, London: Kegan Paul, Trench, 1944.

Blackmore, J. (1972) *Ernst Mach: His Work, Life, and Influence*, Berkeley: University of California Press.

Blose, B. L. (1980) 'The "really" of emphasis and the "really" of restriction', *Philosophical Studies* 38, 2: 183–7.

Boer, S. E. (1979) 'Meaning and contrastive stress', *Philosophical Review*, 88, 2: 263–98.

Boltzmann, L. (1974) *Theoretical Physics and Philosophical Problems*, Dordrecht, Holland: D. Reidel.

Boorstin, D. (1961) *The Image*, New York: Atheneum.

Boring, E. G. (1946) 'Mind and mechanism', *American Journal of Psychology* 59, 2: 173–92.

Born, M. (1949) *Natural Philosophy of Cause and Chance*, New York: Dover, 1964.

Bosanquet, Bernard. (1885) *Knowledge and Reality*, London: Kegan Paul, Trench.

Carnap, R. (1934) *The Unity of Science*, trans. M. Black, London: Kegan, Paul, Trench, Trubner & Co.

—— (1935) *Philosophy and Logical Syntax*, London: Kegan, Paul, Trench, Trubner & Co.

—— (1947) *Meaning and Necessity*, Chicago: University of Chicago Press.

—— (1966) *Philosophical Foundations of Physics*, ed. Martin Gardner New York: Basic Books.

Charlton, W. (1991) *The Analytic Ambition*, Oxford: Basil Blackwell.

Chomsky, N. (1975) *Reflections on Language*, New York: Pantheon.

Cioffi, F. (1970) 'Freud and the Idea of a Pseudo-Science', in R. Borger and F. Cioffi (eds), *Explanation in the Behavioural Sciences*, Cambridge: Cambridge University Press, 471–99.

Clark, S. (1977) *The Moral Status of Animals*, Oxford: Clarendon Press.

Cohen, L. J. (1962) *The Diversity of Meaning*, London: Methuen & Co. Ltd.

—— (1986) *The Dialogue of Reason*, Oxford: Clarendon Press.

Cohen, P. and Cohen, J. (1984) 'The clinician's illusion', *Archives of General Psychiatry* 41: 1178–82.

Collingwood, R. G. (1939) *An Autobiography*, London: Oxford University Press.

Cooter, R. (1980) 'Deploying "pseudoscience" ', in M. P. Hanen, J. Osler and R. G. Weyant (eds), *Science, Pseudo-Science and Society*, Waterloo, Ontario: Wilfred Laurier University Press, 237–61.

Curtis, R. (1989) 'Institutional individualism and the emergence of scientific rationality', *Studies in History and Philosophy of Science* 20, 1: 77–113.

Descartes, R. (1967) *Philosophical Works of Descartes*, trans. Elizabeth S. Haldane and G. R. T. Ross, Cambridge: Cambridge University Press.

Dewey, J. (1938) *Logic*, New York: Holt & Co.

Diderot, D. (1977) 'Letter on the blind', trans. Michael J. Morgan in his *Molyneux's Question*, Cambridge: Cambridge University Press.

Donnellan, K. (1966) 'Reference and definite descriptions', *Philosophical Review* 77: 281–304.

Driver, J. (1984) 'Meta-questions', *Nous* 18, 2: 299–309.

—— (1989) 'The virtues of ignorance', *Journal of Philosophy* 86: 373–84.

Duhem, P. (1974) *The Aim and Structure of Physical Science*, trans. P. Wiener, New York: Atheneum.

Dynes, R. R. and Quarantelli, E. L. (1971) 'The absence of community conflict in the early phases of natural disasters', in Clagett G. Smith (ed.), *Conflict Resolution: Contributions of the Behavioral Sciences*, South Bend, Indiana: University of Notre Dame: 200–18.

Edwards, P. (1967) 'Panpsychism', in P. Edwards (ed.), *Encyclopedia of Philosophy*, vol. 6, New York: Macmillan: 22–31.

Ehrenreich, B. (1984) 'Is abortion really a "moral dilemma"?', *The New York Times*, February 7.

Elster, J. (1979) *Ulysses and the Sirens*, Cambridge: Cambridge University Press.

—— (1983) *Sour Grapes*, Cambridge: Cambridge University Press.

Erwin, E. (1970) *The Concept of Meaninglessness*, Baltimore: The Johns Hopkins Press.

Farr, A. D. (1983) 'Religious opposition to obstetric anesthesia: a myth?', *Annals of Science* 40: 159–77.

Feigl, H. (1952) 'Validation and vindication', in C. Sellars and J. Hospers (eds), *Readings in Ethical Theory*, New York: Appleton-Century-Crofts, 667–80.

Feyerabend, P. (1965) 'Problems of Empiricism', in R. G. Colodny (ed.), *Beyond the Edge of Certainty*, Englewood Cliffs, N.J.: 145–260.

Feynman, R. (1988) *'What do you care what other people think?'*, New York: Bantam.

Flew, A. (1956) 'Facts and "imagination" ', *Mind* 65, 259: 392–9.

—— (1963) *Essays in Conceptual Analysis*, London: Macmillan.

—— (1965) *Logic and Language*, Garden City: Doubleday (originally, First Series 1951, Second Series 1953).

Follesdal, D. and Hilpinen, R. (1971) 'Deontic logic: an introduction', in R. Hilpinen (ed.), *Deontic Logic*, Dordrecht: Reidel: 1–35.

Freud, S. (1949) *Introductory Lectures on Psychoanalysis*, trans. J. Riviere, London: Allen & Unwin.

Galileo (1632) *Two New Sciences*, trans. S. Drake, Madison: The University of Wisconsin Press, 1974.

Gallie, W. B. (1955–6) 'Essentially contested concepts', *Proceedings of the Aristotelian Society*, 56.

Gardner, M. (1981) *Science: Good, Bad and Bogus*, Buffalo, N.Y.: Prometheus.

Gibbard, A. (1990) *Wise Choices, Apt Feelings*, Cambridge, Mass.: Harvard University Press.

Gilligan, C. (1982) *In a Different Voice*, Cambridge, Mass.: Harvard University Press.

Glymour, C. (1990) 'Philosophy and the Academy', in W. Sieg (ed.), *Acting and Reflecting*, Dordrecht: Kluwer, 63–71.

Goldman, A. (1986) *Epistemology and Cognition*, Cambridge: Harvard University Press.

Goldman, H. S. (1980) 'Killing, letting die, and euthanasia', *Analysis* 40, 4: 224.

Goodman, N. (1961) 'About', *Mind* 70, 277: 1–24.

Goodman, N. and Quine, W. V. (1947) 'Steps toward a constructive nominalism', *Journal of Symbolic Logic* 12: 105–22.

Gould, J. and Lewontin, R. (1984) 'The spandrels of San Marco and the panglossian paradigm', in Elliot Sober (ed.), *Conceptual Issues in Evolutionary Biology*, Cambridge, Mass.: MIT Press, 252–70.

Grice, H. P. (1989) *Studies in the Ways of Words*, Cambridge, Mass.: Harvard University Press.

Griffin, J. (1986) *Well-being*, Oxford: Clarendon Press.

Grover, D. (1992) *A Prosentential Theory of Truth*, Princeton: Princeton University Press.

Grünbaum, A. (1976) 'Can a theory answer more questions than one of its rivals?', *British Journal for the Philosophy of Science* 27, 1: 1–23.

Gudmunsen, C. (1977) *Wittgenstein and Buddhism*, New York: Harper & Row.

Hahn, H. (1966) 'Logic, mathematics and knowledge of nature', in Morris Weitz (ed.), *20th Century Philosophy*, New York: Macmillan, 222–35.

Haldane, J. B. S. (1927) *Possible Worlds*, London: Chatto and Windus.

Hall, R. (1963) 'Excluders', in C. E. Caton (ed.), *Philosophy and Ordinary Language*, Chicago: University of Illinois Press, 67–73.

Hanson, N. R. (1958) *Patterns of Discovery*, New York: Cambridge University Press.

Hare, R. M. (1981) ' "Nothing matters" ', in E. D. Klemke (ed.), *The Meaning of Life*, Oxford: Oxford University Press, 241–7.

Harman, G. (1988) 'The simplest hypothesis', *Critica* 20, 59: 23–42.

Hawkins, D. (1969) 'The Safety of the American Automobile', in Garrett Hardin (ed.), *Science, Conflict and Society*, San Francisco: W. H. Freeman, 252–5.

Hempel, C. (1965) 'The theoretician's dilemma', in his *Aspects of Scientific Explanation*, New York: Free Press: 173–226.

Himes, J. S. (1966) 'The functions of racial conflict', *Social Forces* 45: 1–10.

Hintikka, J. (1981) *Scientific Method as a Problem-Solving and Question-Answering Technique*, Dordrecht: Reidel.

Horwich, P. (1990) *Truth*, Oxford: Basil Blackwell.

Hume, D. (1739) *A Treatise of Human Nature*, (ed.) L. A. Selby-Bigge, Oxford: Clarendon Press, 1978.

—— (1777) *Enquiries*, ed. L. A. Selby-Bigge, Oxford: Clarendon Press, 1951.

James, W. (1977) *The Writings of William James*, ed. J. J. McDermott, Chicago: University of Chicago Press.

Jennings, B. (1985) 'Legislative ethics and moral minimalism', in B. Jennings and D. Callahan (eds), *Representation and Responsibility*, New York: Plenum Press, 149–65.

Johanson, D. and Shreeve, J. (1989) *Lucy's Child*, New York: Avon Books.

Johnson-Laird, P. N. (1983) *Mental Models*, Cambridge, Mass.: Harvard University Press.

Kagan, Jerome. (1984) *The Nature of the Child*, New York: Basic Books.

Kant, I. (1781) *Critique of Pure Reason*, trans. N. K. Smith, London: Macmillan, 1965.

Kaplan, D. (1989) 'Demonstratives', in J. Almog (ed.), *Themes from Kaplan*, New York: Oxford University Press, 481–566.

—— (1990) 'Dthat', in P. Yourgrau (ed.), *Demonstratives*, Oxford: Oxford University Press, 11–33.

Kitcher, P. (1984) *Abusing Science*, Cambridge, Mass.: The MIT Press.

Kripke, S. (1977) 'Speaker reference and semantic reference', in P. E. French, T. E. Uehling, and H. K. Wettstein (eds), *Contemporary Perspectives in the Philosophy of Language*, Minneapolis: University of Minnesota Press, 6–27.

Kuhn, T. (1970) *The Structure of Scientific Revolutions*, 2nd edn, Chicago: University of Chicago Press.

—— (1977) *The Essential Tension*, Chicago: University of Chicago Press.

Lamb, D. (1991) *Discovery, Creativity and Problem-Solving*, Brookfield, New York: Avebury.

Langer, E. J. (1982) 'The illusion of control', in D. Kahneman, P. Slovic and A. Tversky (eds), *Judgment Under Uncertainty*, Cambridge: Cambridge University Press, 231–8.

Laudan, L. (1977) *Progress and its Problems*, Los Angeles: University of California Press.

—— (1981) 'Peirce and the trivialization of the self-corrective thesis', in his *Science and Hypothesis*, Dordecht: D. Reidel, 226–51.

Lazerowitz, M. (1968) *Philosophy and Illusion*, London: George Allen & Unwin.

Lehrer, K. and Wagner, C. (1981) *Rational Consensus in Science and Society*, Dordrecht: D. Reidel.

Levin, M. (1984a) 'Why homosexuality is abnormal', *Monist* 67, 2: 251–83.

—— (1984b) 'Why we believe in other minds', *Philosophy and Phenomenological Research* 44, 3: 343–59.

Lewicki, P., T. Hill, and E. Bizot (1988) 'Acquisition of procedural knowledge about a pattern of stimuli that cannot be articulated', *Cognitive Psychology* 20: 24–37.

Lewis, C. S. (1946) *The Great Divorce*, New York: Macmillan.

Lewis, D. (1976) 'The paradoxes of time travel', *American Philosophical Quarterly* 13, 2: 145–52.

—— (1982) 'Logic for equivocators', *Nous* 16, 3: 431–41.

Locke, D. (1967) *Perception and our Knowledge of the External World*, London: Allen & Unwin.

Locke, J. (1690) *An Essay Concerning Human Understanding*, New York: Dover, 1951.

Lorenz, K. (1966) *On Aggression*, New York: Harcourt, Brace, & World.

—— (1973) *Behind the Mirror*, London: Methuen.

Luker, K. (1984) *Abortion and the Politics of Motherhood*, Berkeley: University of California Press.

Lyons, D. (1965) *Forms and Limits of Utilitarianism*, Oxford: Clarendon Press.

Mach, E. (1911) *History and Root of the Principle of the Conservation of Energy*, trans. P. E. B. Jourdain, Chicago: Open Court.

—— (1942) *The Science of Mechanics*, trans. T. J. McCormack, London: Open Court.

—— (1948) *Popular Scientific Lectures*, trans. T. J. McCormack, London: Open Court.

—— (1976) *Knowledge and Error*, trans. C. M. Williams, Dordrecht: D. Reidel.

—— (1984) *Contributions to the Analysis of the Sensations*, trans. C. M. Williams, LaSalle, Illinois: Open Court.

—— (1986) *Principles of the Theory of Heat*, trans. P. E. B. Jourdain, Dordrecht: D. Reidel.

McGinn, C. (1991) *The Problem of Consciousness*, Oxford: Basil Blackwell.

Machina, K. (1987) 'Evaluating student evaluations', *Academe* 73, 3: 19–22.

MacIntyre, A. (1967) 'Being', in P. Edwards (ed.), *The Encyclopedia of Philosophy*, vol. 1, New York: Macmillan, 273–7.

—— (1981) *After Virtue*, Notre Dame, Indiana: University of Notre Dame Press.

Malcolm, N. (1969) 'Defending common sense', in E. D. Klemke (ed.), *Studies in the Philosophy of G. E. Moore*, Chicago: Quadrangle Books, 200–19.

Martin, R. M. (1980) 'Suicide and false desires', in M. P. Battin and D. J. Mayo (eds), *Suicide*, New York: St Martin, 144–50.

Merton, R. (1973) *The Sociology of Science*, Chicago, Illinois: University of Chicago Press.

Mill, J. S. (1859) 'On Liberty', *Three Essays*, Oxford: Oxford University Press, 1975.

Montaigne, M. E. (1965) *The Complete Essays of Montaigne*, trans. D. M. F. Stanford, California: Stanford University Press.

Moore, G. E. (1903) *Principia Ethica*, Cambridge: Cambridge University Press.

—— (1922) *Philosophical Studies*, London: Kegan Paul.

—— (1953) *Some Main Problems of Philosophy*, New York: Macmillan.

Nagel, T. (1979) *Mortal Questions*, New York: Cambridge University Press.

Newell, A. and Simon, H. A. (1972) *Human Problem Solving*, Englewood Cliffs, N.J.: Prentice Hall.

Nietzsche, F. (1886) *Beyond Good and Evil*, trans. H. Zimmern, Buffalo, N.Y.: Prometheus Press, 1989.

—— (1882/7) *The Gay Science*, trans. W. Kaufmann, New York: Random House, 1974.

Nozick, R. (1981) *Philosophical Explanations*, Cambridge, Mass.: Harvard University Press.

Oldenquist, A. (1967) 'Choosing, deciding, and doing', in P. Edwards (ed.), *Encyclopedia of Philosophy*, vol. 2, New York: Macmillan, 96–104.

Owen, D. (1980) *Camouflage and Mimicry*, Chicago: University of Chicago Press.

Parfit, D. (1984) *Reasons and Persons*, Oxford: Oxford University Press.

Passmore, J. (1970) *Philosophical Reasoning*, 2nd edn, London: Duckworth.

Paulos, J. (1985) *I Think, Therefore, I laugh*, New York: Columbia University Press.

Payne, S. S. (1950–1) 'Thoughts about meaningless questions', *Public Opinion Quarterly* 14, 4: 687–96.

Peirce, C. S. (1931–5) *The Collected Papers of Charles Sanders Peirce*, ed. C. Hartshorne and P. Weiss, vols. 1–6, Cambridge, Mass.: Harvard University Press.

—— (1940) 'Some consequences of four incapacities', in J. Buchler (ed.), *The Philosophy of Peirce*, London: Kegan Paul, Trend, Trubner.

Pitcher, G. (1964) *The Philosophy of Wittgenstein*, Englewood Cliffs, N.J.: Prentice-Hall, Inc.

Planck, M. (1949) *Scientific Autobiography and Other Papers*, trans. F. Gaynor, New York: Greenwood Press.

Plantinga, A. (1974) *The Nature of Necessity*, Oxford: Clarendon Press.

Popper, K. and Eccles, J. (1977) *The Self and its Brain*, New York: Routledge & Kegan Paul.

Price, R. (1758) *A Review of the Principal Questions in Morals*, ed. D. D. Raphael, Oxford: Clarendon Press, 1947.

Quine, W. V. (1987) *Quiddities*, Cambridge, Mass.: Belknap Press.

Quinton, A. (1962) 'Spaces and times', *Philosophy*, 37: 130–47.

Rachels, J. (1986) 'Egoism and moral scepticism', in E. D. Klemke, A. D. Kline, and R. Hollinger (eds), *Philosophy: The Basic Issues*, New York: St Martin's Press, 387–94.

Rescher, N. (1984) *The Limits of Science*, Berkeley: University of California Press.

—— (1985) *The Strife of Systems*, Pittsburgh, Pennsylvania: University of Pittsburgh.

Reznek, L. (1987) *The Nature of Disease*, London: Routledge.

Rhees, R. (1969) *Without Answers*, New York: Schocken Books.

Robinson, D. S. (1924) *The Principles of Reasoning*, New York: D. Appleton-Century Company.

Russell, B. (1912) *The Problems of Philosophy*, London: Oxford University Press.

—— (1957) *Mysticism and Logic*, New York: Doubleday.

—— (1964) *Why I am Not a Christian*, London: Allen & Unwin.

Ryle, G. (1949) *The Concept of Mind*, London: Hutchinson.

—— (1967) 'Plato', in P. Edwards (ed.), *Encyclopedia of Philosophy*, vol. 6, New York: Macmillan, 314–33.

Sartre, J. (1956) *Being and Nothingness*, trans. H. E. Barnes, New York: Philosophical Library.

Schiller, F. C. S. (1934) *Must Philosophers Disagree?*, London: Macmillan.

Searle, J. (1969) *Speech Acts*, Cambridge: Cambridge University Press.

—— (1984) *Minds, Brains and Science*, Cambridge, Mass: Harvard University Press.

Shepherd, R. (1987) 'Evolution of a mesh: mind and world', in J. Dupre (ed.), *The Latest on the Best*, Cambridge, Mass.: MIT Press, 251–76.

Simonton, D. K. (1988) *Scientific Genius*, Cambridge: Cambridge University Press.

Singer, P. (1973) 'The triviality of the debate over "Is–Ought" and the definition of "Moral" ', *American Philosophical Quarterly* 10, 1: 51–6.

Slote, M. (1980) 'Inapplicable concepts and sexual perversion', in R. Baker and F. Elliston (eds), *Philosophy & Sex*, Buffalo, New York: Prometheus, 261–7.

—— (1989) *Beyond Optimizing*, Cambridge, Mass.: Harvard University Press.

Smullyan, R. (1978) *What is the Name of this Book?*, Englewood Cliffs, New Jersey: Prentice Hall.

Sorensen, R. (1988) *Blindspots*, Oxford: Clarendon Press.

—— (1991a) 'Vagueness and the desiderata for definition', in J. Fetzer, D. Shatz, and G. Schlesinger (eds), *Definitions and Definability*, Dordrecht: Kluwer, 71–109.

—— (1991b) 'Debunkers and assurers', *Australasian Journal of Philosophy*, 69, 4: 469–91.

—— (1992a) *Thought Experiments*, New York: Oxford University Press.

—— (1992b) 'The egg came before the chicken', *Mind*, 101, 403: 541–2.

Speer, A. (1970) *Inside the Third Reich*, trans. R. and C. Winston, New York: Macmillan Company.

Stebbing, S. (1937) *Philosophy and the Physicists*, London: Methuen & Co. Ltd.

Stevenson, C. (1944) *Ethics and Language*, New Haven: Yale University Press.

—— (1963) *Facts and Values*, New Haven: Yale University Press.

Stocker, M. (1987) 'Emotional thoughts', *American Philosophical Quarterly* 24, 1: 59–69.

Stove, D. (1991) *The Plato Cult and other Philosophical Follies*, Oxford: Basil Blackwell.

Strawson, P. (1950) 'On referring', *Mind* 59, 1: 320–44.

—— (1951) *Introduction to Logical Theory*, London: Methuen.

—— (1985) *Skepticism and Naturalism*, New York: Columbia University Press.

Sumner, L. W. (1986) 'Review of *The Case for Animal Rights*', *Nous* 20, 3: 425–34.

Suzuki, D. T. (1956) *Zen Buddhism*, New York: Doubleday.

Thagard, P. (1980) 'Resemblance, correlation, pseudoscience', in M. P. Hanen, J. Osler, and R. G. Weyant (eds), *Science, Pseudo-Science and Society*, Waterloo, Ontario: Wilfred Laurier University Press, 17–25.

Thalberg, I. (1962) 'False pleasures', *Journal of Philosophy*, 59, 3: 65–74.

Thomson, J. J. (1971) 'A defense of abortion', *Philosophy and Public Affairs*, 1, 1: 47–68.

Turner, E. S. (1964) *All Heaven in a Rage*, London: Michael Joseph.

Unger, P. (1984) *Philosophical Relativity*, Minneapolis: University of Minnesota Press.

Urmson, J. O. (1950) 'On grading', *Mind* 59, 234: 145–69.

—— (1956) *Philosophical Analysis*, Oxford: Clarendon Press.

—— (1974) 'Some questions concerning validity', in R. Swinburne (ed.), *The Justification of Induction*, Oxford: Oxford University Press: 74–84.

Vaihinger, H. (1924) *The Philosophy of 'As if'*, trans. C. K. Ogden, London: Routledge & Kegan Paul.

Waismann, F. (1965) *The Principles of Linguistic Philosophy*, ed. R. Harre, New York: Macmillan.

Warnock, G. J. (1969) *English Philosophy Since 1900*, Oxford: Oxford University Press.

Weldon, T. D. (1953) *The Vocabulary of Politics*, London: Penguin.

Werth, F. L. (1978) 'Normalizing the paranormal', *American Philosophical Quarterly* 15, 1: 47–58.

Whewell, W. (1837) *History of the Inductive Sciences*, London: Parker.

Williams, C. J. F. (1974) 'False Pleasures', *Philosophical Studies*, 26, 3 & 4: 295–7.

Wisdom, J. (1969) *Philosophy and Psycho-analysis*, New York: Barnes & Noble.

Wittgenstein, L. (1922) *Tractatus Logico-Philosophicus*, trans. D. F. Pears and B. F. McGuinness, London: Routledge, 1961.

—— (1953) *Philosophical Investigations*, trans. G. E. M. Anscombe, New York: Macmillan.

—— (1966) *Lectures and Conversations on Aesthetics, Psychology and Religious Belief*, ed. C. Barrett, Berkeley: University of California Press, 27–8.

—— (1967) *Zettel*, ed. G. E. M. Anscombe and G. H. von Wright, trans. G. E. M. Anscombe and D. Paul, Oxford: Blackwell.

—— (1969) *On Certainty*, ed. G. E. M. Anscombe and G. H. von Wright, trans. D. Paul and G. E. M. Anscombe, Oxford: Basil Blackwell.

Woodward, H. B. (1978) *The History of the Geological Society of London*, New York: Arno Press.

Subject Index

Name Index